# Ethics and Integrity of Governance

NEW HORIZONS IN PUBLIC POLICY

**Series Editor: Wayne Parsons**
Professor of Public Policy, Queen Mary and Westfield College,
University of London, UK

This series aims to explore the major issues facing academics and practitioners
working in the field of public policy at the dawn of a new millennium. It seeks to
reflect on where public policy has been, in both theoretical and practical terms,
and to prompt debate on where it is going. The series emphasizes the need to
understand public policy in the context of international developments and global
change. New Horizons in Public Policy publishes the latest research on the study
of the policymaking process and public management, and presents original and
critical thinking on the policy issues and problems facing modern and post-
modern societies.
    Titles in the series include:

The Internationalization of Public Management
Reinventing the Third World State
*Edited by Willy McCourt and Martin Minogue*

Political Leadership
*Howard Elcock*

Success and Failure in Public Governance
A Comparative Analysis
*Edited by Mark Bovens, Paul t'Hart and B. Guy Peters*

Consensus, Cooperation and Conflict
The Policy Making Process in Denmark
*Henning Jørgensen*

Public Policy in Knowledge-Based Economics
Foundations and Frameworks
*David Rooney, Greg Hearn, Thomas Mandeville and Richard Joseph*

Modernizing Civil Services
*Edited by Tony Butcher and Andrew Massey*

Public Policy and the New European Agendas
*Edited by Fergus Carr and Andrew Massey*

The Dynamics of Public Policy
Theory and Evidence
*Adrian Kay*

Ethics and Integrity of Governance
Perspectives Across Frontiers
*Edited by Leo W.J.C. Huberts, Jeroen Maesschalck and Carole L. Jurkiewicz*

# Ethics and Integrity of Governance

Perspectives Across Frontiers

*Edited by*

Leo W.J.C. Huberts

*VU University Amsterdam, the Netherlands*

Jeroen Maesschalck

*Katholieke Universiteit Leuven, Belgium*

Carole L. Jurkiewicz

*Louisiana State University, USA*

with a foreword by John Rohr

NEW HORIZONS IN PUBLIC POLICY

**Edward Elgar**

Cheltenham, UK • Northampton, MA, USA

Published by
Edward Elgar Publishing Limited
Glensanda House
Montpellier Parade
Cheltenham
Glos GL50 1UA
UK

Edward Elgar Publishing, Inc.
William Pratt House
9 Dewey Court
Northampton
Massachusetts 01060
USA

A catalogue record for this book
is available from the British Library

**Library of Congress Cataloging in Publication Data**
Ethics and integrity of governance : perspectives across frontiers / edited by Leo W.J.C. Huberts, Jeroen Maesschalck, Carole L. Jurkiewicz ; with a foreword by John Rohr.
    p.   cm.
    Articles originally presented at the conference 'Ethics and Integrity of Governance: Perspectives Across Frontiers' held in Leuven in June 2005.
    Includes bibliographical references and index.
    1. Political ethics—United States—Congresses.   2. Political ethics—Europe—Congresses.   I. Huberts, L.W.   II. Maesschalck, Jeroen, 1975–
III. Jurkiewicz, Carole L., 1958–
JK468.E7E83   2008
172—dc22

2007047864

ISBN  978 1 84542 854 9

Printed and bound in Great Britain by MPG Books Ltd, Bodmin, Cornwall

# Contents

# Figures

# Tables

# Box

# The contributors

**Guy B. Adams** is Professor of Public Affairs in the Harry S Truman School of Public Affairs at the University of Missouri-Columbia, in Columbia, MO, USA. He is co-editor-in-chief of the *American Review of Public Administration*. His research interests are in the areas of public administration history and theory, public service ethics, and organization studies. He has over 60 scholarly publications, including books, book chapters and articles in the top national public administration journals, and received the 2007 Marshall E. Dimock Award for the best lead article in *Public Administration Review*. He earned his doctorate in public administration in 1977 from The George Washington University in Washington, DC.

**Danny L. Balfour** is Professor of Public and Nonprofit Administration at Grand Valley State University in Grand Rapids, MI, USA. His research and teaching interests are in the areas of organizational theory, social policy, public service ethics, and the Holocaust. He has more than 30 scholarly publications, including two editions of an award-winning book, book chapters, and articles in the top national public administration journals, and received the 2007 Marshall E. Dimock Award for best lead article in *Public Administration Review*. He served as managing editor of the *Journal of Public Affairs Education* from 1995–2000. He earned his PhD from Florida State University in 1990.

**Alex Belling** is a Coordinating Policy Adviser on ethics and integrity issues for the Ministry of the Interior and Kingdom Relations in the Netherlands. He is the former coordinator of the National Office for Promoting Ethics and Integrity in the Public Sector. Belling previously worked for the Ministry of Justice as an HR policy adviser.

**James S. Bowman** is Professor of Public Administration at the Askew School of Public Administration and Policy, Florida State University, in Tallahassee, FL, USA. He is editor-in-chief of *Public Integrity*, a journal of the American Society for Public Administration. His primary research areas are human resource management and professional ethics. He is author of over 100 journal articles and book chapters, in addition to two recent co-authored books. Bowman has also edited five anthologies. He earned his doctorate in political science in 1973 from the University of Nebraska in Lincoln.

**Yves Emery** of the University of Geneva, Switzerland, is a Professor at the Swiss Graduate School of Public Administration in Lausanne (IDHEAP), in charge of the department of Public Management and Human Resource Management. He is a research director and consultant in public organizations. His primary research areas are work motivation, competency management and employability, rewards systems and training strategies in public organizations. He is a member of the board of the Swiss Society for Administrative Sciences.

**Gillian Fawcett** is a Senior Fellow working with the Office for Public Management (OPM) Organisational Development and Policy Team in the UK. She joined OPM from the Audit Commission, where she was a senior policy adviser with expertise in corporate and ethical governance and human rights. Prior to that, she spent a year outside the Commission in Parliament as deputy head of the Scrutiny Unit, responsible for providing professional support to Select Committees in the areas of finance, performance and governance. Fawcett is well-versed in working collaboratively with other agencies to influence policy issues.

**Robert A. Giacalone** is Professor of Human Resource Management at the Fox School of Business and Management, Temple University, in Philadelphia, PA, USA. His research interests focus on the impact of workplace spirituality and changing values on business ethics. He is also recognized as an expert on behavioural business ethics, exit surveying and interviewing, employee sabotage, and impression management. Giacalone has authored over 100 articles on ethics issues, impression management and exit interviewing, edited/authored seven books, and is currently co-editor of the Ethics in Practice book series. He has served on several journal editorial boards and as editor of several special issues. He has consulted and trained for a number of organizations including the FBI, Carter-Wallace Inc., and the US Department of Defense.

**Alain Hoekstra** studied public administration at Erasmus University, Rotterdam the Netherlands. He is a Coordinating Policy Adviser on ethics and integrity for the Ministry of the Interior and Kingdom Relations in the Netherlands. He coordinates the National Office for Promoting Ethics and Integrity in the Public Sector. He has published several articles on integrity and has a special interest in the organizational aspects of managing integrity within the public sector.

**Sylvia Horton** is Honorary Principal Lecturer in the School of Education and Continuing Studies, University of Portsmouth, UK. She is a convenor of the Personnel Policies Study group of the European Group of Public Administration (EGPA) and a member of the EGPA Steering Committee. Her research interests are in the areas of public administration, public management and HRM with special reference to civil services. She has published widely including books, book chapters, and articles in national and international journals. She has worked with European colleagues on a series of comparative studies including public managers, HR flexibilities, competency management, staff participation in public management reform and public service motivation. Her current research is in the area of leadership development and training.

**Leo W.J.C. Huberts** is Professor in Public Administration and Integrity of Governance at the Department of Public Administration and Organisation Science of the VU University in the Netherlands and director of the research group on the Integrity of Governance. From 1997 until 2004 he was professor in Police Studies and Criminal Justice at the same department. His research concerns political, administrative and police power and power abuse (including corruption and fraud). He is author or editor of ten books on integrity, corruption and fraud and published articles in journals such as *Public Integrity* and *Crime, Law and Social Change*.

**Carole L. Jurkiewicz** is the Women's Hospital Distinguished Professor of Healthcare Management in the Public Administration Institute of the E. J. Ourso College of Business at Louisiana State University, Baton Rouge, LA, USA. She has published numerous articles and books in the areas of organizational and individual performance, ethics, power and leadership, bringing to her academic career many years' experience as a key executive in private and nonprofit organizations. She speaks across the US and Europe on issues of ethics and organizational integrity, and has held key leadership roles in the American Society for Public Administration. Jurkiewicz has served as a consultant to many organizations including IBM, US Postal Service, National Public Radio, American Marketing Association, and many governmental departments at the federal, state, and local levels.

**Robert P. Kaye** was Research Officer in Risk and Regulation at the Economic and Social Research Council (ESRC) Centre for Analysis of Risk and Regulation at the London School of Economics in the UK. He completed his doctoral thesis on the regulation of conflict of interest the British House of Commons at the University of Oxford. Kaye has published on standards of public life in the United Kingdom and investigatory mechanisms for allegations of misconduct against government, and on 'innovation' in ethics regulation in the UK and the United States.

**Terry Lamboo** is Research Fellow on Integrity of Governance at the Department of Public Administration and Organization Science at the VU University in the Netherlands. Her research interests include integrity policies and integrity violations within the public sector and most specifically the police. She is primarily focused upon the comparative research approach. Lamboo earned her doctorate in public administration in 2005 at the VU University.

**Karin Lasthuizen** is Senior Researcher on Integrity of Governance at the Department of Public Administration and Organization Science at the VU University in the Netherlands. Her research interests include leadership and ethics, the police and research methodology. She is currently working on a dissertation on leadership and integrity.

**Carol W. Lewis** is a Professor of Political Science at the University of Connecticut, Storrs, CT. Her research specializations are public service ethics and public budgeting. She and Stuart C. Gilman authored *The Ethics Challenge in Public Service: A Problem-Solving Guide*, 2nd edn, San Francisco: Jossey-Bass, 2005.

**Jeroen Maesschalck** is a Lecturer at the Leuven Institute of Criminology in the Law Faculty of the Katholieke Universiteit Leuven in Belgium. His teaching and research interests include public sector ethics, criminal justice administration and policy, and public personnel management. He is also research fellow in Integrity of Governance at the Vrije Universiteit Amsterdam and co-chair of the Study Group on Ethics and Integrity of Governance of the European Group of Public Administration (EGPA). He has published in journals such as *Public Integrity, Public Administration* and *Western European Politics*. He earned his doctorate from the KU Leuven in 2004.

**John A. Rohr** is Professor of Public Administration at the Center for Public Administration and Policy in Virginia Tech's School of Public and International Affairs in Blacksburg, VA, USA. In addition to his doctorate in political science from the University of Chicago, Rohr also holds graduate degrees in philosophy and theology from Loyola and Georgetown universities respectively. He has written and lectured extensively on the constitutional foundations of public administration and on ethical issues that confront the career civil servant. He is the author of seven books and over 100 articles and reviews. He has lectured at many universities and governmental institutions throughout the United States and in Belgium, Canada, the Czech Republic, France, Germany, Portugal and Thailand. Rohr is associate editor of the scholarly journal *Administration and Society* and a member of the editorial boards of *The American Review of Public Administration, Public Integrity, Public Organization Review* and *The Political Science Reviewer*. He received the American Society for Public Administration (ASPA)'s prestigious Dwight Waldo Award in 2002.

**Frédérique E. Six** is Senior Lecturer in the Department of Governance and Organisation at the VU University Amsterdam in the Netherlands. Her research interests are the management of integrity and trust within the public and private sector. She has published several articles, books and book chapters on these topics. She earned her PhD in management in 2004 from Erasmus University Rotterdam. Prior to her academic career she was a management consultant with McKinsey & Company and KPMG for 15 years.

**Wouter Vandenabeele** is a Researcher at the Public Management Institute, Katholieke Universiteit Leuven in Belgium. He is a member of the European Group of Public Administration (EGPA) and American Society for Public Administration (ASPA). His research interests are in the areas of public human resources management and public administration ethics. He has several scholarly publications, including book chapters and articles in local and international public administration journals. He is currently writing his doctoral thesis on public service motivation at the Katholieke Universiteit Leuven.

**Eli van der Heide** is Senior Policy Adviser at the Ministry of Education, Culture and Science in the Netherlands. He studied business economics (cum laude) and law at Erasmus University in Rotterdam. He specialized in the field of ethics and human resource management and has worked in this field at the Ministry of the Interior and Kingdom relations in the Netherlands. His research interests are in the areas of applied ethics, human resource management, organizational change, and the relationship between ethical theory and law.

**Steven Van de Walle** is a Lecturer in Public Management at the Institute of Local Government Studies, School of Public Policy, the University of Birmingham, UK. His research interests are in trust in government, citizens' perception of bureaucrats and the public sector, comparative public administration, and performance measurement. Publications include articles in the *International Review of Administrative Sciences, Public Management Review, International Journal of Public Administration, Public Performance and Management Review, Journal of Comparative Policy Analysis, Public Policy and Administration* and *West European Politics*. He earned his PhD in the social sciences from KU Leuven in 2004, and currently is co-director of the European Group of Public Administration's Study Group on Performance in the Public Sector.

**Jonathan P. West** is Professor of Political Science and Director of the Graduate Public Administration programme at the University of Miami, Coral Gables, FL, USA. He is managing editor of *Public Integrity*. His research interests are in the areas of American politics, public policy, human resource management and ethics. He has over 100 scholarly publications, including books, articles and book chapters. He received his doctorate from Northwestern University and has taught at the University of Houston and the University of Arizona. He served as a management analyst for the US Office of the Surgeon General, Department of the Army.

**Mark Wardman** is a Senior Manager in the Audit Commission in the UK, where he has taken a close interest in governance and accountability in the public sector. He is the author of Audit Commission national study reports on corporate governance, public trust, individual choice in public services, and partnerships. In a predominantly research and policy-based career in both the public and private sectors, he has worked for the National Foundation for Educational Research, the London Borough of Sutton, MORI, and was Head of Policy at the National Lottery Charities Board. He has a Masters in Science in Organizational Behaviour from Birkbeck College, University of London, awarded in 1993.

**Carole Wyser** is a Research and Teaching Assistant at the Swiss Graduate School of Public Administration (IDHEAP). She is involved in a number of research and teaching projects on the post-civil service. Holder of a licence in sociology from the University of Geneva, she has collaborated on various research projects touching thanatology and the sociology of religions, notably through the Observatory of Religions in Switzerland (ORS). Her main research interests are related to the ethics and identity of public agents, the public service ethos, the rupture of the physiological contract, and motivation in the public service.

# Foreword

## John A. Rohr

It was with considerable pleasure that I accepted the kind invitation from the editors of this book to write its preface. My pleasure was doubled by the fact that I had delivered the keynote address at the opening session of the Leuven conference on 'Ethics and integrity of governance: perspectives across frontiers', from which this volume springs.

The chapters in this book are always instructive and at times profound. Despite their many merits, however, they cannot recreate the authentic spirit of international enthusiasm that permeated the conference itself, with its host of scholars from no less than a dozen nations.

The Leuven conference was one of those all-too-rare 'magic moments' in academic life when staid, somber, serious professors set aside their normal reserve and reveal their expertise in a subject with passion to people who really care about what they are thinking.

It would be unfair to ask the fine contributors to this volume to recreate that magic moment in early June 2005. All the props are gone, from the chatty coffee breaks, to the remarkably efficient support staff, to the lovely, old city of Leuven itself.

And yet *Scriptum manet* – the written words remain, as the old Romans told us. This is true, of course, but its obvious truth misses a subtler and more interesting one. To assert that the written word, including the words written in this book, simply remain ignores the dynamic character of writing. The written word does not remain in the flat sense that it simply exists for a long time. Such a pedestrian interpretation of the old Roman adage would rob it of the very richness of its meaning, which, in turn, explains its long-lived relevance. In the context of the Leuven conference, such an interpretation would shortchange the entire enterprise. The essays in this book refresh the faltering memories of those of us who participated in the conference and stimulate the imaginations of those who did not participate. Thus, the written word not only remains frozen in time, but it also projects that moment into the future as it refreshes and stimulates.

I dwell on these points primarily for the sake of those participants in the conference whose papers were not selected by the editors for inclusion in this volume. Time, cost and editorial thematic imperatives demanded that many fine papers presented at the conference could not be included herein. No doubt the authors of the omitted papers are disappointed, as are the editors because they could not include them, but the authors should by no means consider their work as unworthy. They are just as much revered as those whose essays we shall soon be reading because they are vital participants in the same happy, academic event that these printed essays embody.

In examining the essays that follow, the careful reader will surely ponder certain themes and patterns that deserve close attention. For example, the word *governance* appears time and again in this volume, starting with its very title. What does this word add to our analytic tools? Is there a difference between *governance* and *governing?* If so, what is it? Does the same distinction exist in other languages?

Is the discussion of ethics and globalism a bit premature? After all, we still live in an international order based on the nation state. Or, conversely, are we hopelessly late in addressing the ethical aftermath of globalism? The United Nations, for all its warts and wrinkles, has been a significant actor in this international arena for over half a century.

Considerable attention is given to values in this book. Some authors even mention 'main' values, thereby implying some sort of pecking order, with some values more valued than others. How do we make sense of this, objectively?

Taking the argument beyond values, one of the more creative essays addresses the question of 'administrative evil'. Does administrative evil allow for redemption? Is there an administrative equivalent to St Paul's assertion that where sin did once abound now grace does more abound? Does this conceptualization of evil bring administration to the threshold of metaphysical analysis? Recall the medieval distinction between something that was *prohibitum quia malum* (forbidden because it is evil) and *malum quia prohibitum* (evil because it is prohibited).

Perhaps the most interesting aspect of a value-based ethic is its relationship to the rule of law. Values are subjective, whereas law is objective; consequently, the two approaches to ethical decision-making pull in opposite directions. Those who would save the rule of law must explain which law they have in mind – natural law or positive law. If positive law, do they mean constitutional law, statutory law, administrative law, common law, or civil law? And what of the myriad of legal systems and value hierarchies evident from country to country? Although implicitly postulated, is an Aristotelian ethic possible in today's society?

These questions just scratch the surface of the momentous issues that await the reader of this excellent volume. These are issues that will frame the debate for decades to come. Enough of prefaces, introductions, and all the other bookish preliminaries. The main event is now at hand. Let us read, study, and learn.

# 1. Introduction

## Leo W.J.C. Huberts, Jeroen Maesschalck and Carole L. Jurkiewicz

While the media and organizational discussions around the globe have been abuzz with talk of public sector ethics, academic research in the field was, until very recently, dominated primarily by American researchers focusing primarily on American topics. This is of no surprise given that it is only in the US that public sector or administrative ethics has developed as a separate discipline and area of study within public administration. Consequently, the vast majority of textbooks, courses, journals, and professional networks are US-based and reflect the American culture. Yet, this has changed recently as the debates on public sector ethics across the globe have also generated academic interest outside the US. This book represents these changes.

Born from presentations delivered at the first 'Transatlantic Dialogue on Ethics and Integrity of Governance', held at the Public Management Institute of the University of Leuven in Belgium in June 2005, the chapters in this book represent a milestone. The conference was jointly organized by European and American networks (the Study Group on Ethics and Integrity of Governance of the European Group of Public Administration and the Section on Ethics of the American Society of Public Administration, respectively), representing transatlantic dialogue in the truest sense. It is a dialogue of balance, integration, perspective and, ultimately, demonstrates an abiding respect for perspectives from both sides of the Atlantic. A peer-reviewed selection from amongst those myriad voices is presented in this book, challenging current suppositions, confirming mutual concerns, and challenging everyone interested in public sector ethics to move to the next level of inquiry and practice.

The book is organized in four parts. Part I addresses the moral qualities of governance and government, its mission and demonstrated values. Chapters 1 and 2 are empirically-grounded and emanate from a strong theoretical foundation. Vandenabeele and Horton focus on the qualitative aspects of integrity and ethics using historical institutionalism to frame their argument: What is the public ethos of government in the United Kingdom, how has that ethos developed, and which factors or institutions had a significant influence on this evolution? Giacalone and Jurkiewicz pinpoint changes in basic societal values and extrapolate the significance of these measured shifts on organizational values, focusing on the impact to the individual. In the third chapter Lewis paints the ethical landscape with elements that figure prominently in ethical decision-making, including the psychology of moral development, emotions and context. The final chapter of this part is of a more normative nature. Six and Huberts ask what qualifies a public servant to be labeled as ethical or acting with integrity. Can someone be his or her own judge, should the legal framework be decisive, is it the politician's values and preferences that should be followed or is the citizen, in the end, the referee in this game of moral judgment?

Part II of the book addresses the dangers inherent in focusing too tightly on rationality and effectiveness in government. Adams and Balfour suggest that a central tension in present day public administration results when administrators perform rationally in a technical sense but in the process lose conceptions of moral responsibility that are essential for integrity. Emery and Wiser also tackle contradictions between rationality and effectiveness on the one hand, and morality and ethics on the other. They argue that borrowing measures and approaches from the private sector for use in the public sector could lead to unethical behavior, and draw upon empirical data to assess whether that danger is real.

An important developing area in the field of ethics and integrity research focuses upon identifying interventions that will lead to improved organizational integrity; that theme is addressed in Part III of this book. Fawcett and Wardman map the ethical framework of local government in England, reporting unexpected results from a study by the Audit Commission. Hoekstra, Belling, and van der Heide describe the evolution of ethics management in the Netherlands, calling for the current paradigm of compliance to be replaced by a more values-based approach. Finally, Lamboo et al. focus on a single 'instrument' of ethics management: utilizing the case study approach they assess the impact of leadership on unethical behavior.

Part IV addresses the relationship between ethics, integrity, and politics. Bowman and West review appointments in the public sector and question how definitive the criteria of merit and partisanship are, and should be. They conclude that a new politicization of appointments could bode negative consequences for the ethics of governance. Robert Kaye, conversely argues that conflicting demands within a democratic political system are desirable and should be left to their own natural progression in resolving the issues at hand; in other words, politicking is good. Next, Van de Walle concentrates on a key power base of politics: the support and trust of citizens. He tackles the chicken-egg question of whether perceptions of corruption affect the amount of trust citizens have in their government or whether the amount of trust dictates perceptions of corruption. His conclusion challenges the hopes of many in that, in the final analysis, getting things done may be more important to the populace than getting them done with integrity.

The concluding part attempts to frame these multiplicative aspects of ethics, integrity, and governance within the broader context of research and practice. First, the burgeoning interest in ethics and integrity demonstrated by global institutions such as the UN, World Bank and OECD as well as NGO's like Transparency International, is critically examined. The question is addressed point-blank regarding whose interests are best served by all this enthusiasm for ethics management. Second, epistemological and ontological issues surrounding the research literature on ethics and integrity are put into perspective: what do we know, how do we know it, and what does it mean. It concludes with a summary of present research and policy agendas, a challenge to the parochial paradigm which limits our understanding of the truths we seek, and a slew of suggestions for the future of both scholars and players.

The chapters in this book have been selected from over 90 top-notch papers that were presented at the Conference, by a labor-intensive nomination protocol followed by a dual blind peer review process. We would like to thank these thoughtful and attentive reviewers sincerely for their extensive and very useful comments: Guy Adams, Frank Anechiarico, Daryl Balia, Nathalie Behnke, Rob M. Bittick, Mark Bovens, Jim Bowman, Richard Chapman, Gjalt de Graaf, Kathryn Denhardt, Patrick Dobel, Mel Dubnick, Richard Ghere, Robert A. Giacalone, Annie Hondeghem, Michael Johnston, Torben Beck Jorgensen, Emile Kolthoff, Terry Lamboo, Karin Lasthuizen, Alan Lawton, Carol Lewis, Michael Macaulay, Donald C. Menzel, Carel Peeters, James L. Perry, Terrell Rhodes, Robert Schwartz, Frédérique Six, Dennis Smith, Trui Steen, Wouter Vandenabeele, Hans van den Heuvel, Zeger van der Wal, Steven Van de Walle, Kathleen Vanmullem, Patrick von Maravic, and Pieter Wagenaar. We also thank Sonja Wellens and the publisher's team for their administrative and editorial support.

Last, and most important, we want to thank all participants at the 'First Transatlantic Dialogue on Ethics and Integrity of Governance'. Their comments and suggestions were of crucial importance not only to the authors in transforming their presentations into the chapters in this book, but to the beginning of a meaningful, substantive, and truly transatlantic dialogue. One that we hope will be the first of many.

# PART I

# Public service ethos, values and integrity

# 2. The evolution of the British public service ethos: a historical institutional approach to explaining continuity and change

**Wouter Vandenabeele and Sylvia Horton**

## INTRODUCTION

An important aspect of the British Home Civil Service throughout its history has been the continuous presence of the Public Service Ethos (PSE). Woodhouse (1997) describes PSE as 'an amalgam of beliefs and norms or conventions of behaviour [concerning public service]'. This ethos serves as an ethical code for civil servants and public officials (Greenaway, 1995; O'Toole, 1997, 2000). In addition to a guidance function, it also has a motivational aspect (Chapman, 1997; Reeves, 2004). Although some authors contest the idea of PSE, it is generally accepted as a core element of British public administration and its principles are defended by the major political parties in the UK.

The aims of this chapter are threefold: first, to investigate the emergence of PSE since the creation of the modern civil service in the mid 19th century; second, to identify the elements of continuity and change in PSE through-out the twentieth century and third, to explain variations in the content using a historical-institutional theoretical framework. Our analysis spans 150 years from the origins of the modern civil service in 1853 to the present day. The chapter is divided into six sections. Each section describes the historical context and the key events impacting on the PSE, and then seeks to explain the process using our historical, institutional, theoretical framework.

## HISTORICAL INSTITUTIONALISM AS A THEORETICAL FRAMEWORK

The theory of historical institutionalism offers an interesting framework within which to analyse PSE. Peters (2000: 18) defines an institution as 'a formal or informal, structural, societal or political phenomenon that transcends the individual level, that is based on more or less common values, has a certain degree of stability and influences behavior'. Institutions are subject to 'path dependency' or what Peters (2000) calls, 'the legacy of the past', as it focuses on the consequences of earlier events for those that follow. Path dependent explanations make two fundamental assumptions. First, contingent factors trigger a causal chain of events or institutional patterns and, second, this causal chain is relatively deterministic (Thelen, 2003). Therefore, institutions are unpredictable, sensitive to earlier events, demonstrate inertia and are difficult situations from which to exit.

Much of the work on historical institutionalism concentrates on how and why institutions emerge and in particular on how institutions survive (Thelen, 2003). According to historical institutional theory, survival is due to self-reinforcing mechanisms. Once a process has been initiated and invested in, it demonstrates benefits or returns because of coordination effects, diminishing marginal costs, learning effects or adaptive expectations. Consequently, it will be reproduced because of increasing returns (Pierson, 2000) or the utilitarian mechanism. Mahoney (2000) identifies three additional mechanisms that can underpin reproductive processes; these are functional, power and legitimation mechanisms. As in the 'increasing returns' mechanism institutions not only reproduce they also capitalize on the reproduction, causing self-reinforcement.

These positive feedback mechanisms provide an explanation for the persistence of institutions, but the theory also offers an explanation for institutional change. Whenever 'critical junctures' or points of discontinuity occur the path is interrupted and branches appear. This results in disruptive change in the institutional make-up (Cortell and Peterson, 1999). Essentially, critical junctures are disruptions of the positive feedback mechanisms. Examples of critical junctures are: war, changing balances of power, international treaties, technological change, elections and social movements (Hall and Taylor, 1996).

However, this is only a partial explanation of institutional change as institutions change even without the occurrence of critical junctures. In contrast to rapid or radical change, there is a more gradual type of institutional evolution. Hall (1993) describes it as first or second order change, in terms of the magnitude of change. First order change is incremental and the natural response of institutions in adjusting to circumstances and organizational learning but does not disrupt existing power, functional or legitimacy relationships. Second order change involves more significant change, which may involve 'the instruments of policy without changing the hierarchy of goals behind policy' (Hall, 1993: 282) or power relations. Both types of change can be subsumed under what Thelen (2003) defines as 'layering'. This type of change is incremental, does not disrupt the positive feedback mechanisms and is *de facto* in harmony with the institutional setting. Hall's third order change is radical and transformational.

In this chapter, we adopt a single case study method. Although not a valid method for generalizing empirical data to the population, it is valid for judging theoretical propositions on their merits (Yin, 1981; Rueschemeyer, 2003). The theoretical framework acts as a set of hypotheses or a 'thick hypothesis' and is tested by matching with the database patterns found in our case study (Yin, 1994). We also adopt a qualitative approach to our case study that provides far more in-depth information on the actual processes involved than is possible using quantitative methods (Miles and Huberman, 1994).

Our data collection is based on a review of the literature, for both our dependent and independent variables, as we make a historical reconstruction. A problem arises from the fact that our dependent variable (PSE) is an informal institution, so in contrast to a study of formal institutions we cannot refer to substantive records such as legislation and official records especially in the earlier periods. All value-laden elements that point to this institution (set of values) are taken as an operationalizing of variables. In particular norms, attitudes and roles are taken into account in order to provide an overview of the elements that are incorporated in the PSE as reflections of the values upon which PSE is based (Scott, 2001). Our independent variables are historical events stated in terms of our theoretical framework. To identify critical junctures, which fulfil a prime role in explaining institutional change, we rely again on secondary sources referring to disruptions of the positive feedback mechanisms. A major problem implicit in this study is measuring institutional change. Our working assumption is that for our core institution to be altered significantly, at least one value must have appeared or disappeared compared with the previous situation.

## THE BEGINNINGS OF THE MODERN CIVIL SERVICE

In the middle of the nineteenth century central government consisted of a collection of civil offices grouped together into departments of varying sizes. It suffered from various problems including patronage, inefficiency and incompetence (Parris, 1969) and reform was being demanded. Sir Stafford Northcote and Sir Charles Trevelyan were invited to undertake an investigation and report on *The Organisation of the Permanent Civil Service*, which was published in 1854 (Northcote and Trevelyan, 1854).

Their recommendations were radical and challenged the status quo. They knew it would be difficult to get them accepted, because of the resistance by vested interests (Kellner and Crowther-Hunt, 1980; Hennessy, 1989). However, the first step towards implementation of the report was taken by Order in Council in 1855, which created the Civil Service Commission (CSC). It took 70 years before the modern civil service was finally established and with it the ethical framework known as the PSE. The result was a paradigmatic change.

The key characteristics of the new, modern civil service were a unified service, open competition for entry and promotion based on merit; a career service; and separation of private and public life. As the political system evolved in response to the economic and social changes within society the civil service took on a particular institutional form consistent with representative democracy, constitutional monarchy and cabinet government. This included accountability through ministers of the crown, the status of 'servants of the crown', anonymity and political neutrality. The behaviours expected of civil servants were that they would be loyal and serve the government of the day, whatever its political composition, keep all matters of government secret unless authorized to release information, would advise, warn and to some extent influence governments and carry out the policies of the government efficiently.

The Treasury's power and its pivotal role within the civil service increased after 1870 as it worked closely with the CSC and determined the subjects to be examined for entry into the civil service. By the early twentieth century an Oxbridge intellectual elite had emerged (Roseveare, 1968) with the generalist administrators, recommended by Northcote–Trevelyan, dominating. From the outset the higher levels of the civil service were drawn from an exclusive social group not representative of the wider society. It was also drawn from the same social strata as the politicians of the day. This enabled a close symbiotic relationship between the bureaucracy and the political executive to emerge and a ruling elite that was based on class.

Throughout the 70 years over which the modern civil service evolved so too did a distinctive culture. It was within the group of generalist administrators, recruited on merit from the major universities that the PSE grew. It was rooted in the idea of the 'English gentleman' and the playing fields of the English public schools. It was characterized by trust, honesty, integrity, mutual respect between politicians and civil servants (drawn from the same backgrounds), not letting down the team and not least an intellectual rigour in presenting and defending arguments. Fry's (1969) seminal work describes them as 'statesmen in disguise', defenders of the constitution and the public interest. According to Hennessy (1989: 60) by 1914 the civil service was:

A convention bound precedent laden, secretive society . . . dominated by an administrative elite recruited from an exclusive educated class with a strong *espirit d'corps* and sense of its own importance as servants of the crown, loyal to the government of the day, bound by the Official Secrets Acts and committed to a career of service.

From 1900 the changing role of the state, from a night watchman role to a social service role, resulted in a major growth in the civil service (a growth of 140 per cent between 1901 and 1914). This period saw the first challenges to the institutions that had been evolving over the previous 70 years. Men were choosing a career as permanent civil servants to be close to the centre of power and able to influence policy. Because of their expertise, they had as much, if not more, influence than their political masters

It is evident that the Northcore–Trevelyan report represented a critical juncture in the development of the modern civil service. A stream of events, which followed, saw the modern civil service gradually emerge accompanied by the PSE. The report disrupted the existing power feedback mechanism, by shaking up the existing balance of power. It was aided by external events, in the form of the Crimean War, and pressure from the Administrative Reform Association. As permanency, merit based entry and promotion, ministerial responsibility and anonymity of civil servants became institutionalized they were the accepted norms and values of the service. After 1870 the growth of staff associations throughout the service, put pressure on the government to standardize terms and conditions of service across departments and disrupted the power balance in favour of reforms but these changes were internally generated and in fact increased the legitimacy of the system and further contributed to the power of the Treasury. The election of the Liberal government in 1901, with its radical programme caused an external shock to the power mechanism and the civil service expanded significantly. This created a context in which a modern unified bureaucratic civil service became a necessity, reinforced by the further catalytic juncture of the First World War.

## POST-WAR CONSOLIDATION 1920–40

At the end of the First World War, the Haldane Report (1918) on the reconstruction of government confirmed the principles enshrined in the Northcote–Trevelyan Report (Harcourt-Smith, 1920) and the modern civil service was finally established. Three general classes (later called Treasury classes) common to all departments saw the unification of the civil service and this was reinforced by the introduction of joint consultative committees on labour relations known as 'Whitleyism' (White, 1933; Farnham and

Horton, 1996). New departments and ministries were created based on a functional division of labour (Mackenzie, 1957) and reflecting the priorities of the government.

A major development during the interwar years was the gradual increase of Treasury control. Headed by Sir Warren Fisher from 1919 until 1939, who was also Head of the Civil Service, the Treasury had the power to approve expenditure on staff, to set down qualifications for entry and the nature of examinations (although the CSC continued to be responsible for recruitment), and to coordinate and control the work of all departmental establishments (Farnham and Horton, 1996). This enabled Fisher to impose his ideas on the civil service (Pilkington, 1999) and he is generally credited with consolidating the administrative bureaucracy and the PSE.

During this interwar period, we can see that the PSE slowly emerged as a clear set of normative principles or ethics guiding the behaviour of civil servants and the decisions they took. The underpinning principles were political neutrality, loyalty, probity, honesty, trustworthiness, fairness, incorruptibility and serving the public (Farnham and Horton, 1996). It was being consolidated into the culture of the higher civil service and gradually transmitted to the lower levels of the civil service through role models and example as well as the growing establishment code or rules and regulations set down by the Treasury.

During the 1920s and 1930s, higher civil servants became more responsible for policy. The extended role of government compelled politicians/ ministers to leave more and more aspects of policy to their civil servants and to rely more heavily on them for advice. They were anonymous, however, and held accountable for their actions through the principle of ministerial responsibility. This principle, which had emerged during the nineteenth century (Parris, 1969), was defended on the grounds that civil servants would only give free and honest advice to ministers if their positions were safeguarded. In other words anonymity was the price of permanency.

Fisher and Haldane were key figures and change agents. They were also important sources of what the PSE meant at this time. Haldane argued that the function of the civil service was to provide the factors necessary for continuity in administration and to strive always for excellence. The common objective should be the service of the community in the most efficient way practical. He argued that 'virtue is its own reward' (Haldane, 1923). He called for an *esprit de corps* based on the non-economic motive of self-sacrifice, which is inculcated, he maintained, through tradition and education.

Locating this period into our theoretical framework it is clear that the end of war caused a critical juncture in both the functional and power mechanisms. The wartime economy had to be converted back to a peace-time role and the armed forces had to be demobilized. The immediate consequence was the expansion of the civil service (Chester and Willson, 1968), which disrupted the power balance. There was a relative lack of able ministers to control this change and to retain power over the civil service (Brown, 1970). As a consequence new players filled the vacuum. Haldane, who was a key figure in the development of PSE (Haldane, 1923) and Fisher, who controlled the Treasury and the civil service for 20 years, had a power base that enabled them to oversee the gradual standardization and centralization of policy. No critical junctures occurred after 1919 although there were many incremental and internally generated changes while the principles of the PSE became firmly institutionalized and disseminated through the processes of socialization and osmosis.

## WAR AND POST-WAR CONSOLIDATION 1940–60

Once again, in 1939, war was a catalyst for change in the civil service. The economy was quickly put on a war footing and conscription was imposed. New departments and agencies were created and thousands of 'irregulars' were recruited into the civil service to run the command economy and the war effort. The politicians who worked with civil servants during the war were unanimous in their praise and neither Prime Minister Churchill nor his successor Clement Attlee saw any need to disturb the civil service after 1945 and backed the Treasury in fending off reforms (Theakston, 1995). In 1945, a radical Labour Government was elected which nationalized and ran the country's major industries, introduced a welfare state and assumed responsibility for managing the economy. This change in the role of the state led to the creation of new departments and new activities and the recruitment of large numbers of specialist staff. New systems of training were introduced but not for the administrative class. They claimed that, in spite of their extended policy and administrative role, on the job training and development was sufficient. A combination of skill shortages, new technology, and the rapid increase in work in the civil service led to continuous incremental changes although none represented significant departures from the traditional characteristics of the system first established in the 1920s. In retrospect the end of the war was a missed opportunity to restructure the civil service and retain the irregulars, who returned to civil society. The administrative class in fact closed its ranks against reform and reverted to recruiting traditional Oxbridge entrants (Hennessy, 1989).

International crises such as the Suez-crisis in 1956 and mounting economic problems led to criticisms of the civil service. An internal report

(Plowden, 1961) highlighted a lack of economic skills amongst Treasury staff and a general lack of management skills throughout the service. The response was to introduce more training and to review internal procedures. Generally, however, the PSE and the generalist tradition of the administrative class remained undisturbed in the post-war era. Neither Labour (1945, 50) nor Conservative (1951, 55) electoral victories were critical junctures in the path dependent patterns of the civil service as no government saw the need to review the machinery of government or its ethos. The additions to the structures and roles, which accompanied the introduction of the interventionist Keynesian/welfare state were built on the existing arrangement and can be seen as examples of layering or first and second order change rather than radical (Hall's third order) change. At no time was the legitimacy, function or power relationships between civil servants and politicians challenged and each was important in resisting external threats and pressures.

## THE CIVIL SERVICE UNDER PRESSURE DURING THE 1960s

At the end of the 1950s and the first half of the 1960s, criticisms of the civil service grew (Balogh, 1959; Chapman, 1963; Fabian Society, 1964). In 1966, the Labour Government appointed the Fulton Committee to investigate the civil service. As Northcote–Trevelyan had highlighted nepotism, patronage and departmentalism as the hallmarks of the nineteenth-century system in need of reform, so Fulton highlighted the pervasive philosophy of the generalist administrator, the rigid and complex class structure and the isolation of the service from the community it was intended to serve as the major defects. The career service and the social and educational composition of the service were also singled out as possible causal factors of its incompetence. Fulton (1968) argued for a 'new style' civil service based upon a new professionalism, a simplified structure, and the removal of secrecy.

The government accepted Fulton's 158 proposals with the exception of 'preference for relevance'. It immediately created a Civil Service Department (CSD) intended to challenge the power of the Treasury, a Civil Service College to train civil servants especially in management skills, and instructed the new CSD to implement Fulton as quickly as possible. Fulton was clearly a challenge to the legitimacy of the service and to the power of the administrative class. It also questioned the functions of the administrative class stating they should take on a managerial role as well as their traditional policy role. The elite generalists reacted with particular skill in responding positively to those recommendations that posed no threat to their position and allowed to lapse those that they did not agree with. The defeat of the Wilson government in 1970 meant that the reforms were left for the service to implement and the incoming Conservative government had other priorities.

Although the Civil Service was under siege during this period, neither the machinery of government nor the PSE changed significantly. As Garrett observed, 'in general, the civil service of 1980 is not much different to the civil service of 1968' (cited in Theakston, 1995: 107). Although there was a lot of criticism of its competency and its self-perception, the civil service managed to retain the status quo. The Fulton report's attack on the values of the civil service was thwarted because of a lack of political support and therefore was unable to disrupt the existing positive feedback mechanisms. The loss of Wilson's support after the initial changes had been implemented, enabled a coalition of civil servants and mandarins to cooperate against the reforms (Theakston, 1995). After the 1970 election, the Fulton Report's death warrant was effectively signed when Prime Minister Heath left its implementation to the civil service itself. The election of a Labour government in 1974 saw the service continue to evolve but still within its system of 'bounded rationality' and sustained by its positive feedback mechanisms.

## THE CIVIL SERVICE FROM 1979–97

The election of the Conservative Government under Margaret Thatcher in 1979 marked a new era for the civil service. In addition to being committed to radical reform of the public sector she displayed a virulent anti-civil service attitude (Theakston, 1995). She took control of the reform agenda, actively exercised her role as ministerial head of the civil service and provided political clout. Her aim was to reduce the size of the civil service, change its role and managerialize it. The initial assault involved imposing cuts on staffing and expenditure, introducing the financial management initiative (FMI), abolishing the Pay Review Body; facing down the first major civil service strike in 1981; abolishing the CSD and engineering the early retirement of Ian Bancroft, the Head of the Civil Service (Horton and Farnham, 1993, 1996).

A transformation of the civil service unfolded over the 18 years of Conservative governments. There are many accounts of the details (Fry, 1984; Drewry and Butcher, 1988; Metcalfe and Richards, 1990; Horton and Farnham, 1999) but the essential features were the transformation from a system of public administration, with its emphasis on procedures and rules, equity and fairness, mistake avoidance and careful stewardship of public money, to public management with its emphasis on the economic and efficient use of resources to achieve policy outputs. Private business was the model for public management and private business practices, including accountable management, performance management, output budgeting and accrual accounting, were adopted. Where the private sector was cheaper, departments had to contract out.

Between 1979 and 1997 the civil service fell by nearly 40 per cent. Over 150 agencies were created and nearly 80 per cent of civil servants were working in them. The composition of the service had changed as new systems of recruitment were introduced and many posts were openly advertised. Twenty per cent of top posts were filled with people recruited from outside the service. All personnel management responsibilities were devolved to agencies and departments and only the Senior Civil Service of some 3000 posts remained a unified and uniform system.

The response of the civil service to these changes was generally pragmatic. The higher civil servants sought to influence those policies, which threatened their interests but implemented the policies of the government as directed. They continued to defend the traditional principles of the PSE (Butler, 1993; Efficiency Unit, 1993) and the government's consultative white paper *Continuity and Change* (1994) was seen as a victory for the Office of Public Service (successor to the CSD) and top officials in defending their position as mandarins and averting some of the government's more radical proposals for reform (Massey, 1995). Once again there was a commitment to 'sustaining the key principles on which the British civil service is based – integrity, political impartiality, objectivity, selection and promotion on merit and accountability through ministers to parliament' (ibid.: 1).

Not only was the civil service under siege from the government but also its legitimacy was being severely challenged as a result of a series of scandals especially the Arms to Iraq Scandal in 1992. The Scott Inquiry (1996) revealed deceit and hypocrisy by both ministers and high-ranking civil servants (Barker, 1997) and it triggered several responses from Parliament in the form of reports from its various committees including *The Proper Conduct of Public Business* (Public Accounts Committee, 1994), *The Role of the Civil Service* (HC Treasury and Civil Service Committee, 1994) and *Standards in Public Life* (Nolan Committee, 1995). The latter recommended a Civil Service Code of Ethics, in order to preserve the traditional core values of the civil service. The Government responded in a further white paper *Taking Forward Continuity and Change* (1995) by reiterating its commitment to a permanent civil service based on traditional values and accountable through ministers to Parliament. It proposed a Civil Service Code and extended the powers of the CSC to ensure unbiased recruitment.

During the 18 years of Conservative governments there were clearly a number of challenges to the PSE. First there was the impact of agencification, which fragmented the former unified service. Agencification also opened the door to outside recruitment and to limited contracts for senior officials. This resulted in a less permanent Civil Service, as outsiders entered for short periods and 'career' civil servants began to manage their own careers as they increasingly moved in and out of the service (Coxall and Robins, 1998).

The second challenge came with the restriction of their policy role. From the 1980s senior civil servants had to create a *modus vivendi* between their policy role, which consisted increasingly of a gatekeeper function (Campbell and Wilson, 1995) and a managerial role (Theakston, 1995; Barberis, 1998). The use by ministers of policy advisers and their reliance upon external think tanks curtailed the role of senior civil servants as the main source of policy advice.

A third challenge was the introduction of market values into the civil service (Stewart and Clarke, 1987; Butcher, 1997; Bevir and Rhodes, 2003). Efficiency and quality have become the criteria of evaluation of 'good government' and are equated with performance targets and cost savings rather than equity, fairness, procedure and political sensitivity, the traditional criteria associated with public administration.

A fourth challenge has arisen from the greater openness and transparency in the service, which has resulted in civil servants losing their anonymity. Open government and greater transparency has removed much of the secrecy previously associated with the civil service and people now have rights to information and civil servants can be challenged in parliamentary committees, committees of inquiry and the media. This increase in personal responsibility of civil servants has weakened the shield of ministerial responsibility, although that protection was wearing thin before 1979.

A fifth challenge has been to the unquestioned loyalty to politicians. This has altered in part because of soured relationships between civil servants and their ministers (Coxall and Robins, 1998) and the politicization of the service. During the Thatcher governments there were a series of whistle-blowing or leaking incidents, demonstrating how difficult the relationship between civil servants and the government had become and reflecting in part a clash of cultures or a fracture of the psychological contract. The Ponting affair (Ponting, 1985) was only one of several incidents questioning the loyalty of civil servants to their political masters (Chapman, 1993; Theakston, 1995) or to the public interest.

Although the election of the first Thatcher government was a key event, the implementation of the FMI in 1982 could not capitalize on a critical juncture able to disrupt the positive feedback mechanisms that were in place within the civil service. The Treasury was still in a position to impose controls on managers implementing the FMI. Therefore, an increased focus on the management role and the promotion of management values was at first obtained by the process of 'layering' or Hall's second order change. Although managerial efficiency became an additional value, FMI did not disrupt the power mechanism or challenge the existing PSE.

The Next Steps Initiative and the creation of agencies did, however, challenge and change the existing PSE as it promoted markets and economic liberalism and an even stronger focus on management values. The third consecutive Conservative electoral victory in 1987 provided the Thatcher government with enough power to start this new initiative. Not only did the government's power increase but also internal opposition was weakened. The Treasury could no longer impose detailed controls, as it was itself subjected to the reform although it maintained some influence over financial targets. In addition to a shift in the balance of power mechanism, the PSE legitimacy mechanism was becoming more and more out of tune with the prevailing values in society.

The Citizen's Charter (1991) and Major's Market Testing agenda continued the marketization assault but the new Prime Minister's position was relatively weak within an increasingly divided cabinet. The accusations of sleaze and political corruption actually strengthened the position of the civil service, slightly redressing the power balance again. This period was characterized by more continuity than change or punctuated equilibria, diminishing even further the capacity to disrupt the PSE.


## THE MODERNIZED CIVIL SERVICE

In 1997, New Labour came to power. It promised a 'Third Way' of governing between the economic liberalism of the Conservatives and the state socialism of Old Labour (Mandelson and Liddle, 1997; Giddens, 1998). Whilst not rejecting the managerial reforms of the Conservative governments its focus was on better government through creating joined-up government (Richards and Smith, 2004). The *Modernising Government* (1999) white paper set out a programme of radical reform of the senior civil service whilst at the same time acknowledging the importance of the service to the achievement of government policy. Many reforms have taken place since 1997, which appear to be continuing many of the initiatives of the previous Conservative administrations.

Although Labour was committed to valuing the public sector generally, and the civil service in particular, demands for strengthening and safeguarding the traditional values of the civil service and formally institutionalizing them in a Civil Service Act did not abate after the election. The House of Lords Public Service Committee (1998) emphasized the importance and the vulnerability of the traditional PSE. In 1999 the Cabinet Office finally issued the long awaited Civil Service Code but parliament and the civil service unions were demanding a Civil Service Act (HC Public Administration Select Committee, 2002). The Labour Government eventually succumbed and took the unusual step of introducing a bill for consultation in 2004 (CM 6373, 2004). The bill fell when the government resigned in 2005 and the new Labour government elected in May 2005 has not so far reintroduced it.

In the period since 1997, the PSE has undergone two changes. First, there has been a further loss of a policy role for the SCS and their role is now primarily a managerial one. Whenever strategic decisions are made, special advisers from outside the civil service are the main source of policy-advice (Richards and Smith, 2004). Second, traditional civil service values and the PSE have become more prominent again. Both during the final years of the Major government and the first two terms under Blair there was an increased focus on ethical behaviour of civil servants and on the values of impartiality, accountability, trust, equity, probity and service. They are still at the core of the British civil service in spite of the many changes in its structure, composition and activities that have occurred over the last 50 years.

Taking civil servants out of the policy loop began in earnest in 1979 and since 1997 Labour governments have continued the trend and accelerated the process. With three consecutive landslide victories and adopting an increasingly presidential style of government Blair, like Thatcher gained control of the policy process and disrupted the power balance between ministers and their senior civil servants even more than under the Conservatives.

The resurgence of debates about civil service values and PSE, fuelled by the Nolan and Scott reports, however, led Labour to publicly commit to 'value the civil service, not denigrate it' (Cm 4310, 1999: 13). Incrementally, Labour has had to concede a Civil Service Code and a Civil Service Bill. Public and parliamentary pressure and the resilience of the SCS have actually strengthened the legitimacy of the PSE although this has not prevented its continual evolution.

## CONCLUSION

Our first aim was to examine the emergence and evolution of the PSE. Emerging alongside the modern civil service the PSE gradually took form as the values and behaviours required of permanent career civil servants, loyal to the government of the day and exercising a variety of functions as the state grew and took on a more interventionist role, became clear. By 1920 those characteristics of the British constitutional bureaucracy were institutionalized.

Our second aim was to examine the process of continuity and change in the PSE since its institutionalization. Throughout its history, PSE has evolved to accommodate new values in response to the situational context (Keynesian thinking in the 1940s; market values in the 1980s and 1990s). Similarly, values have been removed from PSE as they ceased to fit the context at the time (dominance of the generalists in the 1970s; closed systems of recruitment in the 1980s, secrecy in the 1980s and dominant policy role in the 1990s). However, the essential values of the Northcote–Trevelyan/Haldane–Fisher philosophy are still part of the core PSE: selection and promotion on merit, political impartiality and accountability through ministerial responsibility, integrity, objectivity and service to the public.

Although the higher civil service was the locus of the PSE as it came to reflect the values associated with the elite social and educational backgrounds of its members it gradually cascaded down and was disseminated throughout the growing lower levels. Public service motivation was never as strong in the lower classes, where large numbers of women were employed, but it was clearly in evidence throughout the period from 1920 to the 1960s. Amongst the Treasury classes there was also a strong sense of being part of a unified service as mobility was a condition of membership of the executive and administrative classes However, in the 1980s, agencification disturbed this homogeneity as more and more of the service was fragmented. Nowadays it is not clear to whom the ethos applies, as there are many types of public servants and the boundaries of the civil service have become blurred because of partnerships and contractorization. But with the prospect of a Civil Service Act, this problem may recede and the PSE may become formally institutionalized

Our third aim referred to the value of historical institutionalism as a framework for explaining institutional change. Looking back on the analysis, we can state that the persistence and disruption of positive feedback mechanisms are able to explain a great deal of institutional change. In particular functional, power and legitimation mechanisms proved to be important in pinpointing causal relationships. On the one hand, critical junctures, such as wars (Crimea, Boer, First and Second World Wars) and electoral victories (Liberal 1905, Labour 1945, Conservative 1979) disrupted these mechanisms causing path dependent change. On the other hand, these feedback mechanisms also proved to be responsible for preserving institutional arrangements (interwar period, 1945–79) whilst the concept of layering and Hall's first and second order change explain the process of adding roles, functions and values without disrupting the general structure and content of the organization and its culture.

When applying this theoretical framework, however, we observed that the utilitarian mechanism was never able to disrupt other positive feedback mechanisms, while conversely the power mechanism explains many of the changes. This might be due to the fact that the civil service and PSE are sub-systems of a larger political system. It can, therefore, be argued that in such sub-systems political power prevails over utilitarian motives as the prevailing causal mechanism. Because our research is only based on a single case study, further research is required to test these conclusions.

Historical institutionalism has its limitations. It cannot explain why some changes fail in implementation, why some take longer to achieve than others and why termination of policies is so rare. Further, it cannot explain the process of internally generated cultural change. Nevertheless, it is a useful tool and draws attention to the importance of historical choices in creating boundaries, which constrain subsequent choices and perpetuate power structures, identities and cultures or paradigms that are difficult to overthrow.

# REFERENCES

Balogh, Thomas (1959), *Apotheosis of the Dilettante: The Establishment of Mandarins*, London: Ace Books.

Barberis, Peter (1998), 'The changing role of senior civil servants since 1979', in Michael, Hunt and B.J. O'Toole (eds), *Reform, Ethics and Leadership in Public Service – a Festschrift in Honour of Richard A. Chapman*, Aldershot: Ashgate, pp. 123–41.

Barker, Anthony (1997), 'Practicing to deceive: Whitehall, arms export and the Scott inquiry', *Political Quarterly*, **68**(1), 41–9.

Bevir, Mark and R.A.W. Rhodes (2003), *Interpreting British Governance*, London: Routledge.

Brown, R.G.S. (1970), *The Administrative Process in Britain*, London: Methuen.

Butcher, Tony (1997), 'The citizen's charter: creating a customer-orientated civil service', in P. Barberis (ed.), *The Civil Service in an Era of Change*, Aldershot: Dartmouth, pp. 55–68.

Butler, Robin (1993), 'The evolution of a civil service – a progress report', *Public Administration*, **71**(3), 395–406.

Campbell, Colin and Graham K. Wilson (1995), *The End of Whitehall: Death of a Paradigm*, Oxford: Blackwell.

Chapman, Brian (1963), *British Government Observed*, London: Allen and Unwin.

Chapman, Richard A. (1993), 'Reasons of state and the public interest: a British version of the problem of dirty hands', in R.A. Chapman (ed.), *Ethics in Public Service*, Edinburgh: Edinburgh University Press, pp. 93–110.

Chapman, Richard A. (1997), 'The end of the British civil service ', in P. Barberis (ed.), *The Civil Service in an Era of Change*, Aldershot: Dartmouth, pp. 23–37.

Chester, D.N. and F.M.G. Willson (1968), *The Organization of British Central Government*, London: Allen and Unwin.

CM 2627 (1994), *The Civil Service: Continuity and Change*, London: HMSO.

CM 2748 (1995), *Taking Forward Continuity and Change*, London: HMSO.

CM 4310 (1999), *Modernising Government*, London: The Stationery Office.

CM 6373 (2004), *Civil Service Bill*, London: The Stationery Office.

Cortell, Andrew P. and Susan Peterson (1999), 'Altered states: explaining domestic institutional change', *British Journal of Political Science*, **29**(1), 177–203.

Coxall, Bill and Lynton Robins (1998), *Contemporary British Politics*, Basingstoke: Palgrave.

Drewry, Cavin and Tony Butcher (1988), *The Civil Service Today*, Oxford: Blackwell.

Efficiency Unit (1993), *Career Management and Succession Planning*, London: HMSO.

Fabian Society (1964), *The Administrators*, London: Fabian Society.

Farnham, David and Sylvia Horton (1996), *Managing People in the Public Services*, London: Macmillan.

Fry, Geoffry (1969), *Statesmen in Disguise: The Changing Role of the Administrative Class of the Home Civil Service 1853–1966*, London: Macmillan.

Fry, Geoffry (1984), 'The development of the Thatcher government's "grand strategy" for the civil service: a public policy perspective', *Public Administration*, **62**(3), 322–35.

Fulton, Lord (1968), *Report of the Committee on the Civil Service*, London: HMSO.

Giddens, Anthony (1998), *The Third Way: The Renewal of Social Democracy*, Cambridge: Polity Press.

Greenaway, John (1995), 'Having the bun and the halfpenny: can old public service ethics survive in the new Whitehall?', *Public Administration*, **73**(3), 357–74.

Haldane, Lord (1918), *Report of the Machinery of Government Committee*, London: HMSO.

Haldane, Lord (1923), 'An organised civil service', *Journal of Public Administration*, **1**.

Hall, Peter A. (1993), 'Policy paradigms, social learning, and the state. The case of economic policymaking in Britain', *Comparative Politics*, **25**(3), 275–96.

Hall, Peter A. and Rosemary C.R. Taylor (1996), 'Political science and the three new institutionalisms', *Political Studies*, **44**(4), 936–57.

Harcourt-Smith, Sir (1920), *Opening Address: The Civil Servant and his Profession*, London: Pitman.

HC Public Administration Select Committee (2002), *The Public Service Ethos HC 263-I*, London: House of Commons.

HC Treasury and Civil Service Committee (1994), *The Role of the Civil Service*, London: HMSO.

Helms, Ludger (2000), *Institutions and Institutional Change in the Federal Republic of Germany*, Basingstoke: Macmillan.

Hennessy, Peter (1989), *Whitehall*, London: Fontana Press.

HL Public Service Committee (1998), *Report*, London: House of Lords.

Horton, Sylvia (1996), 'The Civil Service', in D. Farnham and S. Horton (eds), *Managing the New Public Services*, 2nd revised edn, Basingstoke: Macmillan, pp. 155–76.

Horton, Sylvia and D. Farnham (1993), 'The Civil Service', in D. Farnham and S. Horton (eds), *Managing the New Public Services*, Basingstoke: Macmillan, pp. 127–49.

Horton, Sylvia and David Farnham (1999), *Public Management in Britain*, Basingstoke: Palgrave.

Kellner, Peter and Crowter-Hunt, Lord (1980), *The Civil Servants: An Enquiry into Britain's Ruling Class*, London: Macdonald.

Mackenzie, W.J.M. (1957), 'The structure of central administration', in Chester D.N. Campion, W.J.M. Mackenzie, W.A. Robson and A.W.J.H. Street (eds), *British Government since 1918*, London: Allen and Unwin, pp. 56–84.

Mahoney, James (2000), 'Path dependence in historical sociology', *Theory and Society*, **29**(4), 507–48.

Mandelson, Peter and Roger Liddle (1997), *The Blair Revolution: can Blair Deliver?*, London: Faber and Faber.

Marsh, David, David Richards and Martin J. Smith (2001), *Changing Patterns of Governance in the United Kingdom – Reinventing Whitehall*, Basingstoke: Palgrave.

Massey, Andrew (1995), *After Next Steps*, London: Cabinet Office.

Metcalfe, Les and Sue Richards (1990), *Improving Public Management*, London: Sage.

Miles, Matthew B. and Michael A. Huberman (1994), *Qualitative Data Analysis*, Thousand Oaks, CA: Sage.

Nolan Committee (1995), *Standards in Public Life – First Report of the Committee on Standards in Public Life*, London: HMSO.

Northcote, Stafford and Charles Trevelyan (1854), *The Organisation of the Permanent Civil Service*, Parliamentary Papers, Volume XXVII.

O'Toole, Barry J. (1997), 'The concept of public duty', in P. Barberis (ed.), *The Civil Service in an Era of Change*, Aldershot: Dartmouth, pp. 82–94.

O'Toole, Barry J. (2000), 'The public interest: a political and administrative convenience?', in R.A. Chapman (ed.), *Ethics in Public Service for the New Millennium*, Aldershot: Ashgate, pp. 71–91.

Parris, Henry (1969), *Constitutional Bureaucracy*, London: Allen and Unwin.

Peters, B.G. (2000), *Institutional Theory in Political Science: The New Institutionalism*, London: Continuum.

Pierson, Paul (2000), 'Increasing returns, path dependence, and the study of politics', *American Political Science Review*, **94**(2), 251–67.

Pilkington, Colin (1999), *The Civil Service in Britain Today*, Manchester: Manchester University Press.

Plowden, Lord (1961), *Public Expenditure Planning and Control*, London: HMSO.

Ponting, Clive (1985), *The Right to Know: The Inside Story of the Belgrano Affair*, London: Sphere Books.

Public Accounts Committee (1994), *The Proper Conduct of Public Business*, London: HMSO.

Reeves, Richard (2004), 'Don't sell the NHS like shampoo', *New Statesman*, **133**(4695), 24–6.

Richards, David and Martin J. Smith (2004), 'The hybrid state: Labour's response to the challenge of government', in S. Ludlam and M.J. Smith (eds), *Governing as New Labour – Policy and Politics Under Blair*, Basingstoke: Palgrave.

Roseveare, Henry (1969), *The Treasury: The Evolution of a British Institution*, London: Allen Lane.

Rueschemeyer, Dietrich (2003), 'Can one or a few cases yield theoretical gains?', in J. Mahoney and D. Rueschemeyer (eds), *Comparative Historical Analysis in the Social Sciences*, Cambridge: Cambridge University Press, pp. 305–36.

Scott, Sir Richard (1996), *Arms to Iraq Inquiry*, London: The Stationery Office.

Scott, W.R. (2001), *Institutions and Organizations*, Thousand Oaks, CA: Sage.

Stewart, John and Michael Clarke (1987), 'The public service orientation: issues and dilemma's', *Public Administration*, **65**(2), 161–77.

Theakston, Kevin (1995), *The Civil Service Since 1945*, Oxford: Blackwell.

Thelen, Kathleen (2003), 'How institutions evolve: insights from comparative historical analysis', in J. Mahoney and D. Rueschemeyer (eds), *Comparative Historical Analysis in the Social Sciences*, Cambridge: Cambridge University Press, pp. 208–40.

White, Leonard D. (1933), *Whitley Councils in the British Civil Service*, Chicago, IL: Chicago University Press.

Woodhouse, Diana (1997), *In Pursuit of Good Administration – Ministers, Civil Servants and Judges*, Oxford: Clarendon Press.

Yin, Robert K. (1981), 'The case study crisis: some answers', *Administrative Science Quarterly*, **26**(1), 58–65.

Yin, Robert K. (1994), *Case Study Research – Design and Methods*, Thousand Oaks, CA: Sage.

# 3.   A revolution in organizational values: change and recalibration

## Carole L. Jurkiewicz and Robert A. Giacalone

## INTRODUCTION

Inarguably, societal changes over the past 30 years have made the practice of public administration in the twenty-first century dramatically different from what it was in the past (Drucker, 1995). Reacting to and, in fewer instances, preparing for the rapid shifts in technology and globalization, coupled with the political instability challenging leaders and alliances throughout the world has forced upon the public sector a culture that must monitor change as a fact of existence. This monumental shift in traditional bureaucratic orientation has led to numerous changes in the methods and measurements by which we aspire toward the public good, many-well documented in the literature as deriving from specific tangible requirements, such as budgets, transportation and administrative processes. Yet a near invisible and certainly heretofore unarticulated challenge to traditional practices may, it can be debated, have had an even more powerful influence in shifting the practice and promise of public administration and is increasingly worthy of both attention and accommodation.

Dramatic and wide-ranging values shifts have measurably and progressively coalesced among industrialized countries since World War II (Inglehart, 1997), leading some to conclude that we are witnessing a global change in worldview (see Ray, 1996; Ray and Rinzler, 1993) and, concomitantly, the expectations of the citizenry as well as those in the public employ. Empirical evidence indicates that these values are gradually becoming predominant among postindustrial societies and being echoed in developing nations (Abramson and Inglehart, 1992; Inglehart and Abramson, 1994). Inevitably, changing expectations based on these values shifts are having an impact on individual decision making (Conger, 1997) and behavior (Hopkins and Prescott, 1983; Rokeach, 1972) in political, social and institutional settings across the globe (Inglehart, 1999). The label given here to this potent constellation of shifting individual and social stakeholder values (Ray and Anderson, 2000) is expansive values. In comparison to traditional values, which focus on quantifiable, materialistic goals and short-term outcomes, expansive values refer to a constellation of values that transcend materialism and self-interests, focus on the generative and community impact of one's actions, and accentuate the importance of individual self-determination. While expansive values may appear as morally seditious to those individuals and organizations whose stake in power is rooted in the traditional values set, evidence of this more beneficent ethic is welcome news to many.

There is evidentiary confirmation that expansive values are creating new ethical expectations to the extent that they warrant organizational reassessments of ethical standards (Giacalone and Eylon, 2000; McLarney and Chung, 1999), with resultant administrative changes (Hammer and Champy, 1993). As expansive values garner more widespread adherents (Inglehart, 1997), they are creating new social constructions (Eisenstadt, 1990) to define appropriate organizational missions, standards and activities. As the 'context of accountability' redefines accountability procedures and legitimates a broader array of decision-makers and outcomes (McLarney and Chung, 1999), organizations would do well to proactively determine the necessary changes in organizational structures, policies and processes (Daft, 1998; Shenkar *et al.*, 1995) that address and demonstrate an understanding of the ethical issues these expansive values pose (Drucker, 1995). A failure to address these changes in ethical expectations can disadvantage organizations, making their leaders appear avaricious (Hirschman, 1990: 40) and lead the media and the citizenry to question the quality and method of service delivery, integrity of administrative processes, and affect the efficiency and effectiveness of their employees (Quinn, 2000; Thompson, 2000).

But a dearth of theory and research in the organizational sciences demonstrates that management neither recognizes nor understands the far reaching implications of these societal shifts (Abramson and Inglehart, 1992) that other disciplines have wrestled with for more than 30 years (for example Inglehart, 1997). The intention here is to identify how expansive values changes impact the ethical principles and practices enacted in organizations. First, using literature from three different research domains, the content of expansive values will be synthesized and delineated and possible changes in ethical expectations will be outlined. Second, the challenges organizations face in adjusting their ethical standards to these expansive values will be discussed. Finally, recommendations for designing research aimed at determining how scholars might better understand the ethical quandaries in organizations facing expansive values change will be offered.

# THE THREE FOUNDATIONS OF EXPANSIVE VALUES

The content of expansive values is understood through theory and research in three distinct research literatures: political science research on postmaterialism (for example Inglehart, 1997), demographic profiling on integral culture (for example Ray, 1996), and the interdisciplinary literature on changing scientific, social, and organizational paradigms known as new paradigm thought (for example Ray and Rinzler, 1993; Giacalone and Eylon, 2000). Although developed within different intellectual disciplines and traditions, they delineate expansive values and point us toward changes in society's ethical expectations for public sector organizations.

The most consistent explication of expansive values can be found in Inglehart's international values work (1997) at the Institute for Social Research. Inglehart has identified and substantiated shifting individual preferences for postmaterialist values globally. Though often misunderstood, postmaterialism is neither non-materialism nor anti-materialism (Inglehart, 1997: 35), but is instead a value set characterized by an increased emphasis on non-financial, humanistic outcomes for both self and society.

Identification of the postmaterialist trend is based on data covering 70 percent of the world's population, comprised of societies in both industrially developed and developing democracies and non-democratic states (Abramson and Inglehart, 1992; Inglehart, 1997), and with national mean incomes ranging from $300 to $30 000 per year (Inglehart, 1997). The first postmaterialist assessment (1970–1) found that materialists outnumbered postmaterialists four to one, though by 1990, the ratio had shifted to four to three (Inglehart, 1997: 35); essentially, during the period 1972–92, the percentage of postmaterialists doubled (Abramson and Inglehart, 1992). Despite the usual controversies and significant challenges that an emergent trend elicits, models of this values shift projects nearly equal numbers of materialists and postmaterialists in the following decade (Abramson and Inglehart, 1992).

A second literature defining expansive values mirrors postmaterialist data. While Inglehart's work identifies expansive values primarily as social values, the work of Ray (1996) indicates these are personal values changes as well. Using a demographic approach, Ray (1996) found a value structure that he labels 'cultural creatives'. This values group, found in all regions of the United States (but not assessed in other nations) comprises about 24 percent of the adult population, or about 44 million people. Much as the core values of postmaterialism are humanistic social values preferences, cultural creatives share the same values preferences but do so at the intrapersonal and interpersonal level as well, suggesting a deeper integration of professional/personal values among this sample.

New paradigm thought provides a third defining literature. Unlike post-materialist and cultural creative research, new paradigm thought defines the values changes across disciplines, using theory and research in religion (Fox, 1994; Hawley, 1993), biology (Sheldrake, 1981; Sheldrake, 1988), psychology (Frankl, 1962; Valle, 1989), ecological studies (Hawken, 1994), futurism (Henderson, 1991), physics (Wheatley, 1992) and systems theory (Capra, 1993). While adhering to the same humanistic postmaterialist and cultural creative stances, new paradigm thinkers explicitly affirm what is tacit in both postmaterialist and cultural creative values: values that are predicated on individual, societal, and global interconnectedness and interdependence. As such, expansive values are motivated by benevolent humanitarian motives, and a sense of pragmatic mutuality which transcends self-interest and materialism.

## THE CONSEQUENCES OF EXPANSIVE VALUES CHANGE

Changes consistent with expansive values have been demonstrated at different levels. At a societal level, the social movements that brought about increased ecological sensitivity, corporate social responsibility and concern for ethical decision making (for example Hess *et al.*, 2002) surfaced during the expansive values growth period and are consistent with it (Ray, 1996; Inglehart, 1997). At the individual level, growing concern with non-financial aspects of the workplace have employees leaving high paying, pressure-laden jobs for lower-paying, more fulfilling positions, particularly those found in the nonprofit and public sectors, creating what some have labeled a downshifting phenomenon (Cherrier and Murray, 2002). Among those who remain with a proprietary organization, there is a greater emphasis on quality of life, family-work balance, and childcare (Emde, 1998).

From the standpoint of ethics, the adoption of expansive values has changed both what is viewed as ethical issues as well as the moral essentiality (Jones, 1991) of the issues themselves. In much the same way that new ethical concerns emerged over the treatment of factory workers and child laborers at the turn of the nineteenth century, current concerns regarding environmental preservation, the ethical treatment of animals, sustainable logging and living wages across the globe are examples where formerly acceptable behaviors, thought to be fair and humanitarian if given consideration at all, are increasingly viewed as irresponsible and unethical. It is believed this is just the beginning of an increasingly accelerated movement in this direction directly attributable to growth of the expansive values set.

Changing values also make existing ethical issues salient; concerns that had heretofore been given cursory attention are seen as more important; particular ethical issues are more questionable than was first believed. These concerns include availability of healthcare and medicines to all in need, gender equality, same sex partner rights, protection against genocide, proliferation of nuclear weapons and global access to adequate food, water and education. Both Ray (1996) and Inglehart (1997) concur that these values are gaining increasing social consensus, which in turn is stimulating new responses to ethical concerns. Using Jones's (1991) synthesized model of ethical decision making as a guide, the growing social consensus around expansive values facilitates discussion of, and sensitization toward, the globalization of ethical issues whose impact was heretofore considered situational or episodic. It is a pattern echoed in media efforts to analyse, examine, probe and question administrators and that the current US government and less developed non-democratic administrations are trying to quash. The expansive values drive is framing the appropriateness of ethical decision-making, clarifying moral intent, and buttressing values priorities. The result is an increasing likelihood that ethical concerns will be voiced and that decisions consistent with these values will be made. Thus:

*Proposition 1    The global increase in expansive values will require organizations to recalibrate their ethical standards to meet shifting ethical expectations.*

## THE CONTENT AND ETHICAL RAMIFICATIONS OF EXPANSIVE VALUES CHANGE

The three literatures noted here further help us delineate expansive values into three core values classifications driving the change: self-oriented core values (general individual values, values regarding individual voice, individual outcome variables); other-oriented outcome core values; and social outcome core values.

### Self-Oriented Core Values

Self-oriented core values focus on individual values lifestyle outcome preferences. These can be divided into three sub-categories: general individual values, individual voice values and individual outcome values.

**General individual values**

The essence of expansive values lie in the individual's transcendent values of spirituality (Giacalone and Jurkiewicz, 2003) self-actualization (for example Ray, 1996), and idealism (see Ray, 1996; Ray and Anderson, 2000). For expansive values adherents, the ethics of a decision are defined in assessments that go beyond financial concerns and short time foci. Expansive values adherents gauge the desirability of an action based on its long-term systemic consequences for all stakeholders (Ray and Rinzler, 1994). Essentially, the framework which judges temporal immediacy (Jones, 1991) is enlarged. That is, while most discount the impacts of the longer-term consequences of an act, emerging values adherents take into account the consequences of an act within a longer time period. Thus:

*Proposition 2     In contrast to those holding traditional values, expansive values adherents will gauge the ethical propriety of a decision or outcome on long-term and non-financial ramifications for stakeholders.*

Those adhering to expansive values are relatively less affected by external forces designed to control their ethical judgment through persuasion and manipulation (for example Lutz, 1989). Indeed, they are reticent to focus disproportionately on social constructions of what is right or important and instead value and nurture internal (versus external) rewards (Block, 1993), and assess their behaviors and success via a process of self- (versus comparative) valuing (Ferguson, 1993). Because expansive values adherents see themselves apart from the mainstream (Ray, 1996), they are less likely to take into account information that the general public believes to be appropriate behavior or respond favorably to attempts by organizations to spin-doctor ethically questionable behavior as more acceptable (Payne and Giacalone, 1990). Thus:

*Proposition 3     Expansive values adherents' responses to the ethical issues surrounding organizational decisions will be based more on their own values and less on social consensus or manipulative social constructions.*

**Individual voice values**

Over the past three decades, what has characterized expansive values adherents is an increasing desire for greater voice in both personal and social decisions (Inglehart, 1997; Ray and Anderson, 2001). While many point to the fall of communism and the newfound motivation for self-expression and freedom, the increasing value of personal voice has increased globally, and most dramatically in industrialized economies (Inglehart, 1997).

Progressively more of the world's population is expecting and demanding greater involvement in decisions that impact their lives, leading to new political parties, new social movements (Ray and Anderson, 2000: 217), lobbying, and the formation of non-governmental organizations targeting questionable business practices (Goeksen *et al.*, 2002). The value placed on voice is paralleled by increased valuation of personal freedom (Inglehart and Abramson, 1994), resulting in more freedom-focused movements (Ray and Anderson, 2000: 112–25).

But the value of personal voice is about more than 'big picture' freedom and environmentalism issues. For many, voice demonstrates one's authenticity as a human being (Ray and Anderson, 2000: 8). Expansive values adherents have a strong proclivity to express who they are, both to demonstrate their values (Ray, 1996), and to live their lives with meaning (Inglehart, 1997). At work, the values of personal voice manifest as an increasing desire for involvement in both self-relevant and socially relevant issues. Thus:

*Proposition 4    The increasing concern for voice among expansive values adherents creates an ethical expectation for organizations to encourage and foster increased participation and to respond to the issues raised.*

### Individual outcome values

Expansive values adherents' unwillingness to accept socially endorsed values on which there is social consensus (Ray, 1996) is particularly acute in the case of positive, individual materialistic outcomes. While expansive values do not dismiss positive, individualistic outcomes, their primary strivings are not materialistic (Ray and Anderson, 2000).

Socially sanctioned outcomes are not valued by expansive values adherents unless they are consistent with their life values and personal (generally less financially defined) goals (Ferguson, 1993). They find socially prized materialistic values unsatisfactory, and are not 'consumption friendly'. Their values warrant a balancing of materialistic and economic, quality of work life, and social responsibility concerns (DeFoore and Renesch, 1995; Inglehart, 1997; Ray, 1996). They are willing to trade money for quality of life, (as witnessed by the downshifting phenomenon), and spend money for causes that are altruistic and community-focused. An ethically desirable outcome, therefore, does not have as strong a financial component (for example stockholder rights) as would those holding more traditional materialistic values. Thus:

*Proposition 5a    Expansive values adherents will make ethical decisions based less on materialistic values and more on quality of life impact and non-economic social responsibility concerns.*

*Proposition 5b    Expansive values adherents will weigh the ethical appropriateness of a decision more heavily on non-economic factors.*

## OTHER-OUTCOME VALUES

The demarcation of self and others is less clear for expansive values adherents, largely because they see a natural, recursive relationship between self and other outcomes. As a result, they construe personal outcomes and the outcomes of others as interconnected and have salient expectations for the welfare of others. Expectations for good childcare, for example, result from a keen sense of how poor childcare impacts families, community and overall well-being, regardless of their personal circumstances.

Expansive values adherents value and work for positive outcomes for others, using their values to bring these about. They believe that their decisions and those of others must be founded on a procedural assumption: mutually beneficial goals can be achieved through supportive rather than manipulative relationships (Greenleaf, 1977). They bring about outcomes by engaging in cooperate (rather than competitive) relationships and expect that the preferred ethical outcome is one which is founded on a win/win (versus win/lose) system (Maynard and Mehrtens, 1993). As a result, they expect leaders to hold values that promote inclusive processes for decision making, to shift from autocratic to inspirational and servant-centered approaches (Block, 1993; Greenleaf, 1977). Thus:

*Proposition 6a    Expansive values adherents will judge an action as ethical when a positive decision or outcome for internal and external stakeholders is achieved through cooperative means and the possibility of win-win outcomes.*

*Proposition 6b    Expansive values adherents will evaluate a leader's integrity based on the leader's ability to bring about expansive values-based outcomes through cooperative means that maximize win-win outcomes.*

## SOCIAL OUTCOME VALUES

Concern for others is also manifested in macro-level concerns for societal outcomes. Success is simultaneously defined by personal and social expansive values-based outcomes that are inclusive and focus on common needs (Eisler, 1987). In contrast to individualistically and materialistically driven values, expansive values are less concerned with outcomes which achieve individualist/materialist gains and more concerned with group/values oriented gains (Capra *et al.*, 1991; Fox, 1994). For expansive values adherents, ethical decisions are characterized by generativity: a balance of individual and community needs (Gozdz, 1995) across generations (Fox, 1994).

### Responding to Expansive Values: The Challenging Road to Recalibrating Standards

Because changing values are preconditions for behavioral changes and social action, the increase in expansive values adherents is transforming political, social and economic life (Inglehart, 1997), consumer choices and shifts (Ray, 1996), expectations of what individuals want from their lives (see Ray and Rinzler, 1993), medical choice (Ray, 1996,) family lifestyle (Inglehart, 1997; Ray, 1996), and has altered the cultural composition of our world (see Inglehart, 1997).

Despite downward shifts in economic prosperity, the increase in expansive values adherents has shown no substantive reversal (see Inglehart, 1997). Given their growth, organizations would be remiss to ignore the changing ethical expectations they bring. The growing concern with unethical administrative practices has taught organizations that if they ignore stakeholder values, they will be saddled with damaged reputations and widespread and entrenched distrust. These core expansive values, in turn, are changing perceptions and expectations that require organizations to begin recalibrating their ethical standards to align with these changes.

As changes in education and growing economic development result in increased attention toward non-economic goals values, expansive values became and continue to become more important than economic goals and values (Inglehart, 1997). As more and more citizens shifted priorities, aggregate social values were reapportioned, focusing away from economic goals and values toward expansive goals and values. This reapportionment of values priorities created a shift in both what is important and what actions are ethically acceptable. Within a monetized values structure, the desire to increase wealth takes on a direction that will accept ecological destructiveness and even self-destructive activities (see Kasser and Ryan, 1993). As expansive values are given greater priority, such actions are seen as unacceptable both individually and institutionally (Ray and Anderson, 2000), thereby creating new expectations for organizations.

## THE CHALLENGE OF ETHICAL RECALIBRATION

The nature and scope of the values shifts necessitate more than a simple, piecemeal response; it requires ethical recalibration: a reassessment of how values priorities can be translated into ethical standards and goals. The concept of recalibration is introduced here as an extension of the expansive values literature. It is predicated on the assertion that the forces driving changes in values-based decisions at a personal and societal level are impacted by two pivotal concerns: the reordering of values priorities and the motivators that drive decisions toward adherence to expansive values.

### Reordering Ethical Decision Making Priorities

Because expansive values adherence does not result in an abandonment of materialist goals, organizations will be challenged to recalibrate toward an integration of the two (Ray, 1996). Although the general 'master values' of economizing (energy seeking to use in production of something valuable to itself) and power-aggrandizing (power seeking) now dominating organizations will remain, the growth of expansive values forces decision makers to enlarge their consideration of moral responsibilities, integrating new ethical concerns into daily considerations.

The relative importance of expansive values (in comparison to more traditional values) is unclear. Some futurist research predicts an inversion of people and financial organizational priorities (see Maynard and Mehrtens, 1993) over the coming century. While such an inversion may appear extreme there is evidence that it has already started: a majority of citizens feel that organizations owe something to both employees and communities, even if it requires organizational sacrifice (Vamos, 1996). As the relative priority of people and financial outcomes shifts, the reordering will change perceived moral responsibilities. Accordingly, behaviors that are seen as irresponsible to an internal or external community (Inglehart, 1997; Gozdz, 1995) are seen as morally questionable by stakeholders at large. The result is that we are seeing a moral expectation that organizations move away from interest in stakeholder groups driven by financial impact estimates alone. For example, relationships between and among employees will create 'quality standards' that are directed at employee quality of life rather than output quality (for example Eisler, 1995). The expectation of improvement, long associated with continuous improvement, takes on a humanistic meaning that resembles what Giacalone and Jurkiewicz (2003) have labeled workplace spirituality.

### Motives in Recalibration

With expansive values becoming more pervasive, ethical recalibration becomes crucial to organizational legitimacy, survival and success. Because a failure to recalibrate to changing stakeholder values could endanger an administration, an organization's motives for recalibration may differ, driven by pragmatic financial or political concerns, authentic alignment with expansive values, or both.

Appropriately, Giacalone and Eylon's (2000) typology provides two continua on which decision-maker motives can be classified for instituting emerging values-driven ethical recalibration: Goals (Profits/Morals) and Mindset (Business/Global). The 'goals continuum' reflects a motivation based on relative priority of financial advancement or moral convictions. At one extreme, recalibration is driven to increased concern for financial or political advancement, while at the other end, it is strictly for ethical reasons. On the 'mindset continuum', the motivation reflects a relative priority to have a positive organizational impact or a positive broad world impact. In crossing these continua, four recalibration motivations emerge. Darwinists, driven by efficiency and concerns for political longevity, are motivated to recalibrate to achieve organizational effectiveness, legitimacy, and survival in response to a growing stakeholder market segment; they remain unattached to the expansive values themselves. Thus, when values shift back and forth (as will be noted later), the Darwinist recalibrates amorally according to projected personal reward.

Pragmatists, also driven by financial and political advancement as well as efficiency, recognize and respect their interconnectedness to other global social and ecological issues, apart from the pressing current financial or political needs for resources and citizen approval. Ethical recalibration is deemed important because expansive values show a demonstrable and discernable impact on the organization in the long term. Expansive values become a 'necessary evil' when specific expansive values warrant new ethical parameters that will bolster favorable output.

Missionaries' motivation for recalibrating is also a function of the return on investment mindset and in so doing, introducing new workplace values with the goal of improving the overall quality of work life, educating others regarding the environmental responsibilities of the organization, and so on. While ROI-focused and outcome-centered, they see organizations as a vehicle to create some greater good. Missionaries recognize that when meaning and purpose is lost, there are negative productivity, social and physical consequences (see Frankl, 1962); recalibration is based in a mindset that makes meaning and purpose paramount for ethical and practical reasons.

Humanitarians' motivations are based on an expansive values-driven desire to improve the larger world context, regardless of borders and distinctions (cultural, national, ethnic, religious and so on) that may separate people (see Maynard and Mehrtens, 1993). They espouse the ethics of a metanoic organization (Fox, 1994), where there is a sense of collective empowerment, vision, and focus on the individual. Humanitarians prefer building a better world than a more financially efficient or political expedient system, which they see as secondary. Futurist researchers predict such expansive values-focused organizations will become the norm in the future (see Maynard and Mehrtens, 1993, for a complete discussion).

Understanding these motives is important, for recalibration motivated by authentic values alignment or pragmatic financial concerns moderates long-term commitment to recalibration (see Ray and Anderson, 2000). Recalibration for values alignment or pragmatic financial concerns may be both instrumental in nature (to achieve the goal of living one's values or protecting the financial or political interest of the administration), but because values alignment is transcendent, there is a greater likelihood that relevant behaviors will not be swayed very much by economic or political fortunes (Inglehart, 1997). Thus:

*Proposition 7    Although expansive values may necessitate ethical recalibration within organizations, the extent to which organizations and their employees do so will be a function of moral, financial, and political motivations.*

## THE PROBLEM OF DISCONTINUITY AND NARROWING CHOICES

But while reordering priorities and motivations are choices in response to expansive values impacting recalibration, some factors are not chosen and make recalibration more difficult.

### Temporal (Pedomorphic) Discontinuity

Recalibrating organizational ethical standards is predicated on a substantive discernment (see Gamson, 1975) of the magnitude and direction of expansive values. But the organization's discernment is significantly constrained by information access (Diani, 2000) which limits its ability to correctly interpret direction. In the case of expansive values, organizational discernment is complicated by the non-linear growth of, and commitment to, expansive values.

Henderson (1994) characterizes this non-linear growth and commitment as a temporally discontinuous three-stage process. In the first stage, either in response to the realization that increasing economic gains do not lead to increased subjective well-being (Inglehart, 1997) (or alternatively as a function of environmental concerns (Capra, 1993), or spiritual development

(Giacalone and Jurkeiwicz, 2003)), individuals shift their values and consider behavioral changes to align with these values. Change is at an individual level, making organizational recognition difficult.

In the second stage, these nascent values' attempt to 'live their values' result in discordant, confusing behavioral responses. Salient motives for the values change direct the scope of the behavioral changes seen. For example, those driven to increase subjective well-being might move toward more meaningful work and a moral responsibility to society, while those driven by sustainability would shift from consumption toward voluntary simplicity as a moral choice (Fox, 1994; Gozdz, 1995). This individual attempt to align establishes the first signals to others that new values are being explored.

But individuals find some alignments satisfying and others not so much. The resulting frustration leads some back to stage one behaviors inconsistent with expansive values, a process known as pedomorphosis (Henderson, 1994). This pedomorphic process can recur repeatedly until expansive values adherents' actions comfortably align their values with ethical actions.

Sensing the stark contrast to dominant social values, expansive values adherents often remain silent about their values, searching quietly for others who share them. This reticence results in a slower coalescence as a group and obscures the magnitude of change (Ray and Anderson, 2000) over a long period.

What organizations discern is activity 'on the radar screen', but given pedomorphosis, and the slow coalescing of adherents, they are unsure what these actions signify, the extensiveness of the change, and how best to respond. Pedomorphosis in particular sets a confusing tone because it prevents a coherent information flow, leading organizations to incorrectly attribute these behaviors to capriciousness, laziness or other individual-level aberrations.

Identification of and recalibration toward these values under such conditions is difficult, particularly given the growth rate. Even now, with evidence pointing to a slow, steady growth rate of about one percentage point each year (Inglehart and Abramson, 1994), the number of expansive values adherents does not yet exceed the number of traditional materialists. But by 2010, this imbalance will shift when the number of expansive values adherents worldwide is expected to outnumber materialists (Abramson and Inglehart, 1992: 227). Thus:

*Proposition 8    Pedomorphosis undermines organizational recalibration of ethical principles and expectations, making appropriate responsiveness more difficult.*

**Demographic Discontinuities**

As a sizable social majority adheres to expansive values and behaves accordingly, organizations will recognize expansive values patterns (Ray and Anderson, 2000). Organizational leaders become interested in ethical (and other) issues related to expansive values, ignore others, leading them to make ethical decisions that foster or prevent particular outcomes and activities consistent with expansive values (Brunsson, 1982).

The values demographics (percentage who adhere to expansive values) and their level of power in the organization will impact organizations' ability to recognize these values changes, making demographic discontinues in the adherence to expansive values by power holders a factor in how administrators respond. Outside the organization, leading and lagging groups of expansive values stakeholder groups sensitize and frame ethical concerns for organizational leaders. The organization's ability and desire to recalibrate is therefore predicated on complex framing and counterframing among expansive values adherents, non-adherents, the press, influential 'spin doctors' and the organization (Wisler and Giugni, 2000). A recursive process develops in which organizational leadership learns and responds to the information framed before them. The values demographics of organizations whose internal and external stakeholders, particularly those at Henderson's second stage, will dictate whether there are issues advocates who will push these values in self-interested ways (Scully and Creed, 1998) to management. Framing leads to perceptions that expansive values are pro-institutional (when the demands of the new values fit or can fit into the organization), counter-institutional (when the demands of the new values do not fit or cannot fit into the organization) or unrelated to organizational functioning. Subsequent institutional selectivity then legitimizes or represses expansive values (Wisler and Giugni, 1996) and uses political posturing to vilify or justify their recalibrations, often through the application of sophisticated impression management strategies (Rosenfeld *et al.*, 2002,). Organizations without a strong sense of where they stand may argue to a more limited recalibration, a process that Giacalone and Eylon (2000) label 'partial paradigm myopia', resulting in selective responses to some issues while ignoring others. Thus:

*Proposition 9a     An organization's willingness to recalibrate will be a function of whether internal gatekeepers and leaders expect expansive values-based ethical decisions are in their best interests.*

*Proposition 9b     When the values of internal gatekeepers or external stakeholders are inconsistent with expansive values, organizational decision makers will delegitimize expansive values-based ethics.*

The composite framing that results as a function of demographic discontinuity, coupled with Henderson's (1994) temporal discontinuities, make ethical choices complex for organizations are forced to operate in an environment where ethical acceptability is impacted by pedomorphosis: a behavior may be ethically acceptable behavior today but potentially inappropriate six months later (Henderson, 1994). Such an erratic pattern of acceptability creates considerable difficulties for administrators who are trying to calibrate their organizational responses in alignment with expansive values. Where psychological contracts with particular implicit values were pivotal, the organization is left in an ethical quandary: Keep promises made under previous values assumptions or adhere to the dominant moral standard at the time of the decision.

These discontinuities make employee ethical socialization very difficult, particularly when there is a reliance on the interpretation and understanding of normative principles such as ethical codes. An environment of evolving values mandates repeated contextual re-evaluation, precluding ethical consensus in the organization, and increasing the likelihood of personalized or phantom codes of conduct and impression management strategies (Rosenfeld *et al.*, 2002) that recast decisions in a more self-serving light and allow employees to achieve organizational rewards. Thus:

*Proposition 10    Discontinuities will create values inconsistencies resulting in the development of an extended period of 'transition ethics.'*

**Non-Temporal Discontinuity: Uniqueness**

Non-temporal discontinuity, based on the unique aspects of each organization (for example, structural, behavioral and service differences) will create specific ethical challenges (Giacalone and Eylon, 2000) that will vary according to organizational type. For example, organizations whose service provision results in higher levels of pollution will have a more difficult time responding to the more stringent environmental ethics that characterize expansive values. Organizations and departments entrenched in traditional values, such as those in accounting and finance, will experience greater difficulty in understanding the ethical parameters of a worldview that does not weigh financial concerns are predominant above all others. Further, a larger set of organizations will likely be impacted due resultant to the influence of the consumer economy. Thus:

*Proposition 11    The degree of ethical recalibration will be a function of the organization's products/services tied to traditional values.*

## ACTION STEPS FOR THE FUTURE

These propositions are both reactive, in that they are formulated articulations of publicly-voiced concerns, and proactive in that they frame these issues in a manner that facilitates scholarly inquiry. The directions for future research in this area can be clustered into five action items.

First, is the degree to which the national culture is reflecting these new values at a rate that exceeds the organization's ability to cope. The focus here is not that the organization lacks the means or skills to make these changes, but that entrenched leadership, promotional and resource distribution patterns cling to a reward system that benefited them in the past, but does not fit with the new set of environmental challenges, technological advancements and a dramatically different labor pool. Consequently, these organizations are experiencing productivity declines, hiring and retention problems, reputational deterioration, and increasing costs due to employee alienation. The scope of these issues encompasses all sectors, industries, and services, and speaks to a culture neither predisposed to learning or change. Teasing apart the contributing factors as well as the anticipated consequences would advance both our understanding of organizations and provide insight to those who are called to effectively lead them.

Second, and an extenuation of the first action item, is an examination of the values shift in organizations that are attempting to learn and grow in concordance with the external environment. Examining what organizations are doing this well, and poorly, and how each approaches the task would be highly illuminating. In addition to the basic questions of how, where, who, is the weighted concern of when: at what point does an organization discern the difference between a fad or a true cultural values shift, and how do they make this decision? Such a perspective is crucial in moving this field of inquiry into the practical realm as organizations cannot and should not reconfigure to reflect a passing sentiment, but must and should transform to stay vital in a newly configured economic and social order.

The third item for research is rooted in basic change theory but requires an extension into the long-term consequences of an organization's approach to instituting a new value system. The degree to which the effort is comprehensive, or implemented only in certain segments of the organization and the impact of these variations on organizational success is a key area for inquiry. How does the organization develop the model for change, at what level is the change initiated, and how is it communicated throughout organizations large and small? Does the model for systemic value change differ from change theory in general, and why? These are concerns of great value to academics and practitioners alike.

The fourth area focuses on measurable impacts of the change for the organization. Quantifying these outcomes, both for the short and long terms, is critical in understanding both the impact of the current values shift as well as other environmental catalysts for widespread organizational change that are sure to come in the future in various forms. Standard measures of productivity and performance; human resource acquisition, distribution and retention; and fiscal strength need to be examined alongside issues of citizen satisfaction, consequences for the environment and humanitarian impact. The establishment of criteria to measure success is itself a process of reflecting the new values set to go beyond the limited definition of successful organizations that defined mere existence as proof of viability.

The fifth and final area of future research proposed here targets the individual within the organization. What role does the individual play in instigating, promoting, effecting, and incorporating the new cultural shift in values? What idiosyncratic or demographic differences account for variations in both the roles adopted and the degree to which they are adopted? What is the impact on the individual's performance for the organization as well as their physical and mental health? Once these causes and effects are explicated, what type of model can be built for understanding this aspect of organizational shift both in theory and as a guide for future practice?

Certainly the scope of inquiry is not limited to the foci listed here. Rather, it is hoped they will serve as a compass for others to expand our collective knowledge of this key and increasingly vital area in mapping the post-modern organizational terrain.

# REFERENCES

Abramson, P.R. and R. Inglehart (1992), 'Generational replacement and value change in 8 West European societies', *British Journal of Political Science*, **22**, 183–228.

Block, P. (1993), *Stewardship: Choosing Service over Self-interest*, San Francisco, CA: Berrett-Koehler.

Brunsson, N. (1982), 'The irrationality of action and action rationality: decisions, ideologies, and organizational actions', *Journal of Management Studies*, **19**, 29–44.

Capra, F. (1993), 'A systems approach to the emerging paradigm', in M. Ray and A. Rinzler (eds), *The New Paradigm in Business*, New York: Tarcher Books, pp. 230–7.

Capra, F., D. Steindl-Rast and T. Matus (1991), *Belonging to the Universe*, San Francisco, CA: Harper.

Cherrier, H. and J. Murray (2002), 'Drifting away from excessive consumption: a new social movement based on identity construction', *Advances in Consumer Research*, **29**, 245–7.

Conger, J.A. (1997), 'How generational shifts will transform organizational life', in F. Heselbein, M. Goldsmith and R. Beckard (eds), *The Organization of the Future*, San Francisco, CA: Jossey-Bass.

Daft, R.L. (1998), *Organization Theory and Design*, Cincinnati, OH: Thomson.

DeFoore, B. and J. Renesch (1995), *Rediscovering the Soul of Business*, San Francisco, CA: New Leaders Press.

Diani, M. (2000), 'Simmel to Rokkan and beyond: towards a network theory of (new) social movements', *European Journal of Social Theory*, **3**, 387–406.

Drucker, P.F. (1995), *Managing in a Time of Great Change*, New York: Dutton.

Eisenstadt, S.N. (1990), 'Functional analysis in anthropology and sociology: an interpretative essay', *Annual Review of Anthropology*, **19**, 243–60.

Eisler, R. (1987), *The Chalice and the Blade: Our History, Our Future*, San Francisco, CA: Harper & Row.

Emde, E. (1998), 'Employee values are changing course', *Workforce*, **77**, 38–84.

Feather, N.T. (1985), 'Attitudes, values, and attributions: explanations of unemployment', *Journal of Personality and Social Psychology*, **48**(4), 867–89.

Ferguson, M. (1993), 'The transformation of values and vocation', in M. Ray and A. Rinzler (eds), *The New Paradigm in Business*, New York: Tarcher.

Fox, M. (1994), *The Reinvention of Work: A New Vision of Livelihood for Our Time*, San Francisco, CA: Harper Collins.

Frankl, V. (1962), *Man's Search for Meaning: An Introduction to Logotherapy*, New York: Washington Square Press.

Gamson, W.A. (1975), *The Strategy of Social Protest*. Homewood, IL: Dorsey Press.

Giacalone, R.A. and D. Eylon (2000), 'The development of new paradigm values, thinkers, and business: initial frameworks for a changing business worldview', *American Behavioral Scientist*, **43**, 1217–30.

Giacalone, R.A. and C.L. Jurkiewicz (2003), 'Toward a science of workplace spirituality', in R.A. Giacalone and C.L. Jurkiewicz (eds), *The Handbook of Workplace Spirituality and Organizational Performance*, Armonk, NY: M.E. Sharpe.

Goeksen, F., F. Adaman and E.U. Zenginobuz (2002), 'On environmental concern, willingness to pay, and postmaterialist values: evidence from Istanbul', *Environment and Behavior*, **3**, 616–33.

Gozdz, K. (1995), *Community Building: Renewing Spirit and Learning in Business*, San Francisco, CA: Sterling and Stone.

Greenleaf, R.K. (1977), *Servant Leadership*, New York: Paulist Press.

Hammer, M. and J. Champy (1993), *Reengineering the Corporation: A Manifesto for Business Revolution*, New York: HarperBusiness.

Hawken, P. (1994), *The Ecology of Commerce*, New York: HarperCollins.

Hawley, J. (1993), *Reawakening the Spirit at Work: The Power of Dharmic Management*, San Francisco, CA: Berrett-Koehler.

Henderson, H. (1994), *Paradigms in Progress*, Indianapolis, IN: Knowledge Systems.

Henderson, H. (1995), *Paradigms in Progress*, Indianapolis, IN: Knowledge Systems.

Hess, D., N. Rogovsky and T.W. Dunfee (2002), 'The next wave of corporate community involvement: corporate social initiatives', *California Management Review*, **44**, 110–25.

Hirschman, E.C. (1990), 'Secular immortality and the American ideology of affluence', *Journal of Consumer Research*, **17**, 31–42.

Hopkins, G. and S. Prescott (1983), 'Instrumental and terminal values and attitudes of preservice and experienced teachers', *Educational and Psychological Research*, **3**(3).

Ingelhart, R.F. (1997), *Modernization and Postmodernization*, Princeton, NJ: Princeton University Press.

Ingelhart, R.F. and P.R. Abramson (1994), 'Economic-security and value change', *American Political Science Review*, **88**, 336–54.

Inglehart, R. and P.R. Abramson (1999), 'Measuring postmaterialism', *American Political Science Review*, **93**, 665–77.

Jones, T.M. (1991), 'Ethical decision-making by individuals in organizations', *Academy of Management Review*, **16**, 366–95.

Kasser, T. and R.M. Ryan (1993), 'A dark side of the American dream: correlates of financial success as a central life aspiration', *Journal of Personality and Social Psychology*, **65**, 410–22.

Lutz, W. (1989), *Doublespeak*, New York: Harper/Perennial.

Maynard, H.B. and S.E. Mehrtens (1993), *The Fourth Wave: Business in the Twenty-first Century*, San Francisco, CA: Berret-Koehler.

McLarney, C. and E. Chung (1999), 'Post-materialism's silent revolution in consumer research', *Marketing Intelligence and Planning*, **17**, 288–97.

Payne, S.L. and R.A. Giacalone (1990), 'Social psychological approaches to the perception of ethical dilemmas', *Human Relations*, **43**, 649–66.

Quinn, R.E. (2000), *Change the World*, San Francisco, CA: Jossey-Bass.

Ray, P.H. (1996), *The Integral Culture Survey: A Study of Transformational Values in America*, Sausalito, CA: Institute of Noetic Sciences.

Ray, P.H. and S.R. Anderson (2000), *Cultural Creatives*, New York: Random House.

Ray, M. and A. Rinzler (1993), *The New Paradigm in Business*, New York: Tarcher.

Rokeach, M. (1972), *Beliefs, Attitudes, and Values*, San Francisco, CA: Jossey-Bass.

Rosenfeld, P., R.A. Giacalone and C.A. Riordan (2002), *Impression Management: Building and Enhancing Reputations at Work*. New York: Thomson Learning.

Scully, M.A. and W.E.D. Creed (1998), 'Switch persons on the tracks of history: situated agency and contested legitimacy in the diffusion of domestic partner benefits', paper presented at the annual meeting of the Academy of Management, San Diego, CA.

Sheldrake, R. (1981), *A New Science of Life: The Hypothesis of Formative Causation*, London: Blond and Briggs.

Sheldrake, R. (1988), *The Presence of the Past: Morphic Resonance and the Habits of Nature*, New York: Vintage Books.

Shenkar, O., N. Aranya and T. Almor (1995), 'Construct dimensions in the contingency model: an analysis comparing metric and non-metric multivariate instruments', *Human Relations*, **48**, 559–80.

Thompson, C.M. (2000), *The Congruent Life*, San Francisco, CA: Jossey-Bass.

Valle, R.S. (1989), 'The emergence of transpersonal psychology', in R.S. Valle and S. Halling (eds), *Existential-Phenomenological Perspectives in Psychology*, New York: Plenum, pp. 257–68.

Vamos, M.N. (1996), 'America: land of the shaken, *Business Week*, 11 March, pp. 64–5.

Wheatley, M. (1992), *Leadership and the New Science: Learning about Organization from an Orderly Universe*, San Francisco, CA: Berrett-Koehler.

Wisler, D. and M.G. Giugni (1996), 'Social movements and institutional selectivity', *Sociological Perspectives*, **39**, 85–110.

# 4. Ethical norms in public service: a framework for analysis

**Carol W. Lewis**

## INTRODUCTION

The purpose here is to construct a multi-dimensional framework for ana-lysing ethical decision making by integrating the disparate literatures on ethical norms and behavior in public service. Because the empirical evi-dence from developmental management, psychology, decision theory, nor-mative theory, and more suggests that ethical decision making is multi-dimensional and variable across time and context, the synthesis goes beyond an exclusive reliance on any single discipline or model. Depicted graphically as the ethics landscape, the proposed framework shows vari-ations in ethical decision making based on four bundles of variables (cog-nitive development, grounding, normative basis and saliency) across individuals, organizations and situations. The ethics landscape then is applied in a development setting to an ethical dilemma in public service.

## SOURCES OF ETHICAL NORMS

What is ethical behavior and, in particular, good conduct in public service? There are numerous formulations of good behavior (drawing on, for example, motivation or purpose, harm or benefit or mode of reasoning) and its negatives, corruption (Huberts, 2003) and poor moral judgment. These formulations include both empirical, behavioral models from the social sci-ences that explain how and why decisions are made and normative or pre-scriptive models that specify what decisions should be made and why. When categorized by source or field, moral values and behavioral norms cluster by source into six categories. (The Appendix shows the classifications in detail.)

1. Human universals, innate or natural, derived from natural rights theory (for example, the US Declaration of Independence); develop-mental psychology associated with, for example, Lawrence Kohlberg;[1]

sociobiology and bio-behavioralism; and evolutionary psychology and genetics.[2]

2.  Cultural/social perspectives structured relative to experience with the environment and represented by behavioral psychology (conditioning; I. Pavlov, B.F. Skinner); situationalism (conditioning; J. Doris); developmental psychology (innate; J. Kagan); and socialization mechanisms in anthropology, sociology, theories of civic virtue and moral character (for example, the ancient Greeks); and, in its vulgar version, cultural relativism.[3]

3.  Rational analysis and cognitive processes that stress thought, reason, and education are associated with deontology[4] (I. Kant's categorical imperative, for example); teleology[5] (John Stuart Mill, for whom utility entails minimizing pain broadly defined and Jeremy Bentham, whose calculus focuses on pleasure broadly defined); and vulgar teleology or simplistic egoism with an exclusive focus on short-term self-interest and sometimes deteriorating into self-indulgence.

4.  Non-rational and needs-based perspectives include David Hume's critique of moral rationalism; cognitive psychology's emphasis on empirically identifiable universal principles with action related to perception, anchoring, categorization, pattern matching and risk assessment ('Prospect Theory' of D. Kahneman and A. Tversky, 1979); behavioral social psychology (A. Maslow, J. Turiel), and human resource management.

5.  Theological perspectives that posit moral values and behavioral norms are god-given and therefore universal and immutable among believers or adherents and knowable through revelation or natural law (Saint Augustine).

6.  Professional and bureaucratic roles and associated expectations of appropriate conduct that are expressed in public-service ethics systems, public opinion (for example, Transparency International, World Values Survey (Inglehart, 2000 and Welzel *et al.*, n.d.), and career aspirations and secondary hierarchical relationships (Max Weber) that generate both the potential for conflict of interest and its prohibition and common core public-service values (Gilman and Lewis, 1996; Lewis and Gilman, 2005a, Chapter 9; Lewis and Gilman, 2005b).

## UNIVERSALS AND CONTEXT AS EXPLANATORY VARIABLES

Clusters 1 and 5 listed above offer universals as the explanatory variable. Some views in the normative tradition search for universal modes of reasoning generalizable to all people, and its empirical counterpart similarly proposes a universal view.[6] Denying that ethics is relative or subjective, ethicist Peter Singer (1979: 10–11) tells us, 'Ethics takes a universal point of view' and that 'the notion of ethics carries with it something bigger than the individual'. Altogether another approach denies that a universal perspective is either desirable[7] or observable.[8]

Clusters 2, 3, 4 and 6 draw on contextual factors such as experience and culture to explain ethical decision making and behavior. Behavioral psychologist John Doris (2002) and his 'situationalism' and behavioral social psychologist Elliot Turiel (2002) represent this contextual perspective as does John Rohr's formulation (1989) that stresses the importance of regime values for defining good conduct in public service. Because context is often defined in terms of culture (Kagan, 1998, 2000), these disparities make inescapable the question of whether cultural differences induce differences in ethical values and behavior.[9] Overall, the evidence now tilts toward a perspective that argues culture and situation play central roles in defining moral norms and behavior.

A view of culture as 'the entire interactive symbolic environment in which humans live and communicate' (Donald, 2000: 23) makes culture particularly important to an understanding of ethical norms and behavior in public service for three reasons. First, public service itself may be considered as a subculture in which symbolic communication is both common and crucial (for purposes of, for example, mobilization or compliance). Second, organizations are the context for decision and action in contemporary public service and organizational norms and standard operating procedures frame decision making by individuals. Third, public service is affected by the advent of professionalism (included in the roster above). This third factor suggests that, although tradition is enduring, it is not immutable, and newly emerging trends may be moral traditions in their formative stages.

## MORAL TRADITION AND EMPIRICAL FINDINGS

What we know and/or believe we know about ethical norms derives from two broad sources: moral traditions and emerging empirical findings. Moral traditions – enduring, systematic, and widely held systems of thought about right and wrong – are drawn from those sources designated as normative, cultural or religious in formulation. The normative sources of moral tradition include the philosophical perspectives associated with using human reason (rationalism). Foremost among these are perspectives primarily defining ethics either by: (a) universal principles and duties of good conduct; or (b) proper effects on others and the community.[10] On the roster of other normative sources is thinking grounded in natural rights, virtue and moral character, and some approaches relating to common sense and human emotion. Each tradition may generate different answers or different reasons for similar answers to problems posed by ethical dilemmas that demand judgment, and it is the gray, problematic arena of moral judgment that poses the most significant challenges to individual and organizational integrity in today's public service.

What is known about ethical norms draws on sources other than long-standing moral traditions. As Table 4.1 suggests, research in developmental and cognitive psychology and economics has contributed a good deal to our view of ethical norms in general and in public service more specifically. For example, Kohlberg (1980: 92; 1981) identified the fifth stage as the 'official morality' of the US government and Constitution. Later research sought to establish a 'baseline measurement of moral reasoning' among public managers (Swisher *et al.*, 2001). While some studies show a tendency among US public managers toward the law and duty orientation of conventional reasoning (Stewart *et al.*, 2001), other research shows a tendency toward post-conventional moral reasoning (Swisher *et al.*, 2001). Some scholars see continued research on moral reasoning among public servants as especially important. 'The first, and in some sense the most basic, continuing issue in assessing the moral stage theory approach in public administration relates to whether the underlying assumption of "principled reasoning" as the normative ideal is the right assumption for public administration' (Stewart *et al.*, 2001: 473). Although many scholars acknowledge the impact of selected empirical research on our thinking about ethical norms in public service (White, 1999; 2003), other bodies of empirical research in psychology and economics has yet to be brought to bear directly. The framework presented below addresses this gap.

## MULTI-DIMENSIONAL FRAMEWORK

Given the pressing challenges, complex environment, and multiple sources of ethical values and behavioral norms, how do public servants sort through them, weigh them and exercise an ethical choice? Analysing decisions and behavior in terms of the sources of ethical norms is a fruitful enterprise. It is widely accepted that decision makers use a framework to sort and accept ethical claims. Analytic frameworks for moral reasoning and behavior from psychology include: (a) focusing on universals in human development as the key explanatory factor;[11] (b) drawing on universals from genetics and adaptation;[12] (c) stressing contextual factors such as

*Table 4.1    Landmark publications in the psychology of morality*

---

1891    First publication, *On Aphasia*, by Sigmund Freud (1856–1939, Austrian), founder of psychoanalysis, who revolutionizes understanding of personality with its unconscious mental processes including repression and resistance and profoundly influences intellectual developments in ethics and many other fields

1921    Publication of first article on intelligence by Jean Piaget (1896–1980), Swiss cognitive psychologist, whose groundbreaking work on children's intelligence and moral development influenced Lawrence Kohlberg

1979    Publication of *Prospect Theory* by cognitive psychologists Daniel Kahneman and Amos Tversky, whose findings undermine the rational-actor model of decision making under conditions of uncertainty and relate decision making to categorization, pattern matching and choice heuristics

1981    Publication of Lawrence Kohlberg's *The Philosophy of Moral Development: Moral Stages and the Idea of Justice*, an influential work of developmental psychology that details moral reasoning at various stages of cognitive development

1982    Publication of *In a Different Voice* by Carol Gilligan influences study of women's moral development and offers critical response to justice perspective associated with Immanuel Kant, John Rawls and Lawrence Kohlberg; critique developed by Martha Nussbaum, Susan Okin and others; inspires development of ethics of care based on relationships, contrasted with ethics of justice based on rights and principles

1984    Publication of *Caring: A Feminine Approach to Ethics and Moral Education* by educator Nel Noddings, proponent of caring as basis for moral action and relationships rather than principles as basis for moral development, and inspiration for perspective termed *ethic of care*

1994    Journalist Robert Wright's *The Moral Animal*, a work of popular science, draws on evolutionary psychology to explain altruistic behavior

1998    Publication of *Three Seductive Ideas* by Jerome Kagan, the developmental psychologist who refutes fallacies such as 'infant determinism' and argues on behalf of humans' capacity for change and growth and that humans are motivated by a biologically-based concern for right and wrong and empathy

2002    In *The Culture of Morality*, Elliot Turiel provides an empirical basis for heterogeneity of social judgments with moral content and refutes the dichotomy between collectivist and individualist cultures

2002    Publication of John M. Doris's *Lack of Character: Personality and Moral Behavior*, in which empirical studies support 'situationalism' and refute moral character as basis of ethical behavior

---

experience and culture to explain behavior;[13] and (d) centering on cognitive processes.[14]

## THREE KEYS TO ANALYSIS

The analysis suggests three keys to understanding ethical reasoning in many formulations. Universals are one key. Denying that ethics is relative or subjective, Peter Singer (1979: 11) tells us, 'Ethics takes a universal point of view' and that '[f]rom ancient times, philosophers and moralists have expressed the idea that ethical conduct is acceptable from a point of view that is somehow universal' (p. 10). Deontology is another example. Cognitive processes and developmental psychology also offer a universal viewpoint. Building on the work of Jean Piaget to examine moral reasoning, Lawrence Kohlberg (1981) framed his theory of moral development solely in terms of reasoning, which he saw as the basis for ethical conduct. Building on a construct quite different from Kohlberg's, Jerome Kagan (1998) 'identifies the most powerful motive for human beings as the desire to gain and maintain a feeling of virtue, the desire to be "good"' (Shweder, 1999: 798). 'We inherit, because we are humans, a concern with right and wrong, and empathy with others. But the specific actions that we regard as moral can vary with culture', Kagan explains (2000).

A non-rational dimension is a second key to explaining decision making. According to 'Prospect theory', people confronting uncertainty do not make decisions the way linear models of rational decision making would have it (Kahneman and Tversky, 1979). There is something going on other than analytic processing and cognitive operations – something different from a straightforward calculus of costs, benefits, probabilities and risks (Kahneman et al., 1982). Decision makers bias their judgments and remembrances in predictable, systematic ways. 'People edit their judgments with moral criteria . . . they give more weight to losses than to gains of the same amount; they bias remembered experiences by remembering peaks and end points but not duration; they employ a positivity bias – and much more' (Lane, 2000: 17–18).[15] 'Irrationally, people feel differently about losing than they do about gaining, even if either choice produces the same outcome' (Olin, 2003). Their decision biases toward seeking or avoiding risk depend on their understanding of a situation. Because of this bias in decision making, framing the issue as a gain or a loss affects the decision.[16]

Context is a third key to understanding decision making. Overall, the evidence tilts toward central roles for culture, situation and experience in defining moral norms and behavior. Because decision makers use categories drawn from their experience and pattern matching ('anchoring'), it is imperative to recognize the 'powerful impact of contextual factors on decision making. . . . Risk taking, time discounting, and interpersonal decision making . . . are much more a function of how people construe situations than of how they evaluate and weigh attributes' (Loewenstein, 2001: 500–1, notes omitted). Decision makers draw on their experience and expertise first 'to figure out what kind of situation they are in and then adopt choice rules that seem appropriate for that situation' (Loewenstein, 2001: 503). In effect, decisions can be altered by altering or reframing the situation from, for example, personal relationships to organizational or professional obligations and by reducing risk by shifting from prospective loss to retained gain.

Individuals make decisions and take action in a context rich with varied interrelationships, responsibilities, perceptions, inferences, experiences and interpretations. The context may be defined as the constructed situation (along the lines of Prospect Theory) or organizational norms and procedures and hierarchical rank that, coupled with cognitive limits, structure decision making (Herbert Simon, 1948). As noted above, context often is defined in terms of culture.

## RELEVANCE TO PUBLIC SERVICE

Because of public service's emphasis on separating the personal from the public (reflected in the prohibition against conflict of interest, for example) and its taking place in public organizations, two observations from social psychology are especially meaningful for ethics in public service. Rejecting both extremes – that culture wholly dictates or has no effect whatsoever on moral development – and that societies and individuals are culturally monolithic, Elliot Turiel (1994: 237) notes 'several sides to cultural practices stemming from the different perspectives of people in different positions in the hierarchy'. Also, he finds, 'In-group moral commitments are often as important as the moral idea of general applicability. However, one does not negate the other' (Turiel, 1994: 4).[17]

Recognition of the determining influence of situations means that inconsistent behavior across situations is more likely than not (Doris, 2002: Chapter 2).[18] The recognition that individuals' judgments and behaviors are inconsistent or fragmented across situations leads to the rejection of 'general evaluative categories such as "good person" and "bad person"' and to questioning the usefulness of character education that aims at creating 'global character structures' (Doris, 2002: 115, 122–5). Nonetheless, because virtue 'can be "socially sustained"' (Doris, 2002: 90), organizations can promote ethical behavior.

Every framework has its strengths, weaknesses and problems. One approach, erroneously associated with social psychology or anthropology, may encourage some confusion between morality and convention and a failure to recognize that all that is practiced need not be good. As they center on moral reasoning, cognitive frameworks tend to downplay emotional aspects of behavior. The rationalistic, normative frameworks may be suitable for self-conscious analysis but are less useful for analyzing individual and organizational decisions and behavior.

## SYNTHESIS

Instead of opposing seemingly contradictory frameworks – irrationality versus cognitive development or universals versus contextual factors, for instance – and then dismissing the less preferred, it is possible to bring into play the many different frameworks supported by empirical evidence. Melding these frameworks into a flexible decision-making model highlights the multi-dimensionality of ethical decision making and accounts for the (a) inconsistency over time or across decision-making domains (that an observer may label as hypocrisy), and (b) principled reasoning (that nonetheless may appear erroneous or disingenuous).

Research on the effects of uncertainty, decision biases, social interactions, experience and culture shows that ethical behavior draws on feeling and thinking; emotion and reason both influence decisions and behavior;[19] the ethical agent employs both emotion and reason (Cooper, 1987).[20] Therefore, rather than dichotomizing emotion and reason and relying solely upon one or the other, it is more useful to harmonize them when possible, recognize that both are in play, and to acknowledge that the ethically mature person brings both to bear in making moral judgments.

Kagan (2000) says to policy makers that 'at the moment, the gap between the policies that legislators must make and science is so large that wisdom on the part of the legislator is probably the most important ingredient'. The more cautious approach to public policy may be to integrate them.

## ETHICS LANDSCAPE

Figure 4.1 integrates step by step the numerous frameworks and suggests interactions among four central factors. The figure progressively builds an ethical landscape in three steps. First, in Figure 4.1a, moral development brings to bear the stages of moral reasoning and is marked as variable no. 1. Situational differences are represented by saliency (variable no. 2). Saliency

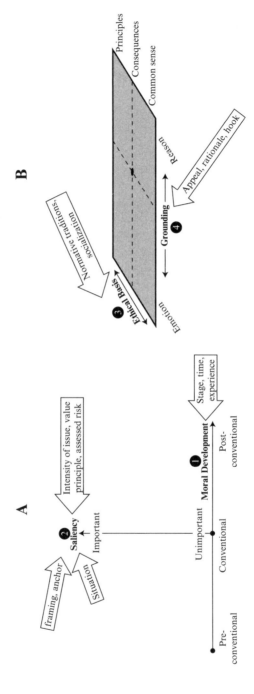

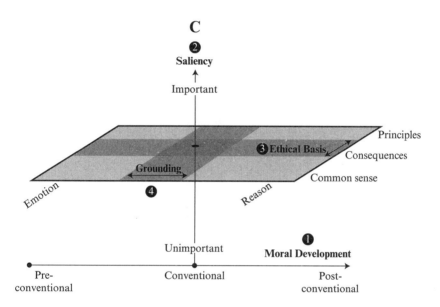

*Figures 4.1 A–E:    Building the ethics landscape. (Page 52) A, first set of variables in ethics landscape; B, second set of variables in ethics landscape; (above) C, integrated view of ethics landscape; (page 54) D, alternative integrated view of ethics landscape; E, comparative views of ethics landscape*

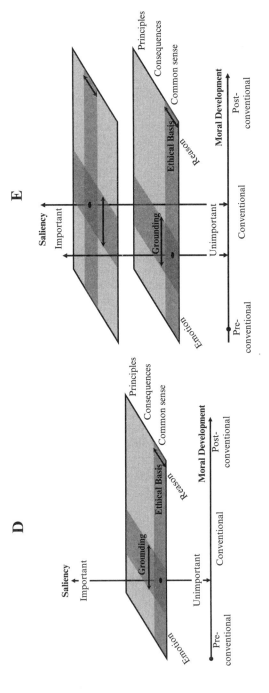

*Source:* © 2005. Carol W. Lewis. Reprinted by permission. Graphics by Brian Baird Alstadt.

54

captures intensity (or triviality or significance of issues), value, principle, or assessed risk.[21] Alternatively, saliency may be taken to refer to the price tag associated with a particular decision or behavior, and includes considerations of career, cost, convenience, competence, commitment, and courage (Lewis and Gilman, 2005a). In either case, the greater the saliency, the more demanding is the question to be answered or the more pressing is the issue to be resolved. Individuals, including those of moral character, are shown sliding along a saliency vector as they attribute difference degrees of saliency to an issue or principle or in response to their different assessments of risk. Finnish experience illustrates this fluidity in practice: 'the central principles of civil service ethics in fact cannot be defined clearly and unambiguously; they differ according to official status and administrative sectors' (OECD, 2004: 232). Such experiences, coupled with Doris's arguments (Doris, 2002: Chapter 2) on behalf of inconsistent behavior across situations, make saliency a central concern.

Figure 4.1a reveals how moral development and saliency might interact to begin forming a decision-making landscape in which a specific decision simultaneously turns on the decision maker's moral development and the saliency the decision maker attributes to the issue. Different places on this landscape may be held by the same person at different times and under different circumstances. Alternatively, these places may be held by different people at the same time.

Two other factors – ethical basis and grounding – interact in the second step to form another landscape. In Figure 4.1b, ethical basis (variable no. 3) represents normative and social aspects. while grounding (variable no. 4) accounts for the cognitive versus emotional grounds for ethical decisions and behavior. Figure 4.1b demonstrates how a specific decision depends upon the interaction between these two sets of factors on the part of the decision maker.

The third step is to bring the two landscapes together; Figure 4.1c suggests how the four factors might interact at a particular decision-making point. The aim of the graphic is not to imply rigid relationships among the four variables. Rather, the central point for analysis is that individuals draw on a variety of influential factors when making an ethical decision and an actual decision depends upon the interaction among these factors. Figure 4.1a–e provides a framework for envisioning how those factors might interact for a specific person making a specific decision.

Figure 4.1d shows an alternative landscape for envisioning a different decision or decision maker. The final step shown in Figure 4.1e compares the two landscapes from Figures 4.1c and 4.1d. With its progressive versions, Figure 4.1 admittedly is a complex graphic. The complexity mirrors possible real-world interactions among four shifting variables. The bundling of factors influencing decision making already simplifies the decision-making framework. (Note that Table 4.1 identifies six separate foundations of ethical norms.) To reduce the framework to a factor or two misses the point: ethical decisions and behavior are multi-dimensional and variable across time and context.

## ETHICS PARABLE

Figure 4.1 can be used for probing decision-making dynamics in different organizations and different cultural settings. When used as an analytic tool, Figure 4.1 helps move us from theory to practice and from the individual to the organization. Highlighted behaviors related to specific cultures and customs but antithetical to the public interest and public service values and principles can be identified as candidates for repositioning . . . to be anchored in public service imperatives and linked to universal, professional, and organizational moral claims.

To demonstrate the analytic potential of Figure 4.1, it is useful to draw upon a time-honored tool in ethics, story-telling. Consider a young development officer out in the field with the assigned task of getting a well dug in a remote village. Figure 4.1c locates her place on the ethics landscape. Ascribing more than average salience to her work, the officer frames her task in terms of the norms of doing good (beneficence) and serving the public interest. Keeping her emotional distance, she thinks about what clean water means for the villagers' health. Reasoning at a conventional stage of moral development, the officer defines her work in terms of doing her duty and she seeks approval from her superiors and peers in the development community.

The immediate problem is that the local leader expects the customary gift to express appreciation for his arranging the villagers' cooperation. The salience of giving a small but unauthorized gift is low; the risks are low because no one beyond the village is likely to know. The token gift can be seen as ceremonial rather than as an outright bribe. This reasoning illustrates how convention may be confused with ethics (and recalls the words of the eighteenth-century pamphleteer, Thomas Paine, 'A long habit of not thinking a thing wrong gives it the superficial appearance of being right'). She frames the issue as an isolated event by considering the consequences of contaminated water to the villagers and ignoring the symbolic and financial implications of 'gifting' over many such projects. Confronting an immediate decision, she goes on gut feel and common sense. Figure 4.1d locates her place on the ethics landscape in this situation. Figure 4.1e compares the two scenarios.

## CONCLUSION

Figure 4.1 helps pinpoint the factors that enter into decisions and behavior at different times, in different situations, and/or by different people. Because more research is needed to specify their interrelationships and weights, the proposed framework as yet disregards what is undoubtedly a crucial issue on the future research agenda. The different landscapes possible from the (as yet undifferentiated) factors in Figure 4.1 counsel that there is no single key to unlocking the mystery of the shaping of ethical norms and behavior for all people at all times. The evidence points to a multi-dimensional view; a simplistic view is unrealistic, not fruitful for analytic purposes, and designed for failure in practical applications. In order to confront the complexity depicted in Figure 4.1, public sector ethics needs a multi-faceted approach. H.L. Mencken articulates the alternative: 'For every human problem, there is a solution that is simple, neat, and wrong'.

## ACKNOWLEDGEMENTS

This chapter is excerpted in large part from the author's 2005 report to the World Bank, Poverty Reduction and Economic Management Network. An earlier version was presented at the conference, 'Ethics and Integrity of Governance: a Transatlantic Dialogue', under the auspices of the Study Group on Ethics and Integrity of Governance of the European Group of Public Administration and the Section on Ethics of the American Society for Public Administration and hosted by Public Management Institute of the Katholieke Universiteit Leuven, Belgium, 2-5 June 2005. This work represents solely the views of the author, who is solely responsible for it contents. The author takes this opportunity to express her sincere appreciation to the many colleagues who contributed their thoughtful comments and insightful suggestions to this work. They include Brian Baird Alstadt, Daryl Balia, Bayard L. Catron, Stuart C. Gilman, Jeroen Maesschalck, Morton J. Tenzer, Michael Rion, Richard Vengroff, Cyrus Ernesto Zirakzadeh, and Leo W.J.C. Huberts who contributed detailed suggestions. Any errors and oversights are, of course, the author's.

## NOTES

1. One essay observes that 'cognitive science still proceeds as if culture did not matter. The only major exception to this is developmental psychology' (Donald, 2000: 20).
2. Evolutionary psychology argues that human nature is the result of adaptation and evolution. The idea of a biological basis for morality dates back at least to Charles Darwin

(2004 [1873]), who suggested that 'sympathy', the foundation of moral sentiment, is a social instinct and biological force. E.O. Wilson's *Sociobiology* (1975) sparked considerable controversy with its argument that most of social life including morality is best seen in biological terms. This thesis was developed in a popular version by Robert Wright (1995).

3.  Cultural relativism 'denies that any independent moral facts exist outside of a society . . . all moral beliefs are proper or improper in relation to a society's customs' (Terkel and Duval, 1999: 58, capitalization omitted).

4.  Deontology is a philosophical perspective based on universal principles and duties with intrinsic value and applicable to moral judgment.

5.  Sometimes referred to as 'consequentialism', teleology is a philosophical perspective whereby actions are judged instrumentally by their effects on the community. 'Consequentialists start not with moral rules but with goals. They assess actions by the extent to which they further these goals. . . . The classical utilitarian regards an action as right if it produces as much or more an increase in the happiness of all affected by it than any alternative action, and wrong if it does not' (Singer, 1979: 3).

6.  Some of these ideas about the foundations of ethical norms and behavior run counter to common wisdom but had been percolating for many years before positive social science addressed them. David Hume, the eighteenth century Scottish philosopher, came down on the side of context rather than universals when he proposed 'that causes and effects are discoverable, not by reason but by experience . . .' (Hume, 1980 [1751]: 28, italics omitted). He also anticipated *Prospect Theory* to some degree when he wrote 'all arguments concerning existence are founded on the relation of cause and effect; that our knowledge of that relation is derived entirely from experience; and that all of our experimental conclusions proceed upon the supposition that the future will be conformable to the past' and concluded, 'From causes which appear *similar* we expect similar effects. This is the sum of all our experimental conclusions' (Hume, 1980 [1751]: 35–6). He also addressed uncertainty: 'If there be any suspicion that the course of nature may change, and that the past may be no rule for the future, all experience becomes useless, and can give rise to no inference or conclusion' (Hume, 1980 [1751]: 37–8).

7.  The normative denial often translates into advocating a particular end or conduct as ethical under certain circumstances.

8.  The empirical denial often is supported by mustering evidence for a situational approach. For a classic statement on 'culture-dependent differences in thinking and acting' (p. 8), see *Culture's Consequences* by Geert Hofstede (1980).

9.  On whether cultural differences induce differences in ethical values and behavior, see Khalid al-Yahya *et al.*, 2005; Cooper and Yoder, 2002; Donald, 2000; Doris, 2002; Gilman and Lewis, 1996; Hofstede, 1980; Lewis, 2005; Lewis and Gilman, 2005b; Moreno, 2002; Myers and Tan, 2002; Smith, 2004, Tayeb, 1994; Turiel, 1994, 2002; and Welzel *et al.*, (n.d.). On conceptual problems with 'national culture', see Al-Yahya *et al.*, 2005: 11–13; Myers and Tan, 2002; and Tayeb, 1994. Lewis (2005, Appendix B) examines the literature in development management and psychology (including Turiel, 1994, 2002 and Doris, 2002) and concludes that a definitive verdict is still out as to whether there are meaningful differences in ethical values and behavior across cultures and, if so, whether these differences are culturally determined.

10. Note the emphasis on an inclusive roster of stakeholders. Consequentialism invokes more than exclusive, single-minded devotion to one's self. It is the vulgar version of simplistic egoism that considers only the short-term self-interest.

11. Developmental psychologists Lawrence Kohlberg (1981) and Jerome Kagan (1998) represent this view.

12. See, for example, work in evolutionary psychology as represented by E.O. Wilson and, in its popular version, by Robert Wright (1994).

13. Behavioral psychologist John Doris (2002) and his 'situationalism' and behavioral social psychologist Elliot Turiel (2002) represent this perspective.

14. The *Prospect Theory* of Daniel Kahneman and Amos Tversky (1979) is an example of this approach.

15. This directly counters the rational assessment claimed by utility theory. These findings from cognitive psychology undercut the rational-actor model of decision making under conditions of uncertainty. See Douglas and Wildavsky, 1982; Fischhoff *et al.*, 1981; Green *et al.*, 1994; Green *et al.*, 1998; Kahneman and Lovallo, 1993; and Kahneman *et al.*, 1982.
16. Ethics and anti-corruption programs as well as organizational incentive structures would be well served by taking these findings into account.
17. This suggests that organizations can effectively support ethical behavior by explicitly linking it to moral commitments to organizational and professional colleagues, in addition to obligations to the public.
18. John Doris's evidence for 'situationalism' draws on Western and non-Western cultures (Doris, 2002: 105–6).
19. See Hobson, 2005 for a popular rendition of current psychological research. On emotional support for values, see Gaylin and Jennings (1996).
20. Doris (2002: 164) argues that a capacity for taking responsibility distinguishes the adult: 'Moral maturity has much to do with acknowledging what one has done. . . . This exercise is as much affective as cognitive; it centrally involves a capacity to have a certain sort of emotional encounter with oneself.'
21. Because changing the 'price' (or incentive and disincentive, including risk) affects behavior, both analysis and public policy would benefit from the application of decision-making theory from cognitive psychology that relates risk of loss to the likelihood and size of prospective benefit.

# REFERENCES

Al-Yahya, K., M. Lubatkin R. Vengroff and M. Ndiaye (2007), 'The impact of culture on public sector management: a comparative perspective,' in Ali Farazmand (ed.), *Handbook of Bureaucracy*, 2nd edn, New York: Marcel Dekker.

Bentham, J. (1948 [1780]), *An Introduction to The Principles of Morals and Legislation*, New York: Hafner Press

Bok, S. (1978), *Lying. Moral Choice in Public and Private Life*, New York: Vintage Books.

Cooper, T.L. (1987), 'Hierarchy, virtue, and the practice of public administration', *Public Administration Review*, **47**, 320–8.

Cooper, T.L. and D.E. Yoder (2002), 'Public management ethics standards in a transnational world', *Public Integrity*, **4**(4), 333–52.

Darwin, Charles (2004 [1873]), *The Descent of Man*, London: Penguin.

Donald, M. (2000), 'The central role of culture in cognitive evolution: a reflection on the myth of the isolated mind', in L.P. Nucci, G.B. Saxe and E. Turiel (eds), *Culture, Thought, and Development*, Mahwah, NJ: Lawrence Erlbaum Associates, pp. 19–38.

Doris, J. (2002), *Lack of Character: Personality and Moral Behavior*, New York: Cambridge University Press.

Douglas, M. and A. Wildavsky (1982), *Risk and Culture*, Berkeley, CA: University of California Press.

Fischhoff, B., S. Lichtenstein, P. Slovic, S.L. Derby and R.L. Keeney (1981), *Acceptable Risk*, Cambridge: Cambridge University Press.

Freud, S. (1953), *On Aphasia*, Madison, CT: International Universities Press.

Gaylin, W. and B. Jennings (1996), *The Perversion of Autonomy, The Proper Uses of Coercion and Constraints in a Liberal Society*, New York: Free Press.

Gilman, S.C. and C.W. Lewis (1996), 'Public service ethics: a global dialogue', *Public Administration Review*, **56**(6), 517–24.

Gilligan, C. (1982), *In a Different Voice*, Cambridge, MA: Harvard University Press.

Green, D. Philip, D. Kahneman and H. Kunreuther (1994), 'How the scope and method of public funding affect willingness to pay for public goods', *Public Opinion Quarterly* **58**(1) (Spring), 49–67.

Green, D., K.E. Jacowitz, D. Kahneman and D. McFadden (1998). 'Referendum contingent valuation, anchoring, and willingness to pay for public goods', *Resources and Energy Economics* **20**(2) (June), 85–116.

Hobson, K. (2005), 'Doing the right thing', *Princeton Alumni Weekly*, 26 January, 28–33.

Hofstede, G. (1980), *Culture's Consequences, International Differences in Work-Related Values*, Newbury Park, CA: Sage.

Huberts, L.W.J.C. (2003), 'Global ethics and corruption', *Encyclopedia of Public Administration and Public Policy*, accessed 14 March 2004 at www.dekker.com.

Hume, D. (1980 [1751]), *An Enquiry Concerning the Principles of Morals*, Westport, CT: Greenwood Press.

Inglehart, R. (2000), 'Globalization and postmodern values', Washington Quarterly, **23**(1), 215–28, accessed 5 September, 2003, at www.worldvaluesurvey.org/library/index.html.

Kagan, J. (1998), *Three Seductive Ideas*, Cambridge, MA: Harvard University Press.

Kagan, J. (2000), 'Jerome Kagan', interview with Norman Swan, 1 July, Australian Broadcasting Corporation, Radio National.

Kahneman, D. and D. Lovallo (1993), 'Timid choices and bold forecasts: a cognitive perspective on risk taking', *Management Science* **39**(1) (January), 17–31.

Kahneman, D. and A. Tversky (1979), 'Prospect theory: an analysis of decision under risk', *Econometrica*, **47**, 263–92.

Kahneman, D., P. Slovic and A. Tversky (1982), *Judgment under Uncertainty: Heuristics and Biases*, New York: Cambridge University Press.

Kohlberg, L. (1980), 'Stages of moral development as a basis for moral education', in B. Munsey (ed.), *Moral Development, Moral Education, and Kohlberg*. Birmingham, AL: Religious Education Press, pp. 15–98.

Kohlberg, L. (1981), *The Philosophy of Moral Development: Moral Stages and the Idea of Justice*, vol. 1, New York: HarperCollins.

Lane, R.E. (2000), *The Loss of Happiness in Market Democracies*, Hew Haven, CT: Yale University Press.

Lewis, C.W. (2005), 'Ethical norms in public service', report to the World Bank Poverty Reduction and Economic Management Network, unpublished manuscript.

Lewis, C.W. and S.C. Gilman (2005a), *The Ethics Challenge in Public Service: A Problem-Solving Guide*, San Francisco, CA: Jossey-Bass.

Lewis, C.W. and S.C. Gilman (2005b), 'Normative and institutional currents and commonalities: a global perspective for public managers', *Public Integrity* **7**(4), 331–43.

Loewenstein, G. (2001), 'The creative destruction of decision research', *Journal of Consumer Research* **28** (December), 499–505.

Maslow, A. (1954), *Motivation and Personality*, New York: Harper.

Moreno, Alejandro (2002), 'Corruption and democracy: a cultural assessment', accessed 5 September, 2003 at www.worldvaluessurvey.org/library/index.html.

Myers, M.D. and F.B. Tan (2002), 'Beyond models of national culture', *Journal of Global Information Management*, **10**(1), 24–32.

Noddings, N. (1984), *Caring: A Feminine Approach to Ethics and Moral Education*, Berkeley, CA: University of California Press.

Nussbaum, M. and A. Sen (eds) (1993), *The Quality of Life*, Oxford: Clarendon Press.

Organisation for Economic Co-op and Development (2004), 'Measures for promoting integrity and preventing corruption: how to assess?', Public Governance Committee report GOV/PGC(2004)24, Paris: OECD.

Olin, D. (2003), 'Prospect theory', *New York Times*, 8 June, magazine section, accessed 7 June 2003 at www.nytimes.com.

Rawls, J. (1971), *A Theory of Justice*, Cambridge, MA: Harvard University Press.

Rohr, J.A. (1989), *Ethics for Bureaucrats: An Essay on Law and Values*, 2nd edn, New York: Marcel Dekker.

Shweder, R.A. (1999), 'Three seductive ideas' (review), *Science*, **283**(5403), 798.

Simon, H. (1948), *Administrative Behavior*, New York: Macmillan.

Singer, P. (1979), *Practical Ethics*, Cambridge, UK: Cambridge University Press.

Smith, R.W. (2004), 'A comparison of the ethics infrastructure in China and the United States: should public servants be executed for breaches of ethics – or is a $150 fine enough?', *Public Integrity*, **6**(4), 299–318.

Stewart, D.W., N.W. Sprinthall and D.M. Shafer (2001), 'Moral development in public administration', in T.L. Cooper (ed.), *Handbook of Administrative Ethics*, 2nd edn, New York: Marcel Dekker, 457–80.

Swisher, L.L., A. Rizzo and M.A. Marley (2001), 'Moral reasoning among public administrators', *Public Integrity* **3**(1), 53–68.

Tayeb, M.H. (1994), 'Organizations and national culture: methodology considered', *Organization Studies*, special issue on cross-national organization culture, **15**(3), 429–46.

Terkel, S.N. and R.S. Duval (eds) (1999), *Encyclopedia of Ethics*, New York: Facts on File.

Turiel, E. (1994), 'Making sense of social experiences and moral judgments', *Criminal Justice Ethics*, **13**(2), 69–76.

Turiel, E. (2002), *The Culture of Morality, Social Development, Context, and Conflict*, Cambridge, UK: Cambridge University Press.

van der Wal, Z., L.W.J.C. Huberts, J.H.J. van den Heuvel, and E.W. Kolthoff (2006), 'Central values of government and business: differences, similarities, and conflicts', *Public Administration Quarterly*, **30**(4).

Welzel, C., R. Iglehart and H. Klingemann (n.d.), 'Human development as a theory of social change: a cross-cultural perspective', accessed 14 March 2004 at http://wvs.isr.umich.edu/papers/KRISEJPR.pdf.

White, R.D. Jr. (1999), 'Public ethics, moral development, and the enduring legacy of Lawrence Kohlberg: implications for public officials', *Public Integrity*, **1**(2), 121–34.

White, R.D. Jr. (2003), 'Moral development theory', in J. Rabin (ed.), *Encyclopedia of Public Administration and Public Policy*, accessed 14 April, 2004 at http://marceldekker.com.

Wilson, E.O. (1975), *Sociobiology, New Synthesis*, Cambridge, MA: Belknap Press.

Wright, R. (1994), *The Moral Animal: Why We Are the Way We Are: The New Science of Evolutionary Psychology*, New York: Pantheon Books.

# APPENDIX. SIX MAJOR SOURCES OF MORAL VALUES AND BEHAVIORAL NORMS

| Source | Field | Example | Method of Acquisition | Characteristics |
|---|---|---|---|---|
| **Human Universals** | | | | |
| | Developmental psychology | L. Kohlberg | Moral development | Universal stages of development, morality as generalizable, empirical |
| | Natural rights | US Declaration of Independence | Natural or God-given | Universal, immutable, normative |
| | Sociobiology, bio-behavioralism, evolutionary psychology | Genetics, E.O. Wilson, Robert Wright (popular science) | Innate | Universal, evolutionary, empirical |
| **Cultural/Social** | | | | |
| | Behavioral psychology | I. Pavlov, B.F. Skinner situationalism, J. Doris | Conditioning | Relative to experience with environment, empirical |
| | Developmental Psychology | J. Kagan | Innate motive, not behavior | Desire to be virtuous does not mean behavioral consistency across cultures |
| | Anthropology/ sociology | | Socialization | Relative to society, empirical |
| | Civic virtue, moral character | Ancient Greece | Socialization | Relative to community, normative |
| | Common sense | Nurturer, adult care giver | Socialization | Applicable to moral choices (good vs. bad), normative/empirical |
| | Vulgar version | Cultural relativism | Socialization | Only criterion is immediate social worth |
| **Rational (analysis, cognitive processes)** | | | | |
| | Deontology | I. Kant, S. Bok (popular version) | Thought, reason, education | Universal principles and duties with intrinsic value, categorical |

| | | | | |
|---|---|---|---|---|
| | Vulgar deontology | Trump | Thought, reason, education | imperative, applicable to moral choice and moral judgment (dilemmas), normative Exclusive focus on single principle or duty |
| | consequentialism (teleology) | John Stuart Mill | | Actions judged instrumentally by effects on community; utility entails minimizing pain broadly defined; applicable to moral choice and moral judgment, normative |
| | | J. Bentham | | Calculus focuses on pleasure broadly defined |
| | Vulgar consequentialism | Simplistic egoism | | Exclusive focus on short-term self-interest, self, self-indulgence, and pain, normative |
| Emotional (emotion and/or needs-based) | Normative theory Cognitive psychology | D. Hume D. Kahneman and Tversky's Prospect theory | Experience, expertise | Critique of moral rationalism Empirically identifiable universal principles but action related to perception, anchoring, categorization, pattern matching, risk assessment |
| | Behavioral social psychology | A. Maslow, J. Turiel | Incentives/ disincentives | Hierarchy of relative prepotency of needs, including fear, guilt, shame, pride, honor, attachments |
| | | HR Management, Theories X, Y, Z | Training, incentives, virtue | |
| Religion | Theology | Religious perspectives | God-given, knowable through rational/ | Universal and immutable among believers/adherents, normative |

| Source | Field | Example | Method of Acquisition | Characteristics |
| --- | --- | --- | --- | --- |
| | | Natural Law | emotional processes and/or revelation St Augustine | God-given, universal, immutable, normative |
| Professionalism (role) | Bureaucracy | Max Weber | | Career, separation of primary and primary relationships produces potential for conflict of interest Prohibition against bribery; justice, and public interest |
| | Selected historical illustrations Selected transnational examples | OECD, World Bank, Inter-American Convention (Art. III), United Nations | Training, incentives, virtue | Core values and duties in value statements/codes |
| | Selected models – governmental ethics systems | South African Public Service Commission Finland, Great Britain's Seven principles of public life, other | Training, incentives, virtue | Core values and duties |
| | Public expectations | World values survey, transparency international | | Values and duties |

*Source:* © 2005. Carol W. Lewis. Reprinted by permission.

# 5. Judging a public official's integrity

## Frédérique Six and Leo W.J.C. Huberts

## INTRODUCTION

In most democratic countries the integrity of public officials is occasionally questioned based upon allegations of misconduct or seemingly dubious decisions. Allegations of being corrupt, or at least having acted without integrity, are very serious allegations. They almost always are very damaging for the reputation of the politician or public servant and can lead to the end of his career. Because of this criticality, it could be expected that integrity researchers would have directed their attention to providing theory-based guidelines for judging a public official's integrity. This, however, has not been the case thus far.

The argument here is that the present line of research regarding the integrity of public officials is incomplete. Greater clarity is needed in defining the concept and addressing fundamental issues such as who is judged by whom and on what basis? Menzel's (1999, 2005) insightful reviews of the existing public ethics and integrity literature showed that most research to date has focused on examining public officials themselves, the institutional ethical arrangements they are subjected to, and the broader ethical environment in which they operate. Insofar as these researchers have made judgments about a public official's integrity, they have relied either on legal convictions or on personal criteria/opinions (Dobel, 1999; Holbrook and Meier, 1993). For example, Dobel (1999) presented a set of criteria to be applied in several stages for judging the integrity of a public official prior to his or her appointment to office. Another line of reasoning can be found in public attitude-centered corruption research, which has investigated public attitudes toward political corruption (Malec, 1993). However, the different research perspectives have not been used to develop a more general theory-based framework for judging public officials' integrity.

The purpose of this study is to address this gap in current public integrity research. The main research question is: How to judge the integrity of a public official? We focus our research on the integrity of the individual public official, not organizational or institutional integrity. A public official can be an elected official (for example, a member of parliament or local council), a politically appointed official (for example, a cabinet minister), or an administrative official (for example, a police officer, policy maker or health inspector) (Frederickson, 1993). This study is conceptual in nature, filling the need for an objective and thorough theory-based examination of this important topic.

We address these questions using concepts and results from the literature on trust. The chapter is the result of discussions between integrity and trust researchers. We begin our investigation with a review of the concept of integrity, followed by a review of the way the trust literature deals with similar questions. The latter review has helped sharpen our argument. We proceed by addressing, respectively, who judges an actor's integrity and what criteria for judging integrity should be used. Next, we apply these general terms to various types of public officials and develop propositions for empirical research. We conclude with a summary of our argument and implications for future public integrity research.

## DEFINING INTEGRITY

Even though the focus here is on public officials, integrity is integral to all professions and organizations. This does not mean, however, that the concept of integrity is clear and uncontested (Montefiore, 1999; Chapman, 2000; Blenkert, 2004). The literature on ethics and integrity reveals a number of differing perspectives (Box 5.1; Huberts, 2005).

One perspective defines integrity as 'wholeness' or completeness, a consistency and coherence of a set of principles and values (in line with one of the meanings of the Latin *integras*: intact, whole, harmonious). Montefiore

---

### BOX 5.1   PERSPECTIVES ON INTEGRITY

1. Integrity as wholeness
2. Integrity as a specific value (incorruptibility) or a number of values and norms
3. Integrity as the quality of acting in accordance with laws and codes
4. Integrity as the quality of acting in accordance with relevant moral values and norms
5. Integrity as exemplary moral behavior

states, based on an inventory of the literature on integrity: 'The association with wholeness seems to be dominant' (1999: 9). A disadvantage of interpretations in terms of wholeness and consistency is the lack of what Blenkert calls a moral filter: 'integrity involves more than simply doing what one says; what one says and does must also pass through some moral filter' (Blenkert, 2004: 4). McFall (1987) also points out the argument in her distinction between personal and moral integrity. Many examples exist where a person showed high internal coherence and therefore high personal integrity, yet we would not readily grant him the general distinction of having high integrity (McFall, 1987).

Other perspectives are, more than the consistency perspectives, characterized by the relationship between integrity and what is right and wrong, referring thus to morals. The second perspective sees integrity as either one specific value or a collection of values. When integrity is one of the specific values referred to in codes of conduct, it usually means incorruptibility or righteousness. The official should not be guided by self-interest or group or party interest, but should serve the interests of the organization or of society. According to Dobel, a public official has to deal with three types of obligations 'obligations of office, personal commitment and capacity, and prudence' (1999: 20). Together they add up to 'seven standards that I propose as focal commitments for public integrity', including 'be truthfully accountable to the relevant authorities and publics', 'address the public values of the political regime' and 'demand competent performance effectiveness in the execution of policy' (Dobel, 1999: 21). Still other perspectives view integrity more as an umbrella concept, referring to sets of values that are relevant for the official who is judged.

The third perspective considered here is the legal or constitutional one, summarized by Rohr (1989: 4–5): 'bureaucrats have an ethical obligation to respond to the values of the people in whose name they govern. The values in question are not popular whims of the moment, but rather constitutional or regime values'. The constitutional interpretation of relevant values and norms is attractive because it is clear concerning which matter and which should be applied when we judge the integrity of a public official. The problem, however, is that the law itself is not a very clear guiding principle in actual decision-making and implementation processes in government (let alone in other sectors such as business).

Further, sometimes the law is in conflict with the moral values and norms of the population and, as a consequence, a broader interpretation in terms of 'complying with the moral values and norms' seems more appropriate. In this fourth perspective, integrity is a characteristic or quality of an actor, for example a public official, meaning that what the official does (or does not do) is in accordance with the relevant moral values and norms (and the laws and rules resulting from them) (Fijnaut and Huberts, 2002; Thomas, 2001; Uhr, 1999). This of course resembles 'a general way of acting morally' and 'morality' (Blenkert, 2004, p. 5).

The fifth and final perspective stresses that integrity is something for which one can strive. Van Luijk stated (2004: 39), 'Integrity now stands for complying in an exemplary way with specific moral standards'. Or even stronger, integrity is the 'stuff of moral courage and even heroism' (Blenkert, 2004: 5).

In our research on the integrity of governance we are using the fourth perspective, integrity as the quality of acting in accordance with relevant moral values and norms. Basically, the arguments for that choice have already been put forward. An integrity judgment always also brings in what is considered right or wrong, the moral dimension. This dimension goes beyond comparing the person's behavior with one (or some) specific values; an official can be said to have acted with integrity when it is ethical in a more generic sense. In a democracy, laws and codes are a reflection of those ethics, but the judicial framework is not always applicable to the behavior that is judged. Much behavior is not regulated, for example private behavior, and sometimes the law can contradict the dominant values in society concerning a public official's behavior. As a consequence, the perspective has to include the more informal values and norms that are relevant for the behavior to be judged. These values and norms clarify what is right and wrong in given circumstances. They do not, in our view, state what is exemplary and admirable; to surmise that a person has acted with integrity, it suffices that the behavior is right and defendable.

This fourth perspective is well-supported by a body of literature that considers integrity as synonymous with being moral or ethical. What is less common, however, is the attempt to clarify and specify the concept and perspective by answering a number of aspects or questions, as done in this study. Before we address these questions, attention is paid to the literature on trust and trustworthiness. We use these insights to sharpen our argument regarding how to judge a public official's integrity.

## TRUST, TRUSTWORTHINESS AND INTEGRITY

Largely following the growing consensus among trust researchers (including Hosmer, 1995; Lane, 1998; Mayer *et al.*, 1995; Rousseau *et al.*, 1998), we define trust as a psychological state comprising the intention to accept vulnerability to the actions of another party, based upon the expectation that the other will perform a particular action important to you. Since trust is related to the positive expectation that it will not be taken advantage of, it requires the absence of opportunistic behavior by the trustee so that the trustor can make himself vulnerable to the action(s) of the trustee. An important antecedent of a trustor's trust in a trustee is the trustor's perception of the trustee's trustworthiness. Mayer *et al.* (1995) refer to trustworthiness as a characteristic of a trustee that is responsible for trust. Trust and trustworthiness are thus two concepts that 'belong' to different actors. Trust is an attribute of a trustor and trustworthiness is an attribute of a trustee. The trust literature is very clear regarding who judges an actor's trustworthiness. The trustor's perceptions of the trustee's trustworthiness are what counts (Hardin, 2002; Lindenberg, 2000; Mayer *et al.*, 1995; Six, 2005); thus, an actor's trustworthiness is ultimately determined by the other's perceptions. This has important consequences, because there are bound to be differences in perceptions between the two actors (Hardin, 2002).

How does a trustor determine a trustee's trustworthiness? Trust building is a process in which an actor learns about the other's trustworthiness in different situations (Gabarro, 1978; Six, 2005). An actor's perceptions of the trustworthiness of another actor are thus based on learning, primarily cognitively based and secondarily on forging emotional bonds (McAllister, 1995). Information of any sort, either directly through interaction with the other actor or indirectly from third parties or the context within which the interaction takes place, will be used as the basis for the judgment. The actor probably always has information of some sort available, and at the same time is usually limited in the capacity to ever achieve full knowledge of the other actor and the other actor's motives (Gambetta, 1988). Thus, errors of judgment can occur because knowledge is necessarily incomplete (Hardin, 1993; Gambetta, 1988).

In sum, and applying it to a public official: a public official's trustworthiness is relevant to another actor who is dependent on the public official's future behavior. The other actor is concerned with whether the official is interested in maintaining a relationship. The other actor's perceptions of the official's trustworthiness are what count for the judgment of the official's trustworthiness; not how the official views his or her own trustworthiness. The actor needs information about the other's trustworthiness upon which to base any judgment. This information is related to the actions and motives of the official, and can be obtained through direct interaction or indirectly from third parties, or the context within which the official operates. Errors of judgment can occur because knowledge is necessarily incomplete and the actor may interpret wrongly. If the actor has insufficient information upon which to base a judgment of trustworthiness, this does not imply that the official is untrustworthy. A judgment of untrustworthiness, leading to distrust, needs to be based on information, just like a judgment of trustworthiness.

For trust and trustworthiness, the central relationship is one between two actors and the criteria for judgment are the four dimensions of trustworthiness: ability, dedication, benevolence and norm-acceptability (Six, 2005). A trusts B (or not) and B is trustworthy in A's eyes (or not). A is the judge of B's trustworthiness (Figure 1a). In comparing integrity and trustworthiness, norm-acceptability is a key dimension. If B's norms are unacceptable to A, A's trust in B is undermined. Whether B's norms are acceptable to A is strongly related to A's own norms.

Even though trust and integrity are often used in conjunction with one another, they are different concepts. Integrity is a concept similar to trustworthiness rather than trust. Both integrity and trustworthiness refer to attributes of a specific actor – in trust terminology, the trustee – that make that actor have higher or lower integrity or trustworthiness in the eyes of another actor – again in trust terminology, the trustor. In both cases, it is generally considered good to maximize the amount of each. The relationship between integrity and trust is such that the higher an actor's integrity, the more he will be trusted by another actor.

Both concepts differ in important ways. Trustworthiness is restricted to the specific relationship: is the other actor interested in maintaining a relationship with me? Is the other actor benevolent to me? Are their norms acceptable to me? (Mayer *et al.*, 1995). On the other hand, integrity, as shown above, is based on a 'relevant set of moral values, norms and rules', not what I, personally, may hold as values and norms, nor my personal interests.

### Judging an Actor's Integrity

The review of contemporary trust research points to the importance of the question, who judges an actor's integrity? Can an actor be his own judge or evaluator? Or, can another individual be the judge or evaluator based on his or her own values or norms? The actor whose integrity is in question will usually consider him or herself to be acting with integrity, considering the circumstances; this belief is facilitated by psychological mechanisms such as cognitive dissonance reduction (Dobel, 1999). As Srivastva (1988: 19) noted, 'the intriguing fact is that very few of us see ourselves as lacking in integrity, yet we can readily point to disintegrity in almost every institution in which we are involved'. Part of the explanation, as he proposed, is that the other actor may see things very differently, also due to differences in mental maps, worldviews, expectations and goal definitions (for example, Weick, 1995). These differences, in turn, lead to different values and norms (Schein, 1992). Thus, an actor's integrity is ultimately determined by another's perceptions.

**a**

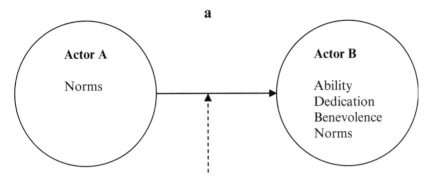

*A's judgment of B's trustworthiness*

**b**

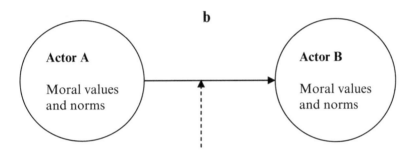

*A's moral judgment about B*

*Figure 5.1    Contrasting A's judgment of B's trustworthiness with A's moral judgment of B: (a) A's judgment of B's trustworthiness and roles of both their norms; (b) A's moral judgment of B*

If it is the perception of the other that ultimately determines an actor's integrity, what are the implications? To elucidate our argument, we contrast trustworthiness and integrity. A is the judge of B's trustworthiness (Figure 5.1a). What is characteristic for integrity and judging integrity? How can actor A judge B's integrity? A first difference is that judging integrity is less reciprocal or mutual than judging trustworthiness. There is no such thing as mutual integrity, whereas there can be, and often is, mutual trust. It is always only one actor's integrity that is at stake or being judged. For A to judge B, it is not very relevant how B judges A's integrity. A second difference between trust (and trustworthiness) and integrity concerns the relevant criteria. Our choice to define integrity as acting in accordance with relevant moral values and norms means that applicable criteria are those that address moral intention and character rather than the resources or capabilities of an actor. When A judges B's morals, A's judgment of B is based on A's own moral values and norms (Figure 5.1b).

Every citizen or journalist can have a moral opinion about a public official's behavior. When the press photographs a cabinet minister as coming out of a brothel, we form an opinion of this cabinet minister. In Figure 5.1b this is called 'A's moral judgment of B'. Does this automatically mean that the cabinet minister's behavior lacks integrity? We think not and this brings us to a last crucial aspect where integrity differs from trustworthiness. Even when actor A, a citizen, condemns actor B, a politician, morally and with the utmost sincerity, this is not sufficient to conclude that B is a public official who failed to show integrity. Somehow, integrity brings in greater numbers of people and broader criteria that overrule one's own morals. The definition says 'relevant' moral norms, values and rules and this introduces the question what, as well as whose, values and norms matter. We discuss those 'categories of integrity criteria' below. Here, it is important to stress the relevance of people other than the actors A and B. A's judgment of the integrity of actor B should take into account the relevant publics. In Figure 5.2 the behavior of actor B, a politician, is judged. The values and norms of 'the public' and of 'organization/party' are mentioned. These seem to be the relevant stakeholders to include. Actor A is more than a judge in the strict sense; actor A is also an interpreter and evaluator of the relevant moral values and norms of the relevant publics as they apply to the behavior of actor B.

Thus, we argue that in contrast to judgments of trustworthiness, integrity judgments need two types of information. First, similar to trustworthiness, information is needed about the actions of the other actor. Second, integrity judgments require information about the content of the 'relevant set of moral values, norms and rules'. This implies that before you can make a statement 'Mary has no integrity', you need to somehow have knowledge of the judgment of the majority of the relevant stakeholder group regarding Mary's actions. Therefore, there are stricter requirements before a judgment of integrity or disintegrity can be passed than are required for a judgment of trustworthy/untrustworthy.

But how to determine what the relevant stakeholder group is when the integrity of an official is judged? A first possible answer is the group that has granted the individual the discretion or power to act in ways that affect others. For an elected official, the electorate is the relevant stakeholder group. If the public official is appointed, then those who appointed him or her are part of the relevant stakeholder group. However, public officials perform a public task and, either directly or indirectly through lines of reporting, have to be accountable for their performance to some

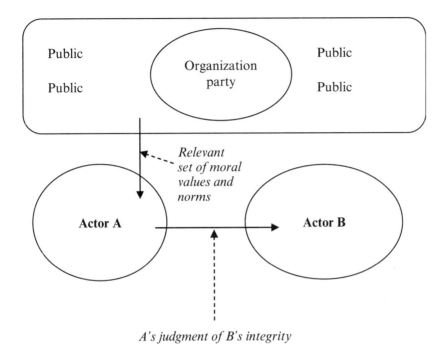

*Figure 5.2    A judging B's integrity*

representative body of the electorate (for example, Parliament). Therefore, one could argue that for all types of public officials, citizens are ultimately the relevant stakeholder group. A second possible answer is that those who are affected by the public official's actions should be part of the relevant stakeholder group. This notion has its limits though. Should the integrity of the US President also be judged by the Iraqi people because they are directly affected by his decision to invade Iraq and oust Saddam Hussein in 2003? It appears safe to state that those actors who are affected by a public official's actions and are part – directly or indirectly – of the group that has granted the discretion or power, should be part of the relevant stakeholder group.

**Criteria for Judgment of Integrity**

Who determines the set of relevant moral values and codes? In the case of a public official performing a public task, 'the public' in principle would have such authority. But referring back to 'the public' – citizens – and surveying their opinion for every allegation of misconduct before passing judgment or before important appointments is impractical and undesirable. Other mechanisms are in place, or can be put in place, through which the relevant set of moral values, norms and rules of the citizens can affect such judgments.

Within the fourth perspective of integrity, three categories of integrity criteria can be distinguished, from very strict and clear-cut to more open to different interpretations and perceptions. First, allegations of misconduct with regard to laws will be dealt with by the judicial system. Provided the judicial system is seen as having high, or at least sufficient, integrity itself, the judgments passed by the system will generally be accepted.[1] Every citizen and holder of a particular office covered by the law is required to comply. In properly functioning democracies over time, laws are reasonably in line with the majority of the moral values and norms of the citizens.

The next integrity criterion consists of the formal codes of conduct or ethical codes produced by an organization or professional association, for example, rules and codes of conduct for parliament or administration. Members of the organization or profession are expected to comply with the code. Allegations of misconduct with regard to the code will be dealt with by either the employee's (organizational) superior or a special committee within the professional association. In the case of politicians, the relevant representative body, such as parliament or local council, will act as judge. Allegations of misconduct in this category are thus dealt with by self-regulation and judgments can therefore be criticized by outside stakeholders. If the code is too far out of line with the moral values and norms of the majority of the citizens, the code cannot be the only framework for judging integrity.

The third criterion is the usually informal moral values and norms by which the stakeholders and citizens expect the public official to abide. Because they are usually informal, they are open to differences in interpretation and perceptions. Also, allegations of misconduct with regard to informal values and norms not covered by the two previous categories have, at present, no explicit platform for discussion or judgment.

The actual content in these three categories of integrity criteria is subject to changes over time and will vary from situation to situation, depending upon the type of public institution or country. Because the content of the two first categories is in written form and has been formally accepted by the relevant representative body, all public officials can be required to abide by these laws, regulations and codes. Because of the usually informal nature of the values and norms in the third category, expectations are likely to vary. Also, as values and norms vary by group of people, it is important to know who will be the judge, evaluating the public official's behavior, and based on which criteria (whose values and norms).

# IMPLICATIONS FOR JUDGING PUBLIC OFFICIAL'S INTEGRITY

As already mentioned, judgments of a public official's integrity are relevant when he or she is elected or appointed and when allegations are made of moral misconduct while the official is in office. At each moment, other criteria will also enter into the final judgment, such as competence and political–administrative considerations.

For each type of public official – elected officials, politically appointed officials and administrative officials – we identify for each category of integrity – laws, rules and codes, and informal moral values and norms – what the criteria are and who the judge is. A summary is provided in Table 5.1. We also reflect on what common practice appears to be in most democracies.

## Elected Officials

Politicians need to abide by election laws and penal laws. Judicial courts are the judge when allegations are made of misconduct regarding these laws. In many democracies, political parties and parliaments (at all levels of government) have, furthermore, formulated codes regarding the conduct that is expected of their members. If a politician is accused of breaching these codes, his or her party or parliament judges the politician's integrity. If a politician is accused of moral misconduct, but has been cleared of breaching the laws and formal rules and codes of conduct, his behavior may still be considered morally wrong. Yet how is it possible to make such a judgment? In most democracies there are no formal procedures for this situation, other than to wait for the next election and let the voters be the judges; or to convince the politician to step down 'voluntarily'. Our argument so far would suggest that the informal moral values and norms of the relevant stakeholder(s) should be the criteria for such a judgment. The relevant stakeholders for an elected official are the citizens and parliament. A systematic inventory of the moral values and norms of citizens and parliament regarding the expected conduct of elected officials is required as the basis for a judgment of a politician's integrity. As far as we know, very few, if any, democracies have such a systematic inventory. Often opinion polls are held after specific allegations are made public against a specific politician, but then the results may be tainted by considerations other than the purely moral (for example, I never liked him anyway, or I love her ideas). In between elections, parliament is, we propose, the appropriate judge basing its judgment on evaluations of the relevant set of moral values and norms of key stakeholders. During elections, citizens will incorporate their

Table 5.1  *Judging a public official's integrity: who is judged, based on what and by whom*

| Type of public official | Category of integrity criteria | | | | | |
|---|---|---|---|---|---|---|
| | Laws | | Rules and codes | | Informal moral values and norms | |
| | Criteria | Judge | Criteria | Judge | Criteria | Judge |
| Elected official | Election and penal laws | Court | Rules and codes of party and parliament[a] | Party, parliament | Moral values and norms of citizens and parliament | Parliament (while in office), voters (during election) |
| Politically appointed official | Administrative and penal laws | Court | Rules and codes of parliament and government[a] | Parliament | Moral values and norms of citizens and parliament | Parliament |
| Administrative official | Administrative and penal laws | Court | Rules and codes of administration | Government, parliament | Moral values and norms of citizens, administration and parliament | Government, parliament |

*Note:*  [a]  Parliament and government can be at any level: national/federal, state, regional or local.

perception of the official's integrity into their considerations when deciding to vote for a candidate. Integrity is an important criterion when deciding whom to vote for, but it is not the only criterion.

## Politically Appointed Officials

Politically appointed officials also need to abide by the relevant laws, which in their case are the administrative and penal laws. As with elected officials, if allegations are made of misconduct, courts are the judge. If a politically appointed official is accused of breaking the codes of conduct of government or parliament, parliament is the judge. Even if both court or parliament clear the appointed official of (moral) misconduct based on the laws and codes, his or her behavior may still be considered morally wrong. Again, in most democracies there are no formal procedures for judging an official's integrity in this situation, other than to wait for the first opportunity to sack the official or to convince the official to step down 'voluntarily'. Our argument in this chapter suggests that the informal moral values and norms of the citizens and parliament, the relevant stakeholders, should be the criteria for such a judgment. Parliament can be considered as the primary interpreter and evaluator of those values and norms and therefore is the appropriate judge of the politically appointed official's integrity. Again, as far as we know, very few, if any, democracies keep a systematic inventory of the moral values and norms of citizens and parliament regarding the (moral) conduct of politically appointed officials.

## Administrative Officials

Civil servants also need to abide by the administrative and penal laws and judicial courts judge any alleged breaches. They are furthermore expected to abide by the codes of conduct of administration and any alleged breaches will first be judged by their politically appointed superiors – government – and in the second instance by parliament. Again, in most democracies no formal procedures are in place for judging a civil servant's integrity in situations where his or her behavior is considered morally wrong, but he or she has been cleared of breaching any laws or codes. The superior may use other criteria or considerations (such as political–administrative ones) to sack the civil servant or convince him or her to step down 'voluntarily'. In these situations the informal moral values and norms of the relevant stakeholders are the criteria for a judgment of the official's integrity. The relevant stakeholders in this situation are citizens, administration and parliament. If a systematic inventory of the moral values and norms of citizens, administration and parliament regarding the (moral) conduct of civil servants is available, then government, as the primary judge, or parliament, as the secondary judge, can form an opinion on the civil servant's integrity.

In sum, courts judge whether the official has acted in accordance with the relevant laws. Acting in accordance with the relevant codes of conduct is judged by political and administrative leadership; the party also has a say in the case of the elected politician; and government has a say in the case of the administrative official. While an official is in office, parliament judges whether he or she has acted in accordance with the informal moral values and norms of the relevant stakeholders – citizens and parliament (and administration for administrative officials). For the administrative official, government is also the judge. For the elected official during elections, the citizens are also the judge.

## CONCLUSIONS AND FURTHER DIRECTIONS

The purpose of this study was to develop a theory-based framework for judging a public official's integrity. The questions we addressed were: Who is the judge? What are the criteria for judging? And what kind of information is required for judging a public official's integrity? These questions were triggered by a comparison between the trust and integrity literatures, which strengthened the analysis. Our argument is based on the assumption that it is only valid in reasonably functioning democracies in which most inhabitants are recognized and participate as citizens. The first part of the argument was that of the five different perspectives on integrity present in the literature, the view is preferable which sees integrity as the quality of acting in accordance with relevant moral values and norms. This triggers the questions: What is this set of relevant moral values and norms? Whose formal and informal norms, values and rules should be included?

Next, we examined the consequences of this view for judging a public official's integrity. First, who is the judge? We argued that it makes no sense that an official should be the judge of his or her own integrity; most of us probably consider ourselves to be acting with integrity, considering the circumstances. Also, another individual basing his judgment on his or her own moral values and norms can only have a personal moral judgment, but not a judgment of the official's integrity. A judgment of a public official's integrity is only possible if the judging actor refers to the set of relevant moral values and norms, as determined by the majority of the relevant stakeholders. In the case of public officials performing a public task, we argued that the relevant stakeholders always include 'the public', citizens.

Thus, we argued that two types of information are required before the integrity of a public official can be judged. First, like judgments of trustworthiness, information is required about the behavior of the public official. Second, information is required about the content of the set of relevant moral values and norms that it is expected he or she would abide. A statement 'Mary has no integrity' is meaningless if it is based only on one's personal moral values and norms. Only if we somehow have knowledge of the judgment of the majority of the relevant stakeholders – particularly the citizens – regarding actions like Mary's, can we make sound judgments of Mary's integrity.

However, surveying citizens' opinions for every allegation of moral misconduct before passing judgment, or before important appointments, is impractical and undesirable. We proceeded to present three categories of integrity criteria that nonetheless enable the relevant set of moral values and norms of citizens to affect such judgments (Table 5.1). The first category consists of the relatively clear-cut laws that are part of the local, national or international legal system. Allegations of (moral) misconduct with regard to these laws are dealt with by the judicial system (courts). The second category consists of the formal codes of conduct produced by the organization or professional association, such as codes of conduct for parliament. Allegations of (moral) misconduct in this category are usually dealt with by the organization or professional association themselves, in other words, by self-regulation. For example, parliament will be the judge of any allegation of misconduct with respect to parliamentary codes of conduct. The third category consists of the informal moral values and norms by which citizens and other relevant stakeholders expect the public official to abide. Due to their informal nature, these are open to differences in interpretation and perception. Also, allegations of moral misconduct with regard to the informal values and norms not covered by the previous two categories usually have no explicit platform for discussion or judgment.

A judgment about a public official's integrity is usually not made in isolation. The situation is often such that the moral judgment (about the official's integrity) is one of several considerations for decisions regarding the official's (continued) appointment. Political and/or administrative judgments are usually also involved. We urge researchers and practitioners to take more care in separating these different judgments. Judgments about someone's disintegrity/corruptness are usually considered quite damaging, while political or administrative considerations can more easily be overcome in future.

We have been somewhat surprised to find that, even though most integrity researchers appear to agree that others should be the judge of someone's integrity, they have not acted on it, as most integrity research to date has focused on studying public officials themselves. The clear implication of this study is that research is needed on the content of the 'relevant set of moral values, norms and rules', that is, what do citizens consider morally acceptable conduct on the part of public officials? In most democracies, the first two categories of integrity criteria (laws, and rules and codes) are formally written down and procedures are in place for dealing with allegations of breaches. The quality of the laws, rules and codes, and the quality of the procedures, across levels of government, across countries, and for each type of public official, need to be studied systematically.

In theory, in a properly functioning democracy, laws, rules and codes of conduct should, over time, be sufficiently in line with the 'relevant set of moral values, norms and rules'. However, when the first two categories are not sufficiently in line with the majority of citizens' expectations, discontent may grow. And as a consequence, the third category of integrity criteria may be invoked more often. This category of integrity criteria requires that a systematic inventory is present of the (informal) moral values and norms of citizens, parliament and administration regarding the expected (moral) conduct of public officials. As far as we know, few, if any, democracies have made such a systematic inventory, let alone update it regularly. Public opinion polls abound after specific allegations have been made against a specific public official, but these results are likely to be tainted by considerations other than the purely moral. Corruption research focused on public attitudes may provide a valuable starting point for creating such systematic inventories, and making them operational for judgments of public officials' integrity.

Thus, systematic empirical research is needed into citizens' perceptions of public officials' integrity, distinguishing at least the three types of officials included in this study and the different levels of government. Related to this, it is necessary to determine citizens' expectations regarding public officials' integrity. What is the content of this 'relevant set of moral values, norms and rules' for the different types of official in different situations (across levels of government and across countries)?

## NOTE

1.  The arguments in this chapter assume that a democracy is in place and no large groups of inhabitants are excluded from citizenship (for example, the black inhabitants in South Africa under the Apartheid regime, or slaves during the centuries that slavery was not banned).

## REFERENCES

Blenkert, G.G. (2004), 'The need for corporate integrity', in G.G. Blenkert (ed.), *Corporate Integrity and Accountability*, Thousand Oaks, CA: Sage, pp. 1–10.

Chapman, R.A. (ed.) (2000), *Ethics in the Public Service for the New Millennium*, Aldershot: Ashgate.

Dobel, J.P. (1999), *Public Integrity*, Baltimore, MD: Johns Hopkins University Press.

Fijnaut C. and L.W.J.C. Huberts (2002), *Corruption, Integrity and Law Enforcement*, The Hague: Kluwer Law.

Frederickson, H.G. (1993), 'Introduction', in H.G. Frederickson (ed.), *Ethics and Public Administration*, Armonk, NY: Sharpe, pp. 3–12.

Gabarro, J.J. (1978), 'The development of trust, influence and expectations', in A.G. Athos and J.J. Gabarro (eds), *Interpersonal Behavior, Communication and Understanding in Relationships*, Englewood Cliffs, NJ: Prentice-Hall, pp. 290–303.

Gambetta, D. (1988), 'Can we trust trust?', in D. Gambetta (ed.), *Trust, Making and Breaking Cooperative Relations*, New York: Basil Blackwell, pp. 213–38.

Hardin, R. (1993), 'The street-level epistemology of trust', *Analyse & Kritik*, **14**, 152–76.

Hardin, R. (2002), *Trust and Trustworthiness*, Russell Sage Foundation series on trust, vol. IV, New York: Russell Sage Foundation.

Holbrook, T.M. and K.J. Meier (1993), 'Politics, bureaucracy, and political corruption: a comparative study analysis' in H.G. Frederickson (ed.), *Ethics and Public Administration*, New York: M.E. Sharpe, pp. 28–51.

Hosmer, L.T. (1995), 'Trust: the connecting link between organizational theory and philosophical ethics', *Academy of Management Review*, **20**(2), 379–403.

Huberts, L.W.J.C. (2005), *Integriteit en integritisme in bestuur en samenleving* [Integrity and Integritism in Governance and Society], Amsterdam: Vrije Universiteit.

Lane, C. (1998), 'Introduction: theories and issues in the study of trust', in C. Lane and R. Bachman (eds), *Trust Within and Between Organizations, Conceptual Issues and Empirical Applications*, Oxford: Oxford University Press, pp. 1–30.

Lindenberg, S. (2000), 'It takes both trust and lack of mistrust: the workings of cooperation and relational signaling in contractual relationships', *Journal of Management and Governance*, **4**, 11–33.

Malec, K.L. (1993), 'Public attitudes toward corruption: twenty-five years of research', in H.G. Frederickson (ed.), *Ethics and Public Administration*, Armonk, NY: M.E. Sharpe, pp. 13–27.

Mayer, R.C., J.H. Davis and F.D. Schoorman (1995), 'An integrative model of organizational trust', *Academy of Management Review*, **20**(3), 703–34.

McAllister, D.J. (1995), 'Affect- and cognition-based trust as foundations for interpersonal cooperation in organizations', *Academy of Management Journal*, **38**(1), 24–59.

McFall, L. (1987), 'Integrity', *Ethics*, **98**, 5–20.

Menzel, D.C. (1999), 'A review and assessment of empirical research on public administration ethics: implications for scholars and managers', *Public Integrity*, **1**, 239–64.

Menzel, D.C. (2005), 'Research on ethics and integrity in governance. A review and assessment', *Public Integrity*, **7**(2), 147–68.

Montefiore, A. (1999), 'Integrity: a philosophers introduction', in A. Montefiore and D. Vines (eds), *Integrity in the Public and Private Domains*, London, Routledge.

Rohr, J.A. (1989), *Ethics for Bureaucrats, an Essay on Law and Values*, New York: Marcel Dekker.

Rousseau, D.M., S.B. Sitkin, R.S. Burt and C. Camerer (1998), 'Not so different after all: a cross-discipline view of trust', *Academy of Management Review*, **23**(3), 393–404.

Schein, E.H. (1992), *Organizational Culture and Leadership*, 2nd edn, San Francisco, CA: Jossey-Bass.

Six, F.E. (2005), *The Trouble with Trust, the Dynamics of Interpersonal Trust Building*, Cheltenham, UK and Northampton, MA, USA: Edward Elgar.

Srivastra, S. (1988), 'The urgency for executive integrity', in S. Srivastra (ed.), *Executive Integrity: The Search for High Human Values in Organizational Life*, San Francisco, CA: Jossey-Bass, pp. 1–28.

Thomas, R.M. (2001), 'Public trust, integrity and privatization', *Public Integrity*, **3**, 243–61.

Uhr, J. (1999), 'Institutions of integrity, balancing values and verification in democratic governance', *Public Integrity*, **1**, 94–106.

Van Luijk, H. (2004), 'Integrity in the private, the public and the corporate domain', in G.G. Blenkert (ed.), *Corporate Integrity and Accountability*, Thousand Oaks, CA: Sage, pp. 38–54.

Weick, K.E. (1995), *Sensemaking in Organizations*, Thousand Oaks, CA: Sage Publications.

PART II

The integrity, rationality and effectiveness of governance

# 6. Ethical leadership and administrative evil: the distorting effects of technical rationality

## Guy B. Adams and Danny L. Balfour

## INTRODUCTION

This is a tale of two leaders. Both owe their reputation and careers to their membership in the Nazi party and their participation in the tragedy of the Holocaust, yet they are remembered fondly, albeit for very different reasons. One, Wernher von Braun, engaged in acts of administrative evil, but managed to achieve considerable success in his career as a rocket scientist. The other, Oskar Schindler, failed repeatedly in his professional and personal life but is remembered as an ethical exemplar, a hero who saved many lives. Their stories poignantly illustrate the paradox of ethical leadership in modern organizations, in which 'good' leaders and managers need not be ethical, and ethical leaders run the risk of being marginalized and even ostracized. These cases show that how society judges an individual's ethical behavior is less a result of the behavior itself than of the social and cultural context in which it occurs.

## THE CHALLENGE OF ADMINISTRATIVE EVIL

We have written extensively on the nature and characteristics of what we call administrative evil (Adams and Balfour, 2004). The central issue for this chapter is that despite an extensive literature on public service ethics, there is little recognition of the most fundamental ethical challenge in modern organizations: that is, one can be a 'good' and responsible professional or administrator and at the same time commit or contribute to acts of administrative evil. As Harmon (1995) has argued, contemporary professional ethics has difficulty dealing with what Milgram (1974) termed the 'agentic shift', where the professional or administrator acts responsibly toward the hierarchy of authority, public policy and the requirements of the job or profession, while abdicating any personal, much less social, responsibility for the content or effects of decisions or actions. There is little in the way of coherent justification for the notion of a stable and predictable distinction between the individual's personal conscience guided by higher values and the socialized professional or administrator who internalizes agency values and obedience to legitimate authority. In the dominant model of both public service and business ethics, the personal conscience is always subordinate to the structures of authority. The former is 'subjective' and 'personal', while the latter is characterized as 'objective' and 'public'.

We believe that the ethical failures of leadership in modern organizations are rooted in the unquestioned dominance of technical rationality (Adams and Balfour, 2004: 29–36). Technical rationality is a way of thinking and living (a culture) that emphasizes instrumental problem-solving based on the scientific-analytic mindset and faith that technological progress will lead to a better world for all (Barrett, 1979; Ellul, 1954). Donald Schon (1990: 21) and others have argued that technical rationality has been the most powerful influence on thinking both about the professions and the institutional relations of research, education, and practice. Technical rationality has unquestionably brought many benefits to humanity. At the same time, the lack of any countervailing authority in professional practice, public affairs and business has made it difficult to perceive its shortcomings, especially as a basis for ethical behavior.

Administrative and professional ethics in the technical-rational tradition draw upon both teleological and deontological ethics, and focus on the individual's decision-making process in modern, bureaucratic organizations and as a member of a profession. In the public sphere, deontological ethics are meant to safeguard the integrity of the organization by helping individuals conform to professional norms, avoid mistakes and misdeeds that violate the public trust (corruption, nepotism, and so on), and assure that public officials are accountable to the people through their elected representatives. At the same time, public servants are encouraged to pursue the greater good by using discretion in the application of rules and regulations and creativity in the face of changing conditions (teleological ethics). The 'good' public servant and administrator should avoid both the extremes of rule-bound behavior and undermining the rule of law with individual judgments and interests. It is fairly self-evident that public (and private) organizations depend on at least this level of ethical judgment in order to function efficiently and effectively, and to maintain public confidence in government (and business).

Yet confusion remains within the professions over behavior which benefits a profession or an organization, yet can also be defined as ethical behavior. As both MacIntyre (1984) and Poole (1991) have argued, modernity, thoroughly infused with technical rationality, has produced a way of thinking – an epistemology – that renders moral reasoning superfluous. Note how ethics is simply subsumed in professionalism in this statement by Kearney and Sinha (1988: 575):

> In a sense, the profession provides the professional administrator with a Rosetta Stone for deciphering and responding to various elements of the public interest. Professional accountability as embodied in norms and standards also serves as an inner check on an administrator's behavior. . . . When joined with a code of ethics or conduct and the oath of office, professionalism establishes a value system that serves as a frame of reference for decision making . . . and creates a special form of social control conducive to bureaucratic responsiveness.

Professionals do not see the technical rational model of professionalism as eschewing ethics, quite the contrary: They see the role model of 'professional' as satisfying the need for a system of ethical standards. To be professional – that is, to be technically and rationally proficient – is to be ethical.

The ethical failure, and moral vacuity, of this way of thinking is starkly illustrated in the Third Reich and the Holocaust. Many of the administrators directly responsible for the Holocaust were, from the technical-rational perspective, effective and responsible administrators who used administrative discretion to both influence and carry out the will of their superiors. Professionals and administrators such as Adolph Eichmann and Albert Speer obeyed orders, followed proper protocol and procedures, and were often innovative and creative while carrying out their assigned tasks in an efficient and effective manner (Keeley, 1983; Hilberg, 1989; Harmon, 1995; Lozowick, 2000). Ironically, the *Schutzstaffel* (SS) was very concerned about corruption in its ranks, and with strict conformance to the professional norms of its order (Sofsky, 1997).

As Rubenstein (1975) points out, no laws against genocide or dehumanization were broken by those who perpetrated the Holocaust. Everything was legally sanctioned and administratively approved by a legitimated authority, while a number of key programs and innovations were initiated from within the bureaucracy (Browning, 1989; Sofsky, 1997). Even within the morally inverted universe created by the Nazis, professionals and administrators carried out their duties within a framework of ethics and responsibility that was consistent with the norms of professionalism and technical rationality (Lifton, 1986). The professions were 'everywhere' in the Holocaust (Hilberg, 1989). Lawyers, physicians, engineers, planners, military professionals, accountants all contributed to the destruction of the Jews and other 'undesirables'. Scientific methods were used in ways that dehumanized and murdered innocent human beings. The moral vacuity of professional ethics is clearly revealed by the fact that the vast majority of those who participated in the Holocaust were never punished, and many were placed in responsible positions in post-war West German government or industry, and even within public and private organizations in the US.

If the Holocaust teaches us anything, it is that individual administrators and professionals, far from resisting administrative evil, are most likely to be either helpless victims or willing accomplices. The ethical framework within a technical rational system posits the primacy of an abstract, utility-maximizing individual, while binding professionals to organizations in ways that make them into reliable conduits for the dictates of legitimate authority, which is no less legitimate when it happens to be pursuing an evil policy. An ethical system that allows an individual to be a good adminis-trator or professional while committing acts of evil is necessarily devoid of moral content, or even morally perverse. No public servant should be able to rest easy with the notion that ethical behavior is defined by doing things the right way. Norms of legality, efficiency and effectiveness – however 'pro-fessional' they may be – do not necessarily promote or protect the well being of humans, especially that of society's most vulnerable and superfluous members. We turn now to two historical cases which we believe help illuminate how significant the public context is for understanding these paradoxes of ethical leadership.

## TWO NAZI LEADERS

Wernher von Braun became a leader as well as perhaps the world's premier rocket scientist during the 1930s and 1940s in Nazi Germany. The origins of the Nazi rocket program were in the early 1930s. Walter Dornberger, an Army ordnance officer, saw in the rocket a potentially fearsome weapon, and importantly, a weapon system not banned by the Treaty of Versailles, which ended World War I. Dornberger discovered the young von Braun, who became one of the world's pioneers of rocket science, made him a civil-ian employee of the army, and financed his education, including the com-pletion of his PhD in physics in 1934 from the University of Berlin which he completed in a remarkable two years. In the mid-1930s, von Braun and a staff of 80 worked on rocket development at Kummersdorf West, near Berlin, Germany's first facility for the development of rocketry.

In 1937, the rocket development facility at Peenemunde opened and the entire team moved north to the Baltic coast (McElheran, 1995). It was there that the design and testing of the V-1 cruise missile and V-2 rocket were accomplished (Kennedy, 1983). Many other projects were pursued during

Peenemunde's eight year life; among them was the conceptual design of an intercontinental ballistic missile (Klee and Merk, 1965). Dornberger, who was to become a major general by the end of the war, commanded the facility, and von Braun was the technical director. The group of engineers and scientists, later to be known as the von Braun team and who would follow von Braun to the United States, was first assembled there.

As the V-2 rockets grew more successful and the Luftwaffe began to lose effectiveness through continual attrition, attention at Peenemunde began to shift from development to production (Garlinski, 1978). The first V-2 (or A-4, as it was known in Peenemunde) rocket launch was in 1942, but numerous problems delayed its readiness for full production. However, the 'A-4 Special Committee' was formed to ensure that full production could get underway just as soon as the rocket was ready. The Peenemunde production facilities had used prisoner of war (POW) labor from two camps in the immediate area, Karlshagen and Trassenheide, whose prisoners were primarily Polish and Russian POWs.

Throughout German industry from 1941 on, there were increasingly severe labor shortages. The Russian front demanded more and more manpower for the German army. In such difficult circumstances, the use of POW forced labor – although lamentable – seems predictable enough. This was the initial choice at Peenemunde for rocket production. The use of slave labor was an entirely different issue. These were concentration camp prisoners (*Haftlinge*) under the control of the SS, and a part of the whole SS system of concentration and death camps. It is important to note here that other Nazi leaders, such as Albert Speer, Hitler's Minister of Armaments, were convicted of war crimes for the intentional use of slave labor. Wernher von Braun was fully aware during this time of the use of SS-provided slave labor in the production of rockets; indeed, the management team led by Dornberger and von Braun explicitly discussed and adopted as policy the use of SS-provided slave labor in rocket production (Neufeld, 1996: 187). Slave labor had been investigated, promoted and then requisitioned by Arthur Rudolph, a key member of the von Braun team (Piskiewicz, 1995: 96–7). Based on this policy decision, slave labor was also requisitioned for the other V-2 production facilities, in particular the underground Mittelwerk factory at the Mittelbau-Dora concentration camp.

Mittelbau-Dora was the last SS concentration camp to be formally established, and it was the only one exclusively formed for the purpose of weapons production. Dora was the site of the huge, underground Mittelwerk factory that built the V-2 rockets for the Reich. Mittelwerk produced just about 6000 rockets and 20 000 deaths in its less than two years of operation (Neufeld, 1996). Each V-2 rocket thus carried, at least symbolically, three corpses with it to its final destination. During the beginning and then again at the end of its short life, it was arguably among the worst of the living hells produced by the SS concentration camps.

Dora was initially a minor appendage of the better-known Buchenwald concentration camp. Only in 1943, when Hitler decided to make V-2 rocket production the top armament priority, did Dora mushroom. In August 1943, after the extensive British air raid on Peenemunde, V-2 production had to be moved to a place as secure from air attack as possible. An underground location had become the preferred choice for all of German armament and industrial production at this time. All told, Mittelwerk incorporated about 35 million cubic feet (9 91 090 cubic metres) of space. At its peak, 10 000 slave laborers at a time lived and toiled in this massive complex.

Later, after V-2 production was shifted to Mittelwerk, Dornberger, Rudolph and von Braun attended a May 1944 meeting in which the use of additional slave labor because of labor shortages was discussed and agreed upon (Neufeld, 1996). Von Braun traveled a number of times from Peenemunde to Mittelwerk, as did Dornberger and other members of the team. Arthur Rudolph was among a number of personnel who moved full time to Mittelwerk; he became the chief production engineer, with an office on one of the main tunnels. Magnus von Braun, Werner's brother, worked under Rudolph on site. Another dozen members of the von Braun team who eventually moved to the US also staffed Mittelwerk. No one could have any illusions about a factory whose production mode during most of its existence was quite simply to work its labor force to death, although their roles may not have involved some of them directly in decisions about, or relationships with, *Haftlinge*. Von Braun's substantial involvement, however, is quite clear (Neufeld, 1996: 228):

> there is no doubt that he remained deeply involved with the concentration camps. On August 15, 1944, he wrote to Sawatski (director of Mittelwerk) regarding a special laboratory he wanted to set up in the tunnels. . . . The letter begins: 'During my last visit to the Mittelwerk, you proposed to me that we use the good technical education of detainees available to you and Buchenwald to tackle . . . additional development jobs. You mentioned in particular a detainee working until now in your mixing device quality control, who was a French physics professor and who is especially qualified for the technical direction of such a workshop. I immediately looked into your proposal by going to Buchenwald, together with Dr Simon, to seek out more qualified detainees. I have arranged their transfer to the Mittelwerk with Colonel Pister (Buchenwald camp commandant), as per your proposal.

In August 1945, the US initiated Operation Overcast, the aim of which was to bring selected Germans over to participate in the production of German-inspired weapons, including V-2s, to be used against the Japanese.

Overcast included an assurance that if any committed Nazis were inadvertently brought to the US, they would be returned to Europe for trial. In September 1945, von Braun and 118 members of his team moved to the US under Operation Overcast, which was renamed as Operation Paperclip in March 1946. Michael Neufeld notes that (1996: 271):

> security reports for a number of individuals, including von Braun, had to be revised or fudged to circumvent the restrictions that still existed. Some writers have seen those actions as evidence of a conspiracy in the Pentagon to violate a policy signed by President Harry Truman, but it really reflected a conscious choice by the US government, approved up to the level of the Cabinet at least, to put expediency above principle. The Cold War provided ample opportunity after 1947 to rationalize that policy on anti-Communist grounds, but the circumvention of restrictions on Nazis and war criminals would have gone ahead at some level anyway, because the German's technical expertise was seen as indispensable.

In spite of the fact that the Paperclip policy explicitly barred committed Nazis and even more obviously, war criminals, the goal of technical superiority was all the justification needed to move at least a handful of individuals to the US, including von Braun, who participated in activities for which others were convicted of war crimes.

## WERNHER VON BRAUN AND 'ETHICAL' LEADERSHIP

Wernher von Braun's subordinates, by all accounts, ranked him very high as a manager and leader (Bilstein, 1980). Among members of the von Braun team, this is perhaps not surprising, since it was his leadership that rescued the group from the dead-end of post-war Germany, brought them to a new land, and led them forward to great accomplishments. His knowledge of technical detail was legendary, and he was a successful leader both at Peenemunde and later within the National Aeronautics and Space Administration (NASA). From his mid-20s until his retirement in 1972, von Braun held increasingly responsible management positions and exercised clear leadership in all of them. His leadership inspired a *Festschrift* in honor of his 50th birthday in 1962 (Stuhlinger *et al.*, 1963).

Von Braun's leadership style was expansive, and although quite functional in the context of developing the Saturn and other rockets, it was also a very controlling, even narcissistic, approach. He accepted large numbers of public speaking engagements during the 1950s and 1960s; during the latter decade, the number of engagements at least was in apparent violation of NASA regulations. James Webb, the NASA administrator at the time, is said to have told von Braun to limit these engagements (McConnell, 1986). Von Braun, during the 1950s, developed a relationship with Walt Disney, and even served as a consultant on three Disney, space-related films from those years. He clearly saw himself as a visionary for space and its exploration. We explore von Braun's career as a leader in the United States to a greater extent after introducing our second Nazi leader.

## OSKAR SCHINDLER AS ETHICAL LEADER

Oskar Schindler was the Czech-born German entrepreneur who saved about 1200 Jews from the Holocaust, most of whom worked for him in his enamelware factory in Kracow, Poland. While historical research on the Holocaust has uncovered numerous examples of 'rescuers' – those who in one way or another saved Jews from the fate of the concentration camps, only Oskar Schindler is known to have rescued such a large number of Jews (Rittner and Myers (eds), 1986). Schindler's family was both prominent and prosperous in their home town of Zwittau, in the ethnically German Sudetenland region of Czechoslovakia, however, the economic depression of the 1930s bankrupted their farm machinery plant. Like von Braun and many other Germans, Oskar Schindler joined the Nazi party; he did so in 1938 after the Sudetenland was annexed into Germany. Sensing business opportunities, he followed the German army into Poland in 1939.

Living in an apartment vacated by a Jewish family which had been relocated to the Kracow ghetto, Schindler became an insider with the Gestapo and was enlisted by German Intelligence (*Abwehr*) to spy on the Poles. Schindler was quite successful in black market trading, and participated actively in the system of bribery that determined one's success as an entrepreneur within the Army-run General Government of Poland (Keneally, 1982). His early successes in this environment enabled him to become the owner and operator of a formerly Jewish-owned, enamelware factory, *Deutsch Emaliawerken Fabrik* – known as Emalia to the Jews who would work there. Schindler's connections and bribes won Emalia a contract to produce mess kits and field kitchenware for the German army.

Emalia was located very close to the Jewish ghetto, where most of Kracow's Jews had been moved by March, 1941. Because of their proximity and because he would not have to pay them much in wages, Schindler employed Jews at Emalia. Oskar Schindler became rich, as do some entrepreneurs in a wartime environment, and he was very visible in the local social circles of the German military and SS in (and through his German Intelligence/*Abwehr* bosses, had access to Berlin society as well). By all accounts (Blair, 1983), Schindler had an expansive personality and loved a good time; he was a heavy drinker and having left his wife Emilie back in Czechoslovakia, a frequent and unrepentant adulterer. As an individual, it is an understatement to note that Oskar Schindler was far from a moral exemplar.

Perhaps because of his family's active Catholic faith, perhaps because his best childhood friends were the two sons of the Jewish rabbi who were the Schindler's closest neighbors, or perhaps for other reasons we cannot fathom, Oskar Schindler become increasingly and deeply uncomfortable with the horror that was descending on the 25 000 Jews of Kracow, including those who worked at Emalia. Concentrated first in the ghetto, these men and women were removed in March, 1943 to Plaszow, a slave labor camp similar to Mittelbau-Dora and run by the brutal SS officer, Amon Goeth. The Emalia Jews were among those who lived within Plaszow, but were transported to work every day at the factory. Schindler convinced Goeth, perhaps through persuasion, perhaps through bribes, to allow the Emalia Jews to live in a new subcamp, to be built within the compound of the factory.

Living at Emalia was very different from Jewish existence in other places controlled by the Nazis. At Emalia, the barracks were more like uncrowded dormitories, and daily meals consisted of 2000 calories instead of 900 or less in Plaszow. When it became clear that industry had to be redirected to the war effort, Schindler 'transformed' Emalia to a 'munitions' factory, which intentionally did not produce a single usable munition during its seven-month run. He reclassified his Jews, including women and children, as metal workers and machinists, 'essential' for the war industry. When people died at Emalia, they were accorded a Jewish burial service.

In October, 1944, as the Russian army began to overrun Poland, Schindler accomplished his most improbable feat. He was able to negotiate and bribe German officials for permission to move not only his factory to Brunnlitz in Czechoslovakia, but also his 'essential' workers, who were written down onto 'Schindler's List'. When some 300 of Schindler's women were accidentally transported to Auschwitz, he succeeded in getting them back out – the only such shipment to Auschwitz-Birkenau that was more than 'one way'. Those Jews who remained from the 25 000 in Plaszow were transported to the death camp at Auschwitz-Birkenau 60 km away, and theirs was indeed a one-way trip. The best available estimates are that Schindler spent about four million marks either directly or indirectly providing for and eventually rescuing Jews; it was his entire fortune from the war (Furrow, 1988).

Schindler's life after the war demonstrated none of the entrepreneurial or leadership successes he had during the war. Interestingly, and in contrast to von Braun, he applied for an entry permit to the US, and was denied because he had been a member of the Nazi party. By 1949, he and his wife Emilie had settled on a farm in Argentina. In 1957, he was bankrupt once again, and leaving Emilie behind again, returned to Germany. In 1962, he was honored as a 'Righteous Gentile' in Israel, and came to enjoy yearly reunions in Israel with 'his' Jews, where he could once again be the old, expansive Oskar Schindler who loved a big party. By contrast, he was reviled and mistreated in Germany by those who recognized him. He died in Frankfurt in 1974 at the age of 66. He had requested burial in the Catholic cemetery in Jerusalem, and hundreds of 'his' Jews attended his funeral in the Catholic Church in Jerusalem.

Oskar Schindler and Wernher von Braun had much in common as leaders, all the more so when viewed from the technical-rational perspective of professional ethics. Both were expansive, larger-than-life personalities and both were opportunists (or more kindly, entrepreneurs), who cut many corners. Still, by conventional – or technical rational – ethical standards, von Braun was seen as the more ethical leader of the two. Von Braun continued to meet those standards during the American leg of his career, while Schindler's fortunes were declining.

## VON BRAUN IN THE US

Within a few years of the end of World War II, the uncomfortable moments for the von Braun team had largely passed. The Army clearly had a vested interest in them, and had shielded a number of them from having to testify at the Mittelbau-Dora war crimes trial, held at Dachau in 1947 (Gimbel, 1986; 1990). Von Braun himself and other team members successfully maintained the fiction that the use of slave labor had been the exclusive province of the SS, and that they were rocket scientists interested in space flight who had been forced to take a temporary detour into wartime weapons development on the way to their real goal (Stuhlinger and Ordway, 1994). They enjoyed a better than half-hearted acceptance, after a time, by their adopted community of Huntsville, AL, and their colleagues within NASA. Still later, they were rewarded for their great achievements in the Apollo Program. Arthur Rudolph eventually received NASA's highest civilian honor, the Distinguished Service Award.

While stories and rumors persisted regarding the pasts of some members of the von Braun team, it was only after most of them had left government service in the early 1970s that the facts about their pasts were acknowledged. Survivors of the French resistance who had been imprisoned at Dora knew and spoke the truth all along (Michel, 1979). Americans were much slower to recognize the unsavory history of some of these Germans.

Still, based on the information we now have, it would be equally mistaken to issue a blanket condemnation of all of the Germans who came over with von Braun.

Of the 118 who originally came with von Braun, somewhere between half and three-quarters had been members of the Nazi party (Piskiewicz, 1995). Certainly, most of these were only nominal members. Most also had no direct involvement with slave labor and the policy decision to use it. Only four were known to have joined the SS (Neufeld, 1996). Von Braun himself was one of these, receiving his commission in 1941; put in context, this is not an early membership which ordinarily would mark a 'committed Nazi'. He is reported to have worn his SS uniform only once, on the day that Heinrich Himmler, the head of the SS, visited Peenemunde to see for himself how rocket development was going. Himmler rewarded von Braun with a promotion to major. In this action and in many others, von Braun appears as more an opportunist than a committed Nazi (much like Schindler). Another SS member and an earlier Nazi adherent was Kurt Debus who reportedly wore his SS uniform regularly at Peenemunde and at one point denounced a colleague as anti-Nazi to the Gestapo (Piskiewicz, 1995: 237). Debus eventually became the first Director of the Kennedy Space Flight Center in Florida. Arthur Rudolph was a seriously committed Nazi who joined the party in June, 1931 and had other early Nazi affiliations (Neufeld, 1996).

## THE MARSHALL SPACE FLIGHT CENTER

The National Aeronautics and Space Administration was widely regarded in the 1960s as the paradigmatic example of the successful, high-performing organization, and especially so for a public sector organization (McCurdy, 1993: 2). The Apollo program and its great success punctuated by the moon landing was clearly the principle reason (Brooks *et al.*, 1979). The Marshall Space Flight Center was created in 1960 and von Braun became its first director. The von Braun Team at the Marshall Space Flight Center was an integral part of this success; it was their Saturn rockets which boosted all of the crews into orbit and on to the moon (Graham, 1995).

The project manager in charge of the Saturn V Program Office was Arthur Rudolph. Much as von Braun established himself as an outstanding manager and leader in the US, Arthur Rudolph demonstrated outstanding leadership with the Saturn Program Office. He developed the concept of the 'Program Control Center', which essentially gathered relevant information about all of the Saturn subsystems in one large conference room, and made them visually accessible. The Saturn Program Office was used as a model for the Apollo Program Office at NASA headquarters in Washington, as well as for other NASA centers and for prime contractors. James Webb, the NASA administrator during the Apollo program, was so impressed that he sent a procession of academics and executives from business and government to Huntsville to see the operation that Arthur Rudolph put together (Bilstein, 1980: 291).

Arthur Rudolph, a clearly outstanding leader in perhaps the most successful American public organization in modern times and earlier at the Mittelwerk factory in the Third Reich, retired from NASA with its highest civilian award. He was living quietly in retirement in San Jose, CA, collecting his government pension, when he was confronted in the early 1980s by the Office of Special Investigations, the Justice Department unit created by Congress in 1979 for the express purpose of pursuing Nazi war criminals living in the United States. Unsurprisingly, surviving members of the von Braun team (von Braun himself died in 1977) were an early subject of OSI investigations; some investigations continued over the next two decades (Rosenbaum, 1997). In 1984, at the age of 77, Arthur Rudolph voluntarily renounced his US citizenship and left the country after signing an admission that he could not contest the OSI charges; in effect, he admitted his guilt.

## ETHICAL LEADERSHIP IN A CULTURE OF TECHNICAL RATIONALITY

The von Braun case illustrates the tendency of technical rationality to drive out moral considerations, because it downplays and masks the interactive, relational foundation of ethical behavior as well as its public context. We will probably never know the extent to which those who crafted Operation Paperclip knew of the slave labor and mass murder at Dora when they placed responsibility for the program with von Braun and his compatriots. Regardless of what they knew, once the program was under way, administrative processes and technical achievements – most of them consistent with public service and professional ethics – progressively papered over the wartime activities of von Braun, Rudolph, and others.

With the benefit of hindsight, Operations Overcast and Paperclip appear to be examples of policies and programs absent moral considerations, or at least ones in which those concerns were only rhetorical. While technical superiority is still in evidence as a paramount American goal today, and while national security is more than ever a valid rationale for many actions, a justification for bringing committed Nazis and some individuals who were directly implicated in the use of SS slave labor (a war crime) to the US is not easily provided. While the Cold War provided an after-the-fact rationale for Paperclip, at the time this was primarily an affirmative exercise – we wanted this expertise for ourselves. The principle of denying this expertise to others could have easily been met in other ways. Those who were guilty of war crimes could have been incarcerated, and they would have been prevented from lending their expertise to the Russians or to anyone else. There were plenty of 'clean' Germans to work on rockets for the US, and their lives would not have been conflicted by the knowledge and continuous anxiety of keeping the secret past. Arguably, the US could have done without the Germans altogether. For example, there was a budding group of rocketeers at the Jet Propulsion Laboratory in California (Neufeld, 1996). Granted, they were years behind the Germans, but would it really have mattered in the greater scheme of things if the moon landing occurred not in 1969, but in 1974 or even 1979? Did the US really need to land on the moon carrying the symbolic baggage of 20 000 human beings worked to death at Dora?

## CONCLUSION

The contrasting cases of von Braun and Schindler suggest the moral short-comings of professional and public service ethics under the norms of technical-rationality. They further suggest that ethics has an interactive, relational foundation (beyond the individual practitioner), and that the public context within which they both acted is indispensable in judging their respective cases.

Both von Braun and Schindler had promising starts to their careers in Nazi Germany. Wernher von Braun's successes in developing the rocket program for Hitler were rewarded by the Nazi regime and later by the United States, where he went on to become a leader and visionary as one of the key progenitors of NASA's space program. Both the space shuttle and the space station – the leading-edge programs of the US's current national space policy – were originally a part of von Braun's vision (Neufeld, 1996). His ethical and moral failures while a member of the SS and overseeing the living hell of Mittlebau-Dora did not impede his ascent to the top levels of one of the foremost technical-rational organizations of our times.

Oskar Schindler also began his career as a supporter of the Nazi party and took full advantage of the opportunities afforded him by the Nazi regime. He eventually followed a path very different from von Braun's, becoming an ethical and moral exemplar (although not in his personal and professional life), but a failure as a businessman who was shunned by his peers; even in his postwar years he was unable to sustain a successful business. Yet he was lauded in Israel (and later in books and movies) as a moral and ethical hero for having saved hundreds of Jews from almost certain death while sacrificing his dreams of wealth and success. He was a pre-eminent rescuer of Jews during a time when there were too few rescuers and far too few rescued. But unlike von Braun, Schindler was denied entry to the US and was treated with outright hostility back in Europe. As a practical matter, his ethical behavior and moral courage were of less value than von Braun's scientific contributions to a society bound by its cultural attachments to technical-rational achievements.

These two examples show how modern organizational and professional practice is rife with ethical paradox. A 'good' leader within a technical rational system need not necessarily be ethical. Our admiration and praise of ethical leadership masks the essential moral vacuity of modern, technical-rational organizations. Codes of ethics, rules and regulations are not sufficient to prevent or punish unethical behavior. Individuals who take an ethical stand are too often cast off by society (even as they are being praised), while the unethical – in the rare instances that they are made to account for their actions – are often rewarded with golden parachutes and soft landings back into positions similar to the ones they disgraced. Ethics is too often relegated to the sidelines as an afterthought, invoked only as an antidote to the worst, most visible practices and then put aside as impediments to efficiency and effectiveness until the next abuse is uncovered. In the culture of technical rationality, the ethical leader can quickly fall from favor and become feared and even reviled as unreliable, a non-team player who undermines the organization by not working within the system.

These two historical cases suggest that professionals in public life would do well to reflect on the possibility that their systems and actions can contribute to the worst kinds of human behavior, and that our ethical standards and professional training do not adequately address the potential for administrative evil. There is no easy way out of the social and organizational dynamics that foster administrative evil. Rarely is one confronted with an obvious up or down decision on ethical issues. Instead, it is more common to follow a pathway of smaller, ambiguous choices until a series of commitments and habits drive out ethics in favor of a comfortable mask. Therefore, no profession should be taught, practiced, or theorized about without considering the psychological, organizational and societal dynamics that can lead those in public service to confound the public interest with acts of dehumanization and destruction. Only a conceptual framework for ethics that goes beyond the narrow vision of technical rationality and recognizes the interactive, relational foundation of ethics and its public context can help us better understand and perhaps ameliorate – even if we cannot fully resolve – these moral paradoxes of ethical leadership in modern organizations.

## REFERENCES

Adams, Guy B. (2000), 'Administrative ethics and chimera of professionalism: the historical context of public service ethics', in Terry L. Cooper (ed.), *Handbook of Administrative Ethics*, 2nd edn, New York: Marcel Dekker, pp. 291–308.

Adams, Guy B. and Danny L. Balfour (2004), *Unmasking Administrative Evil*, revised edn, Armonk, NY: M.E. Sharpe.

Barrett, William (1979), *The Illusion of Technique*, Garden City, NY: Anchor Doubleday.

Bilstein, Robert E. (1980), *Stages to Saturn: A Technological History of the Apollo/Saturn Launch Vehicles*, Washington, DC: National Aeronautics and Space Administration.

Blair, J. (1983), *Schindler: The Documentary* (film), London: Thames Television.

Brooks, C.G., Grimwood, J.M., and L.S. Swenson, Jr. (1979), *Chariots for Apollo*, Washington, DC: National Aeronautics and Space Administration.

Browning, Chistopher (1989), 'The decision concerning the final solution', in F. Furet (ed.), *Unanswered Questions: Nazi Germany and the Genocide of the Jews*, New York: Schocken Books, pp. 96–118.

Ellul, Jacques (1954), *The Technological Society*, New York: Vintage.

Furrow, D. (1998), 'Schindler's compulsion: an essay on practical necessity', *American Philosophical Quarterly*, **35** (July), 209–30.

Garlinski, J. (1978), *Hitler's Last Weapons: The Underground War Against the V1 and V2*, New York: Times Books.

Gimbel, John (1986), 'US policy and German scientists: the early cold war', *Political Science Quarterly*, **101**, 433–51.

Gimbel, John (1990), 'German scientists, United States denazification policy and the Paperclip conspiracy', *International History Review*, **12**, 441–85.

Graham, J.F. (1995), *History of Apollo and Saturn*, Washington, DC: National Aeronautics and Space Administration.

Harmon, Michael M. (1995), *Responsibility as Paradox: A Critique of Rational Discourse on Public Administration*, Thousand Oaks, CA: Sage Publications.

Hilberg, Raul (1989), 'The bureaucracy of annihilation', in F. Furet (ed.), *Unanswered Questions: Nazi Germany and the Genocide of the Jews*, New York: Schocken Books, 119–33.

Kearney, Richard C. and C. Sinha (1988), 'Professionalism and bureaucratic responsiveness: conflict or compatibility', *Public Administration Review*, **48**, 571–9.

Keeley, M. (1983), 'Values in organizational theory and management education', *Academy of Management Review*, **8** (3), 376–86.

Keneally, Thomas (1982), *Schindler's List*, New York: Simon and Schuster.

Kennedy, G.P. (1983), *Vengeance Weapon 2*, Washington, DC: Smithsonian Institution Press.

Klee, E. and O. Merk. (1965), *The Birth of the Missile: The Secrets of Peenemunde*, New York: Dutton.

Lifton, Robert J. (1986), *The Nazi Doctors: Medical Killing and the Psychology of Genocide*, New York: Basic Books.

Lozowick, Yaacov (2000), *Hitler's Bureaucrats: The Nazi Security Police and the Banality of Evil*, New York: Continuum.

McConnell, M. (1987), *Challenger: A Major Malfunction*, New York: Doubleday.

McCurdy, Howard E. (1993), *Inside NASA: High Technology and Organizational Change in the US Space Program*, Baltimore, MD: Johns Hopkins University Press.

McElheran, B. (1995), *V-bombs and Weathermaps: Reminiscences of World War II*, Montreal, QC and Buffalo, NY: McGill-Queen's University Press.

Michel, J. (1979), *Dora*, London: Weidenfeld & Nicolson.

Milgram, Stanley (1974), *Obedience to Authority*, New York: Harper and Row.

Neufeld, Michael J. (1996), *The Rocket and the Reich*, Cambridge, MA: Harvard University Press.

Piszkiewicz, D. (1995), *The Nazi Rocketeers: Dreams of Space and Crimes of War*, Westport, CT: Praeger.

Poole, Ross (1991), *Morality and Modernity*, London: Routledge, Chapman and Hall.

Rittner, C. and S. Myers (eds) (1986), *The Courage to Care: Rescuers of Jews During the Holocaust*, New York: Praeger.

Rosenbaum, Eli (1997), personal telephone conversation with author, 4 August.

Rubenstein, Richard L. (1975), *The Cunning of History*, New York: Harper and Row.

Schon, Donald (1990), *The Reflective Practitioner*, New York: Basic Books.

Schon, Donald (1993), 'Generative metaphor: a perspective on problem setting in social policy', in A. Ortony, (ed.), *Metaphor and Thought*, Cambridge: Cambridge University Press, pp. 137–63.

Sofsky, Werner (1997), *The Order of Terror: The Concentration Camp*, Princeton, NJ: Princeton University Press.

Stuhlinger, E., F. Ordway III, J. McCall and G. Bucker (1963), *Astronautical Engineering and Science from Peenemunde to Planetary Space*, New York: McGraw-Hill.

Stuhlinger, E.F. and F.I. Ordway (1994), *Werhner von Braun: Crusader for Space*, Malabar, FL: Krieger.

# 7. The Swiss Federal Administration in the context of downsizing: public servants' perception about their work environment and ethical issues

**Yves Emery and Carole Wyser**

> To tell public servants that they are highly valued at the same time as many of them are being 'let go' may strike at least part of the audience as ironic, or worse.
>
> Pollitt and Bouckaert (2004: 172)

## INTRODUCTION

Long inspired by the Weberian ideal-type (Weber, 1971), the management of public organizations has undergone a profound transformation, notably through the development of *new public management (NPM)* (Pollitt and Boukaert, 2003). The changes that have taken place since the early 1980s are so profound that the foundations of the bureaucratic model are being completely redefined, leading many analysts to speak of a change of paradigm. In many OECD countries (PUMA, 2001; Reichard, 2002; Bossaert, 2005), the traditional conditions of civil service employment have been fundamentally challenged by the application of new public management principles: the abolition of the 'status' of public servants, the introduction of practices geared towards performance and new organizational values emphasizing quality, competitiveness and public entrepreneurialism (du Gay, 2000; Emery, 2000).

In this new environment, which one might call post-civil service (Emery and Giauque, 2005), the added introduction of downsizing programmes makes it difficult for employees to cope with the daily workload. All these changes have a significant impact on the staff, and are likely to lead to various ethical problems. However, there have been very few studies looking at these dynamics (Knudson *et al.*, 2003). There lies the main interest of this contribution.

## BACKGROUND AND LITERATURE REVIEW

The shift towards a post-civil service model which started with the introduction of new public management policies immediately gave rise to numerous critical comments (Hufty, 1992; Merrien, 1998; Knoepfel and Varone, 1999; Pollitt and Bouckaert, 2000). Many fears focused on the reforms themselves and on the potential misuse of redundancies – imposing this new regime on public servants who no longer benefit from guaranteed employment. Meanwhile, a number of OECD countries have had to face a public finance crisis and have started to implement restructuring programmes aimed at cutting the number of employees in the public sector. For Pollitt and Bouckaert (2004), continuous and repeated cuts in the workforce destroy the foundation of trust and commitment. They also curtail institutional memory, reduce the chances of survival of a 'public service ethic' and, finally, result in a less efficient public sector. The promotion of a management ideology (de Gaulejac, 2005) that tends to push civic values into the background, can in fact give rise to major ethical problems (Smith, 2003).

The greater part of the literature on ethical aspects in the public sector, tackles the question from a theoretical rather than an empirical point of view. Thus, the main themes identified by Menzel (2005) show that the most common approach consists of evaluating the impact of ethical practices on the functioning and performance of the organization. The evaluation of the impact of performance on ethics has been far more rarely undertaken. The author argues that the introduction of entrepreneurial methods brings with it a significant ethical risk which should be analysed in more detail (Menzel, 2005: 33). Besides, most prescriptive studies on the management of ethical conduct recognize this problem and its importance for practitioners (Baines *et al.*, 1999).

Wittmer (2005) conceptualizes the influence of contextual variables on ethical conduct, stressing the importance of rewards and sanctions, the key role of the peer group, codes of conduct, and so on. However, other contextual variables such as structural characteristics or those related to the scarcity of resources are only referred to in research that is now quite dated.

The impact of restructuring programmes on the staff has already been the subject of numerous research projects in the private sector, where ethical issues were not of primary importance. From these studies it seems that job security plays a vital role for employees, both in terms of its objective aspects and in the subjective perceptions linked to it (Büssing, 1999; Klandermans and Van Vuuren, 1999). The main impacts of job insecurity are:

- reduced involvement in the work carried out and less organizational commitment (Turnley and Feldmann, 1999; Allen *et al.*, 2001; Knudson *et al.*, 2003);
- feelings of stress, burnout and illnesses that have lasting effects on the well-being of the staff (Kinnunen *et al.*, 1999); and
- a decline in qualitative and quantitative performance (Grunberg *et al.*, 2000).

All these aspects are possibly linked to non-ethical behaviour, although this still remains to be proven. But what happens in public organizations where job security was (and still is in a number of countries) raised to the status of dogma (Bossaert, 2005)?

It has been nearly ten years since the OECD (OCDE, 1997) noted that public servants subjected to modernization programmes suffer from a 'weariness attributable to change', a 'loss of prestige', as well as a feeling of 'insecurity' induced by their new work environment. The first empirical studies focusing on the implementation of NPM-inspired practices and their impact on the employees are now being published (Reichard, 2002; Aubert, 2003; Duvillier, Genard *et al.*, 2003; Giauque, 2003, 2004; Ritz, 2003; Leisink and Steijn, 2004; Pollitt and Bouckaert, 2004; Meyer and Hammerschmied, 2005; Rondeaux, 2005). They portray a reality in which public servants may be motivated in some instances, but are often bewildered when faced with new practices and new values that are, at times, at odds with their previous practices.

Looking at the impact of the abolition of employment security in the State of Georgia (that state's at-will employment system), Kellough and Nigro have observed, on a sampling of some 2000 respondents, that the attitudes towards the various reforms undertaken have generally been negative. It is to note that this negativism was less pronounced for at-will employees than for protected employees. For these two categories of employees, political pressures remain insignificant, even if we would have to analyse this element further. Other aspects, relating to the neutrality and productivity of public sector employees would also need to be explored (Kellough and Nigro, 2005).

A review of the impact of 30 years of reform in different European countries (Lacasse and Thoenig, 1996) shows that ethical aspects are only touched on as peripheral elements,[1] as is the case with regard to the evaluation carried out in Switzerland (see below), or simply mentioned as a particular impediment to reform.[2]

Frederickson is interested in the impact of downsizing programmes on the ethical conduct of public servants. He reiterates the belief that such programmes contribute to a decline in morale, institutional loyalty and collective memory. The author deals with the question by highlighting the relocation of the core bureaucracy away from the centre, and its relocation within more peripheral organizations which may pursue interests at odds with the public interest (Frederickson, 1996).

His conclusions are overtly pessimistic, predicting a period marked by major ethical problems. Smith examines the impact of what he calls the 'neo-liberal agenda' on the problem of ethics. He believes that the impact will be serious, particularly on 'the ability of the public sector and public employees to work according to shared values and a shared sense of purpose . . . and to work collaboratively, effectively and accountably with other sectors' (Smith, 2003). However, the literature remains essentially prescriptive, following the principles of the ethical architecture promulgated by the OECD (OCDE, 1998). Clear empirical research still needs to be carried out on the subject.

The modernization programmes that have been implemented produce a certain amount of confusion regarding the referential values of public servants (Grant *et al.*, 2003; Emery and Giauque, 2005; Meyer and Hammerschmied, 2005; Rondeaux, 2005). These have a tendency to oscillate between opposites:

- the traditional values of the public sector, values of the bureaucracy, the public service ethos (Brereton and Temple, 1999; Farnham and Horton, 2005); and
- the 'market values' inspired by the private sector and the economy (Boltanski and Thévenot, 1991; Pollitt and Bouckaert, 2004).

This hybridization, which is a characteristic feature of the current situation of post-civil service, creates a new frame of reference and legitimization that is hardly free from contradiction. At best, it produces problems when it comes to adopting specific modes of behaviour; at worst, it creates real confusion about what reference values should guide the actions of public sector employees[3] (Jurkiewicz *et al.*, 1998). In this context, the notion put forward by Menzel of 'ethics-induced stress' is an interesting one, in that it is based on a dissonance between the public servant's sense of ethics and the types of values found in the workplace (quoted contribution, p. 26).

We start from the idea that, in a period of profound restructuring, the stress induced by incoherent change is likely to provoke, or intensify, non-ethical behaviours. That is where our main interest lies; understanding the perception of public servants directly involved in service delivery.

# THE SWISS CONTEXT IN AN INTERNATIONAL PERSPECTIVE

In Switzerland, with a large number of public bodies at all hierarchical levels (the Federal administration, the cantons and communes), having implemented major NPM-type modernization programmes and having abolished security of employment, we are now witnessing increasing amounts of job cuts and, in certain cases, redundancies (Mutter, 2004).

The trend noted in Switzerland, characterized by the 'abolition of the traditional status'[4] of civil servants in conjunction with a strengthening of the judicial framework of public law (Emery and Ueberhart, 1999), constitutes a unique framework for analysing these two dynamics. This new statute introduces an objective employee insecurity, which is likely to be fully realized only when restructuring programmes are effectively implemented.

The administrative level chosen for this research, the Federal administration, is undergoing a complete transformation as a result of the joint introduction of reform and cost-saving programmes. The reforms, tested in different agencies since 1997 (Leuenberger, 2005), are broadly inspired by new public management theories: the use of new policy instruments such as performance mandates, global budgeting and delegation of responsibilities to agencies. Moreover, various sectoral reorganizations have taken place. These have been implemented in the form of projects, some of which are cross-departmental (for example, increasing efficiencies in purchasing, reducing legislative density, and so on) and others specific to each of the seven departments that make up the Federal administration. Thus, in the units studied here, where job cuts or redundancies are expected (see methodology), major restructuring programmes are now being implemented. A number of cost-saving programmes, devised by Parliament, have been progressively implemented in recent years. They have added a layer of complexity to the reforms already underway. The current total workforce (37 000 people in 2005) will be cut by approximately 4000 by 2010, mostly by implementing rationalization measures and by abandoning certain tasks.

Our investigation has been conducted in a public-sector organization that is currently engaged in a number of 'reorganization' projects. To date, few evaluations have been carried out on this subject in Switzerland. The study, which evaluates ten years of New Public Management type reforms, has not touched on ethical questions in any meaningful manner (Lienhard *et al.*, 2005). The evolving culture of Swiss administrations towards a more 'client-oriented' approach is noted without raising the ethical questions linked to this particular choice. The 'overall' positive assessment of the reforms must be weighed against the rise of new dynamics weakening the

State and the functioning of the public administrations. These new elements may lead to a deterioration in motivation, commitment and productivity of public servants, although these trends vary greatly depending on the context. This observation is based on the emergence of a large number of paradoxes (Pollitt and Bouckaert, 2004; Emery and Giauque, 2005), raising long-term questions of credibility about the discourse and the objectives pursued by these reforms.

In the conclusion of his study, Schedler points to the potential contradiction between the entrepreneurial logic underlying NPM, which is supposed to give greater autonomy to public servants and the intensification and multiplication of control mechanisms. But even in this last chapter, he does not deal with any ethical problems that might arise out of these contradictions.

## AIMS AND METHODOLOGY OF THE RESEARCH

This research aims at assessing the perception of federal administration employees on the impact of objective employment insecurity (in a context of downsizing) on work environment and ethical behaviour. To evaluate this impact, we selected three units that are being subjected to increasingly large-scale restructuring efforts. These efforts will constitute one of our main independent variables.

Taking our inspiration to a great extent from Grounded Theory (Baszanger, 1992; Strauss and Corbin, 1997; Strauss and Corbin, 2004) we have conducted twelve in-depth interviews lasting on average two hours. This inductive approach, which does not involve validating or invalidating a hypothesis, consists of the systematic collection of empirical data which, in a continuous two-way movement between facts and hypotheses, allows us to build a theoretical construct of the studied subject.

This methodology pays great attention to the context of the action which, according to Strauss and Corbin (Strauss and Corbin, 1998), covers the global and general conditions, both close and distant, that influence actions and strategies of interaction. Thus, the results of this research are not only concerned with the effects of the loss of employment security – experienced as a result of different levels of restructuring – but also with the development of the work conditions which the units studied provide for their employees.

Starting from the idea of constructing a theory based on facts, we proceeded to carry out comprehensive interviews according to the methods developed by Kaufmann (2004). This approach to interviewing opens up the possibility of freer interactions, allowing, among other things, a better understanding of the concerns of the interviewee. This systematic approach enabled us to spontaneously tackle the independent variables mentioned in the literature, but also to look at other variables which emerged through the interview process. This process is carried on until interviewees start repeating themselves in the interviews. This then assures the qualitative validity of the process.

This dynamic approach requires a 'theoretical sampling' (Strauss and Corbin, 1998) which evolves during the research process. In accordance with this principle, we asked the people interviewed to indicate which of their colleagues they believed had a different or contrasting perception of the situation. This approach maximizes the opportunities to compare events and allows us to create clusters that vary according to various characteristics and contexts. It is then possible to look for similarities and differences with other events. This process reaches its conclusion when the commentaries obtained start reflecting each another, thus allowing us to establish a clearer contextual view of the elements under study.

## CHOICE OF THE FIELD OF STUDY

In cooperation with the Federal Office of Personnel (Office fédéral du personnel OPFER), which has a global perspective of the reforms in each department, we selected three units within the Federal administration, an organization that has abolished the traditional civil service statute. The selected units (U) represent contexts that are subject to the growing pressures of reorganization: (U1) no job cuts planned; (U2) job cuts announced or implemented; (U3) redundancies announced or implemented. The stage of implementation of the reforms announced by the Swiss public administration varies greatly from one department to another. Thus, the two units most affected by the restructuring (U2 and U3) in the same department were selected, since the situations had not yet reached a stage of completion in the other departments.

## RESULTS AND DISCUSSION

It is important to recall that this is a piece of exploratory research which focuses on a limited number of individuals. Thus, the trends noted and the analyses that are derived from these cannot by any means be representative of what occurs in the entire organization. Moreover, since the results are based exclusively on the perceptions of those interviewed, they cannot be corroborated with more objective measurements.

First, the most important aspects related to the work environment will be addressed and, in a second section, the consequences as experienced by our interlocutors in terms of ethical behaviour.

## ASPECTS RELATED TO THE WORK ENVIRONMENT

The first observation concerns the loss of reference points, which can be seen by a growing politicization, a confused, sometimes even absent, hierarchy, and the appearance of market-driven values in the work place. In U1, this predominance of the political debate in the management of public affairs can be explained by very direct contacts with the political authority, but also by a new management style that is more interventionist and aims to 'set an example' in the organization. In such a context our interlocutors have the perception that personal sympathies carry an increasing weight in the organization. Also mentioned is a form of blackmail, based in part on the currently poor conditions of the Swiss job market, and leading to the imposing of decisions without any real process of discussion. In U2 and U3, the prevailing feeling is that the political debates have a very direct impact on the future of their units. This perception is all the stronger in that the notion of hierarchy, which until recently represented a fundamental structuring principle in these units, is completely disappearing. Three of our interlocutors were not even able to identify their immediate superior; the civil servants in these two units seem to suffer a form of anomie which is highly disturbing.

We must also note the large-scale introduction of a market-driven approach in the three units, leading civil servants to be concerned, first and foremost, with issues of efficiency, productivity, cost-savings, and more specifically for units U2 and U3, earning power and even profits. This last point is not in itself a problematic element since in these three units, people assert that they can also see positive elements in this frame of reference.

Second, we note a dramatic contraction of the time horizon in management. In the first unit (U1), there are a growing number of uncertainties with regard to the tasks and working conditions that will prevail. In the second unit (U2), the reorganizations lead to a real rupture; the future is reduced to a very short-term horizon (a few months). In unit 3, the future is even shorter.

Third, the clarity and coherence of the working environment tend to deteriorate. In U1, the least affected, people experience an increase of demands being placed upon them, a growing push for flexibility and responsiveness. Nevertheless, the conditions in which the work is being done, the hierarchy and the responsibilities remain clear and are not leading to disruptions. For the people in U2 and U3, the picture is quite different: whereas their duties and immediate work environment remain clearly marked out; the rest of the structure is characterized by a general feeling of chaos. Added to the loss of frame of reference as noted above, this chaotic environment is experienced as highly destabilizing and even perceived as an offence to the professional conscience of our interlocutors. In fact, they are put in a situation where it becomes very difficult to do a good job; the objectives are continuously elevated while the resources needed to carry them out are being constantly reduced.

The dysfunctional nature of the control systems in the units studied must also be pointed out. In fact, in U1 we can find a growing number of controls being carried out on most work related aspects. If this trend continues, these controls could become counter-productive and disrupt work performance. In U2, the controls are carried out mainly in work teams or by the line manager if present. A form of mutual control and self-regulation emerges in line with the very noticeable concern of wanting to 'do a good job' and of being able to retain a form of professional dignity linked to the quality of the work accomplished. The immediate sphere of activity thus becomes a form of protection. As for U3, controls have completely disappeared. Several examples given by our interlocutors show that distinct dysfunctional modes of behaviour exist, and that the hierarchy is in no way intervening to correct the situation.

Finally, we want to refer to the mechanisms by which, based on increased delegation to the operational units, various inequalities are emerging among the staff (salaries, working hours and so on). This phenomenon is amplified by a lack of transparency, which tends to increase the perceived inequalities. All this is happening in an individualistic spirit, where each one acts in its own sphere while being less concerned, or indeed not at all concerned, about what the others are doing.

## ASPECTS RELATED TO THE ETHICAL BEHAVIOUR OF PUBLIC SERVANTS

While in U1, performing the work becomes more difficult because of the changes in the work context; our interlocutors did not mention any new problems of an ethical nature.

In the second unit, despite the absence of an ethical framework, the loss of organizational references, the lack of orientation and of trust in the hierarchy, of demands that are disproportionate to resources, the impossibility of projecting oneself into the future, our interlocutors do not display, to date, unethical behaviours towards clients or in the way they carry out their jobs. Several times, the potentially explosive character of the near future was mentioned. Nevertheless, their professional dedication and their concern to continue to produce good work, prevails and helps to avoid regrettable slippages. In the eyes of our interlocutors, the operational methods that characterize the work environment are leading to a decline in productivity and in the quality of work. In certain cases, the maintaining of professional standards can only be met with difficulty, and with a sense of responsibility that is surprising in people who find themselves in such situations.

Although the conditions described in unit 3 constitute an unfavourable framework for ethical behaviour, non-ethical behaviour is only present in a very marginal way. These exceptions are comprised of individuals who come and 'punch in' for work without actually working. Added to this is a growing alcohol problem, affecting employees and line managers.

Trust in the hierarchy, whether remote or close, has been broken. This is even more apparent as they are now considered as representing a counter-example rather than a model to be emulated. As with unit 2, despite unfavourable conditions the persons interviewed continue to produce high quality work, attributable to their dignity and self-respect.

In contrast with the stability of the Weberian model, we can observe the difficulty public servants have in projecting themselves into the future. This seems to be linked to the seriousness of the reforms they are experiencing.

In each of the units job security and trajectory preoccupy employees, a topic of considerable anxiety under the impetus of various, consecutive restructuring programmes. In the first unit, it is clear that the people project themselves into the future with a growing number of uncertainties. In the second unit (U2) the people we met were unable to project themselves into the future, although the 'future' may be a matter of mere months, employing such phrases as 'disaster', 'charging into the wall', and so on to describe a job scenario dominated by apprehension and fear. As for the individuals in Unit 3, they have similar perceptions to the people in U2, except that their projection into the future is even shorter. The expectations of the people in U2 and U3 are clearly of an existential nature: knowing what will happen to their position, knowing about the decisions that will affect the future of the organization, in short, being able to project themselves into the future.

As regards the commitment of the public servants interviewed, a clear gradation can be observed between the three units, reflecting the degree of the transformations underway. The need for transparency and information, which is felt to be lacking at present, emerges as an issue in all three units. The propensity for individuals to leave the organization can be viewed as resultant of the break up of a stable work relationship that was initially intended to be long-lasting. This was a key element of the former psychological contract between employer and employee. Evident in units 2 and 3, this finding is also beginning to be valid in the first unit.

These last two observations raise the question of a cognitive dissonance emerging between the personal values held by the public servants and those advocated by the organization. This may indeed become a source of future ethical dilemmas.

## DISCUSSION

Despite a significant potential for non-ethical conduct resulting from the organizational context described, we did not discover any real slippage. This suggests that compensatory regulation mechanisms may be at work and in this regard, three interactive levels of regulation are apparent. This observation has special relevance given that our chosen method focuses on the context which influences the actions and strategies of interaction.

### The Level of the Organization

The regulatory influence is diminishing in this global context. It appears that the existence of an ethics charter has almost no practical effect (Igalens and Dehermann-Roy, 2004), especially when it diverges from employees' immediate reality (Argyris and Schön, 1978). By contrast, we can point to the reappearance of the typical problems which were present at the origin of the bureaucratic model, that is, increasing intervention by politicians in the administration and the phenomena of favouritism. In the absence of a control group, it cannot be determined whether these problems are a consequence of the current changes, or whether they existed before and now have intensified following the abolition of the traditional status of public servants. This danger is typically inherent in open civil service systems such as that of Switzerland (Bowman *et al.*, 2001), and has been observed in other studies carried out in the Federal administration (Giauque, 2004).

As regards values, it is worth noting the disparity among the sources included in the literature review. It is interesting to note that these 'new' values do not seem to be problematic in and of themselves, but rather it is in their practical application and implementation that conflicts arise. As pointed out in the Swiss literature regarding administrative modernization, this conflict of values has not yet been really addressed, nor have the associated ethical problems been confronted. An explanation for this may be that the implementation of reforms is still at an intermediate stage (Lienhard *et al.*, 2005).

**The Level of the Immediate Working Environment**

The more immediate working environment takes on greater importance because of the decentralization of responsibilities. This is true of unit 2 in particular, where a type of 'protective bubble' formed, allowing people to partly neutralize the effects of the chaotic organization surrounding the unit. Other research also shows the strengthening of the protective role of the team at a time of restructuring (Büssing, 1999; Knudson *et al.*, 2003).

Added to this is the disappearance of the traditionally strong layer of protection provided by the hierarchy, which used to act as a 'shield', protecting the staff from the higher political echelons. Considered no longer credible, and no longer fully appraised of the realities on the ground, this hierarchy appears like some sort of illusory and unpredictable phantom which has lost its practical relevance. It is clearly no longer seen as a 'model' by its staff (Bass and Moulton, 2002). Lewis and Gilman stress the vital role of managers in establishing a functioning ethical dimension (Lewis and Gilman, 2005: 235ff), but what can be done if, as we have observed, the hierarchy 'disappears' and the basic professionalism and ethics of the staff become the vital element?

Some of the more negative impacts from all the changes described above might have been avoided if control mechanisms had been put in place to ensure that the professional and technical requirements, and also those relating to cooperation and the ethics of public service, were being followed. This is, however, scarcely the case, even though in unit 1, the controls are getting more stringent. When one looks more closely, these controls revolve more around the procedural and contextual aspects of work rather than its precise content. The situation is critical from a professional and ethical point of view, above all in U2 and U3, where the remaining safeguards appear to be limited to a form of 'intervision', or self-control, leaving the field open for all types of behaviours. This is all the more noteworthy in that this is traditionally a unit where control mechanisms have been very much present.

**The Individual Level**

Apparently, no major dysfunction has been observed at this level to date. This may be due to the strong self-control mechanisms exercised by our interlocutors. These mechanisms themselves stem from, and we formulate this as a hypothesis, the strong cultural ethic towards work itself within the Swiss context, since the code of conduct that is in force in the organization was not mentioned by our interlocutors. And since, due to the absence of specific professional socialization for public sector workers in Switzerland, one cannot use the hypothesis of the existence of a form of 'public servant ethos' (Mayntz, 1997), as put forward, for example, by Fisch (2000). This finding would be in line with that made by Turansky and Rousson (2001), who state that one should distinguish between the ethic of work and the ethic towards work. While the former, which reflects the central role work plays in society, is in sharp decline, the second is tending to re-establish itself. The ethic towards work is defined as a 'responsible commitment that is based on a set of beliefs, values and principles such as responsibility, pride, performance etc.' (ibid: 293). Our respondents stressed their need to deliver work they could feel proud of, illustrating a work ethic that compensates for the dysfunctions present in the work environment. Linked with the dimensions investigated by Büssing, who is interested in 'control at work' (Büssing, 1999), the pre-eminence of this level of regulation over and above the others could explain why the people we met maintain, despite the objective difficulty of their situation, an astonishing level of personal control. Equally, as suggested by Jorgensen (2005), one of the key factors in the motivation of public servants is related to the work itself, showing a form of 'professional commitment' which can explain some of the statements collected in the present research.

According to our interlocutors, maintaining professionalism on the job is a means of preserving self-respect, reinforcing an individual's dignity at work. It allows them to finish the day with a feeling of personal satisfaction, having carried out a meaningful activity. As a response to the lack of environmental clarity, this orientation is inherently unpredictable and is rife with expectations that are increasingly difficult to decipher (De Witte, 1999). Both these elements are at the heart of the insecurity of employment, and were found to play an important role in understanding the situation.

Similar to the isolation of certain public servants working 'a long way from the centre', an issue dealt with by Kelso (2003), the public servants we met are left to themselves and to their own codes of conduct. The form of organizational 'anomie' we noted in our research echoes the concluding remarks of Ghere. He underlined the need to develop some general models of ambiguity that could offer predictive insight into circumstances leading the person, as a moral agent, into dissonant, defensive or otherwise problematic behaviours (Ghere, 2005).

Of course, it remains necessary to examine in greater depth the dynamic interaction between these three (systemic) levels of ethical regulations. Dicke and Boonyarak (2005) show that the end of the bureaucratic model represents a major problem with regard to accountability: it was ensured by the hierarchical structure yet is now dependent upon contractual relationships with 'few considerations and discussions about the potentially dangerous consequences' (quoted contribution, p. 187). But this accountability must be based as much on an internalized sense of duty as on an externally imposed set of requirements (p. 188). Monitoring and measurements of performance alone would not be synonymous with accountability, especially as these methods are far from being fully instituted. Doig takes the same view by observing the difficulties inherent in the transition from an ethical system based on (external) control to a system based on accountability, the latter 'often abrogates individual responsibility or ignores the contextual or cultural framework' (Doig, 2003). In fact, a proper balance has to be found between external and internal regulation, this being assumed because of an implicit or explicit interest in public services (Doig, 2003: 113). Clegg and Stokes (2003) go even further when they plead for a return to a curriculum that details the classical tradition with particular emphasis on Aristotle and Weber, to strengthen the character and the purpose of public servants, to supplement the prevailing managerialism. For Switzerland, where socialization geared specifically to public sector organizations is virtually nonexistent, this argument is of fundamental importance.

For Bishop and Connors, a shift from 'government to governance' (Peers, 2003) does not imply a strengthening of ethical standards but rather a different approach that brings together an enterprising spirit, freedom of action and a sense of responsibility. Along with Caiden, we finally want to assert that individual regulation, based on professionalism, expertise and personal integrity, will continue to play a vital role in the State's ethical action (Caiden, 2005).

## CONCLUSION

In this first analysis, we have taken an exploratory approach which has allowed us to refine the method for the second phase of research. It is clear that the research model adopted does not allow one to assess the impact of the change in the status of employees as the principal independent variable – this would require selecting organizations still operating with a traditional personnel statute. The phenomena observed could develop differently in the longer term and are perhaps partly due to the particular difficulties of the current phase of changes. Parker and Hartley (2003) show, for example, that processes of strategic reorganization can end up having a less forceful impact on the staff when they are looked at over a longer period. They are then considered as involving a 'rightsizing' rather than a 'downsizing' approach, helping to clarify roles and to introduce innovative processes in carrying out the work.

It is obvious that at a time of profound change, feelings of insecurity and anguish, which are sometimes of an existential nature, can develop. We nevertheless have the feeling that this is not a transitory state, but rather reflects an enduring situation close to a 'perpetual motion' (Baruch and Hind, 1999), which will no longer include periods of stabilization as defined by Lewin (1951).

Nonetheless, the changes recorded make for a 'post-civil service' situation that is rather worrying – while noting, however, that the statements made by our interlocutors are many and varied. All the changes highlighted create a working context that has a significant potential for being dysfunctional and the source of ethical problems, although to date this potential has not yet really materialized. In the absence of an appropriate ethical framework, the main safeguard seems to be a form of personal ethics in carrying out the work. In the bureaucratic model, the frame of reference is defined above all by the organization, whereas in the situations observed, the standards and references that guide the activities become, in the most critical units, above all personal ones. As Menzel (1996) stresses, public servants are very likely to find themselves in a stressful situation of cognitive dissonance which forces them to choose between their own personal values and those of their employer.

## NOTES

1. Thus A. Matheson (Modernisation du secteur public: un nouveau programme pour les pays de l'OCDE' in Lacasse and Verrier, p. 213) points out that the managerial reforms have underestimated their adverse effects, in particular with regard to corruption; but he does not substantiate his claims.
2. As part of his analysis of the reform of the Italian government apparatus, the author mentions that 'the principles of impartiality and neutrality . . . are often invoked in an unwarranted way to avoid assessing the results and to protect the secure income from the irresponsibility of inefficient senior public servant . . .' Bassanini F.: Réforme de l'Etat: la tronçonneuse ou l'anesthésie? Les leçons de l'expérience italienne, in Lacasse and Verrier (2005), p. 76.
3. To illustrate this point, we refer to the early departure of the two leading managers at the Swiss Federal Personnel Office who could no longer recognize their roles in the reform programmes that were being implemented.
4. Since 1 January 2002, a new personnel statute has been introduced, based on the use of contracts, which makes it easier to terminate working relationships.

## REFERENCES

Allen, T., D. Freeman, J.E.A. Russell, R.C. Reizenstein and J.O. Rentz (2001), 'Survivor reactions to organizational downsizing: Does time ease the pain?', *Journal of Occupational and Organizational Psychology*, **74**, 145–64.
Argyris, C. and D. Schön (1978), *Organizational Learning: A Theory of Action Perspective*, Reading, MA: Addison-Wesley.

Aubert, N. (2003), Les sources de démotivation dans une entreprise publique en mutation, in T. Duvillier, J.-L. Genard and A. Piraux (eds), *La motivation au travail dans les services publics*, Paris: L'Harmattan, pp. 93–108.

Baines, P.R., B. Lewis and B. Ingham (1999), 'Exploring the positioning process in political markets', *Journal of Communication Management*, **3**(3), 325–36.

Baruch, Y. and P. Hind (1999), 'Perpetual motion in organizations: effective management and the impact of the new psychological contracts on "Survivor syndrome"', *European Journal of Work and Organizational Psychology*, **8**(2), 295–306.

Bass, G.D. and S. Moulton (2002), 'The Bush Administration's secrecy policy: a call to action to protect democratic values', OMB Watch working paper, Washington, DC.

Baszanger, I. (1992), 'Les chantiers d'un interactionniste américain', in A. Strauss (ed.), *La trame de la négociation: sociologie qualitative et interactionnisme*, Paris: L'Harmattan, pp. 11–63.

Boltanski, L. and L. Thévenot (1991), *De la justification. Les économies de la grandeur*, Paris: Gallimard.

Bossaert, D. (2005), *The Flexibilisation of the Employment Status of Civil Servants: From Life Tenure to More Flexible Employment Relations?*, Luxemburg: Institut européen d'administration publique, pp. 1–46.

Bowman, J. S., E.M. Berman and J.P. West (2001), 'The profession of public administration: an ethics edge in introductory textbooks?', *Public Administration Review*, **61**(2), 194–205.

Brereton, M. and M. Temple (1999), 'The new public service ethos: an ethical environment for governance', *Public Administration*, **77**(3), 455–74.

Büssing, A. (1999), 'Can control at work and social support moderate psychological consequences of job insecurity? Results from a quasi-experimental study in the steel industry', *European Journal of Work and Organizational Psychology*, **8**(2), 219–42.

Caiden, G.E. (2005), 'An anatomy of official corruption', in H.G. Frederickson and R.K. Ghere (eds), *Ethics in Public Management*, New York: M.E. Sharpe, pp. 277–96.

Clegg, S. and J. Stokes (2003), 'Bureaucracy, power and ethics', in P. Bishop, C. Connors and C. Sampford (eds), *Management, Organizations, and Ethics in the Public Sector*, Burlington, VT: Ashgate, pp. 145–59.

De Witte, H. (1999), 'Job insecurity and psychological well-being: review of the literature and exploration of some unresolved issues', *European Journal of Work and Organizational Psychology*, **8**(2), 155–77.

Dicke, L.A. and P. Boonyarak (2005), 'Ensuring accountability in human services: the dilemma of measuring moral end ethical performance', in H.G. Frederickson and R.K. Ghere (eds), *Ethics in Public Management*, New York: M.E. Sharpe, pp. 184–202.

Doig, A. (2003), 'The matrix of integrity: is it possible to shift the emphasis from compliance to responsibility in changing contexts? Lessons from the United Kingdom', in P. Bishop, C. Connors and C. Sampford (eds), *Management, Organizations, and Ethics in the Public Sector*, Burlington, VT: Ashgate, pp. 101–19.

du Gay, P. (2000), *In Praise of Bureaucracy*, London, Thousand Oaks, CA, and New Delhi: Sage Publications.

Duvillier, T., J.-L. Genard, A. Piraux and Collectif d'auteurs (2003), *La motivation au travail dans les services publics*, Paris: L'Harmattan.

Emery, Y. (ed.) (2000), *L'administration dans tous ses états. Réalisations et conséquences*, Lausanne: Presses Polytechniques et Universitaires Romandes.

Emery, Y. and D. Giauque (2005), *Paradoxes de la gestion publique*, Paris: L'Harmattan.

Emery, Y. and B. Ueberhart (1999), *Tendances dans les statuts du personnel des cantons suisses*, Lausanne: Idheap.

Farnham, D. and S. Horton (2005), *Origins, Development and Decline of the Public Service Ethos in the British Civil Service: An Historical Institutional Analysis*, Bern:

Fisch, S. (2000), 'Beamtenethik und Beamtenethos – Anmerkungen aus historischer Sicht', in A. Hofmeister (ed.), *Brauchen wir eine neue Ethik in der Verwaltung?*, Berne: Société suisse des sciences administratives (SSSA), pp. 163–77.

Frederickson, H.G. (1996), 'Comparing the reinventing government movement with the new public administration', *Public Administration Review*, **56**(3), 263–70.

Gaulejac de, V. (2005), *La société malade de la gestion: idéelogie gestionnaire, pouvoir managérial et harcèlement social*, Paris: Seuil.

Ghere, R.K. (2005), 'Conclusions: ethics and public management: questions and answers', in H.G. Frederickson and R.K. Ghere (eds), *Ethics and Public Management*, New York: M.E. Sharpe, pp. 356–71.

Giauque, D. (2003), *Changements dans le secteur public: vers une redéfinition de la régulation organisationnelle en situation de nouvelle gestion publique*, Lausanne: Institut de hautes études en administration publique, p. 390.

Giauque, D. (2004), *La bureaucratie libérale*, Paris: L'Harmattan.

Grant, D., J. Shields and M. O'Donnell (2003), 'The new performance paradigm in the Australian public service: a discursive analysis', in T. Duvillier, J.-L. Genard and A. Piraux (eds), *La motivation au travail dans les services publics*, Paris: L'Harmattan, pp. 247–60.

Grunberg, L., R. Anderson-Connolly and E.S. Greenberg (2000), 'Surviving layoffs: the effects on organizational commitment and job performance', *Work and Occupation*, **27**(1), 7–31.

Hufty, M. (1992), *La pensée comptable. Etat, néolibéralisme, nouvelle gestion publique*, Paris: Puf.

Igalens, J. and E. Dehermann-Roy (2004), 'Les codes de conduite: une existence légitime, une efficacité contestable', *Revue de gestion des ressources humaines*, **54** (October-November-December), 27–55.

Jorgensen, T.B. (2005), 'Value consciousness and public governance', proceedings of the Ethics and Integrity of Governance: the First Transatlantic Dialogue Conference, 2–5 June, Leuven.

Jurkiewicz, C., T.K. Massey and R.G. Brown (1998), 'Motivation in public and private organizations', *Public Productivity and Management Review*, **21**(3), 230–50.

Kaufmann, J.-C. (ed.) (2004), *L'entretien compréhensif*, Paris: Armand Colin.

Kellough, J.E. and L.G. Nigro (2005), 'Dramatic reform in the public service: at-will employment and the creation of a new public workforce', *Journal of Public Administration Research and Theory*.

Kelso, R. (2003), 'Isolated agents', in P. Bishop, C. Connors and C. Sampford (eds), *Management, Organisation and Ethics in the Public Sector*, Burlington, VT: Ashgate, pp. 201–17.

Kinnunen, U., S. Mauno, J. Natti and M. Happonen (1999), 'Perceived job insecurity: a longitudinal study among Finnish employees', *European Journal of Work and Organizational Psychology*, **8**(2), 243–60.

Klandermans, B. and T. Van Vuuren (1999), 'Job insecurity: introduction', *European Journal of Work and Organizational Psychology*, **8**(2), 145–53.

Knoepfel, P. and F. Varone (1999), 'Mesurer la performance publique: méfions-nous des terribles simplificateurs', *Politiques et management public*, **17**(2), 123–45.

Knudson, H., J. Johnson, J. Martin and P. Roman (2003), 'Downsizing survival: the experience of work and organizational commitment', *Sociological Inquiry*, **73**(2), 265–83.

Lacasse, F. and J.-C. Thoenig (eds) (1996), *L'action publique: morceaux choisis de la revue 'Politiques et management public'*, Paris: L'Harmattan.

Lacasse, F. and P.E. Verrier (eds) (2005), *30 ans de réforme de l'Etat: Expérieces françaises et étrangères: stratégies et bilans*, management public, Paris: Dunod.

Leisink, P. and B. Steijn (2004), *Public Management Reform and Staff Participation: the Case of Civil Service Modernisation in the Netherlands*, Leuven: Public Management Reform and Staff Participation in Public Services International Comparisons.

Leuenberger, D. (2005), 'FLAG für die Bundesverwaltung – eine Standortbestimmung', in A. Lienhard, A. Ritz, R. Steiner and A. Ladner (eds), *10 Jahre NPM in der Schweiz: Bilanz, Irrtümer and Erfolgsfaktoren*, Bern: Haupt, pp. 25–34.

Lewin, K. (1951), *Field Theory and Social Science*, New York: Sage.

Lewis, C.W. and S.C. Gilman (2005), *The Ethics Challenge in Public Service*, San Francisco, CA: Jossey Bass.

Lienhard, A., A. Ritz, R. Steiner, A. Ladner (eds) (2005), *10 Jahre New Public Management in der Schweiz. Bilanz, Irrtümer un Erfolgsfaktoren*, Bern: Haupt.

Mayntz, R. (1997), 'L'administration publique dans le changement sociétal', in M. Finger and B. Ruchat (eds), *Pour une nouvelle approche du management public*, Paris: Seli Arslan, pp. 97–108.

Menzel, D.C. (1996), 'Ethics stress in public organizations', *Public Productivity & Management Review*, **20**, 70–83.

Menzel, D.C. (2005), 'State of the art of empirical research on ethics and integrity in governance', in H.G. Frederickson and R.K. Ghere (eds), *Ethics in Public Management*, New York: M.E. Sharpe, pp. 16–46.

Merrien, F.-X. (1998), *Misère de la nouvelle gestion publique?*, *La pensée comptable*, Paris and Genève: PUF and Les nouveaux cahiers de l'IUED.

Meyer, R. and G. Hammerschmied (2005), *Changing Institutional Logics and its Impact on Social Identities. A Survey of Austrian Public Sector Executives*, Bern:

Mutter, B. (2004), 'Beamter sucht job', *Facts*.

Organisation for Economic Co-operation and Development (OECD) (1997), *Questions et évolution dans la gestion publique*, Paris: PUMA and OECD.

OECD (1998), *Public Management Reform and Economic and Social Development*, Paris: OECD and PUMA.

Parker, D. and K. Hartley (2003), 'Transaction cost, relational contracting and public private partnerships: a case study of UK defence', *Journal of Purchasing & Supply Management*, **9**(3), 97–108.

Peers, A.M. (2003), 'A citizen is more than just a taxpayer', *The Toronto Star*, Toronto.

Pollitt, C. and G. Bouckaert (2000), *Public Management Reform – A Comparative Analysis*, Oxford: Oxford University Press.

Pollitt, C. and G. Bouckaert (2004), *Public Management Reform: A Comparative Analysis*, Oxford: Oxford University Press.

Pollitt, C. and G. Boukaert (2003), 'Evaluating public management reforms: an international perspective', in H. Wollman (ed.), *Evaluation in Public-Sector Reform*, Cheltenham, UK and Northampton, MA, USA: Edward Elgar, pp. 12–35.

PUMA (2001), *Développements récents de la gestion des ressources humaines dans les pays membres de l'OCDE*, Paris: PUMA and OECD, p. 16.

Reichard, C. (2002), *Evaluation de la gestion des ressources humaines axée sur la performance dans certains pays de l'OCDE*, Paris: OECD and PUMA, pp. 1–15.

Ritz, A. (2003), *Die Evaluation von New Public Management*, Bern: Haupt.

Rondeaux, G. (2005), *The Evolution of the Organisational Identity of a Federal Public Service in a Context of Change*, Bern:

Smith, R.F.I. (2003), 'Ethics in a changing state – problems and opportunities, in P. Bishop, C. Connors and C. Sampford (eds), *Management, Organisation, and Ethics in Public Management*, Burlington, VT: Ashgate, pp. 19–41.

Strauss, A. and J. Corbin (1997), *Grounded Theory in Practice*, Thousand Oaks, CA: Sage Publications.

Strauss, A. and J. Corbin (1998), *Basics of Qualitative Research: Techniques and Procedures for Developing Grounded Theory*, Thousand Oaks, CA: Sage Publications.

Strauss, A. and J. Corbin (2004), *Les fondements de la recherche qualitative: techniques et procédures de développement de la théorie enracinée*, Fribourg: Academic Press Fribourg.

Turansky, V.A. and M. Rousson (2001), 'Centralité du travail et éthique(s) chez les cadres suisses romands?', *Revue économique et sociale*, **4**, 291–300.

Turnley, W.H. and D.C. Feldmann (1999), 'The impact of psychological contract violations on exit, voice, loyalty, and neglect', *Human Relations*, **52**(7), 895–922.

Weber, M. (1971), *Economie et société*, Paris: Plon.

Wittmer, D.P. (2005), 'Developing a behavioral model for ethical decision making in organizations: conceptual and empirical research', in H.G. Frederickson and R.K. Ghere (eds), *Ethics and Public Management*, New York: M.E. Sharpe, pp. 49–69.

# PART III

# Ethics and integrity management and instruments

# 8. Ethical governance in local government in England: a regulator's view

## Gillian Fawcett and Mark Wardman

## INTRODUCTION

### Overview

High-profile corporate failures underpinned by poor standards of behaviour and/or corruption ('sleaze') have brought ethical governance into sharp focus in the United Kingdom in both the private and public sectors. The need to increase public trust and hold managers and politicians to account more effectively are recurring topics in debates about publicly-funded bodies in the UK. Low levels of trust, it is argued, are caused or sustained by poor standards of behaviour. There has been, therefore, a growing emphasis on the need for officials and politicians to adhere to the highest ethical standards to help increase the public's trust in public bodies.

> Trust is at the heart of the relationship between citizens and government. It is particularly important in relation to services which influence life and liberty – health and policing. But it also matters for many other services – including social services and education. In these cases, even if formal service and outcome targets are met, a failure of trust will effectively destroy public value (Kelly and Muesrs, 2002).

> The qualities the public looks for in different leaders and professions varies according to the nature of the role. *Honesty* and *trustworthiness* are the most significant personal qualities for public leaders. In contrast, the public looks to Civil Servants to be efficient, competent and honest, while experience in running a business and professionalism are considered more important for business people. Therefore, while honesty and trustworthiness are important qualities for most leaders, they are *more* significant for public leaders (Duffy *et al.*, 2003).

This chapter deals with ethical governance in local government and provides a basis for discussion about the role of regulators in ensuring higher ethical standards in local government in England. The Audit Commission (the

Commission) is an independent body responsible for ensuring public money is well spent and delivers high quality public services. Its remit covers around 11 000 local bodies in England, which between them spend more than £180 billion of public money each year. The Commission challenges poor ethical standards and inappropriate behaviour through its regulatory activities in audit and inspection. Drawing from this work, this chapter explores:

- Benchmarking for ethical standards and behaviour – whether it is possible to benchmark for ethical governance because of the softer cultural issues involved.
- What is different about regulating for ethical governance – contrasting the different approaches used for auditing ethical standards against other auditing practices.
- The impact of ethical change in local government in England – the impact of ethical standards on local government behaviour and practice.

**Research**

The focus of this chapter is the ethical framework operating in local government in England. It draws upon data collected by the Commission in:

- ethical governance audits;
- corporate assessments of local authorities as part of their comprehensive performance assessment (CPA). The CPA assessment framework from 2002–4 led to an overall rating for local authorities of one of the following five categories: Excellent, Good, Fair, Weak or Poor. In 2005 and 2006, the framework was revised and it now gives an overall star rating for an authority's performance: from 0 to 4 stars. Further details of the CPA methodology are given in Appendix 8.1;
- corporate governance inspections (CGIs). Further details of the CGI methodology are given in Appendix 8.1; and
- Public Interest Reports (PIRs).[1] These address matters of importance that need to be brought to the attention of the public.

**Context**

The Audit Commission does not define 'ethical governance'[2] but rather situates it within its overall definition of corporate governance in the public sector: 'the framework of accountability to users, stakeholders and the wider community, within which organizations take decisions, and lead and control their functions, to achieve their objectives'. This definition recognizes that effectively governed organizations combine reliable 'hard' data from robust systems and processes with effective 'soft' characteristics such as leadership, and 'cultural' attributes such as openness and transparency in order to make sound decisions. Within this broad approach, the importance of high standards of behaviour and ethics becomes clear. The Commission assesses both 'hard' and 'soft' attributes when making judgements about a local authority's performance.

The Commission's approach to ethical governance has of course been directly informed by other initiatives. Of the numerous national reports on corporate governance and the proper conduct of public business, the Cadbury report was particularly influential in establishing the principles of openness, integrity and accountability in the governance of publicly quoted companies (Cadbury Committee, 1992). In the public sector, the Nolan Committee's (Nolan Committee, 1995) seven principles of public life – selflessness, integrity, objectivity, accountability, openness, honesty and leadership – remain the benchmark for behaviour and conduct in running any public sector organization.

Part 3 of the Local Government Act 2000 introduced an ethical framework for local government in England, which set out new structures to oversee standards of behaviour based on the Nolan principles. Local authorities are required to:

- adopt a new council constitution;
- adopt a code of conduct regulating the behaviour of elected members, including a register of elected members' interests, with a separate code of conduct for officers; and
- appoint a monitoring officer and a local Standards Committee to advise on the Code, monitor its operation, and promote high standards.

The Act also provided for establishing two new, non-departmental public bodies: the Standards Board for England, responsible for investigating cases of unethical conduct by members; and the Adjudication Panel for England, an independent judicial tribunal which hears and adjudicates on serious matters concerning the conduct of elected members.

More recent developments include: the Department of Communities and Local Government (CLG), previously the Office of the Deputy Prime Minister (ODPM), has completed a review of the effectiveness of the Standards Board for England (House of Commons ODMP, 2005); the Independent Commission on Good Governance published a common standard of governance for public services (Independent Commission on Good Governance for Public Services, 2004); and the Graham Committee (a successor to the Nolan Committee) published the tenth report on standards in public life, *Getting the Balance Right – Implementing Standards of Conduct in Public Life* (Committee on Standards in Public Life, 2005).

Continuing interest in these matters at a national level has inevitably led to regulators like the Commission taking a close interest in ethical standards in the public sector. This chapter sets out the findings and conclusions from the work the Commission has undertaken in this area among local authorities.

## BENCHMARKING FOR ETHICAL GOVERNANCE

> For several years now, leaders have been encouraged to consider the impact of material forces in organizations – culture, values, vision and ethics. Each describes a quality of organizational life that can be observed through behaviour (Wheatley, 2001).

The majority of members and officers working in public services in England adhere to the high ethical standards expected by citizens and the users of services. Incidents of misbehaviour and/or corruption within public services are isolated. Only 21 Public Interest Reports (PIRs) were issued in the period between 1997 and 2005, and not all of these related to poor ethical practice.

Similarly, the Standards Board for England has received 9648 complaints about the conduct of elected members since it was established in March 2001, but these have resulted in only 240 sanctions against individual elected members. Common categories of misconduct resulting in such sanctions include breaches of the code of conduct, bullying behaviour, misuse of council resources, bringing the council into disrepute and using position for personal gain.

It is all too easy to identify the behaviours and factors that contribute to corporate failure after the event, and to learn the lessons and benchmark for them. For example, it is now recognized that the conditions which led to the failure of public officials to prevent the death of an eight-year old girl (Laming, 2003), the removal of body parts from deceased patients without family consent (Redfern, 2000), and the high rate of death in children's heart surgeries (Bristol Royal Infirmary Inquiry, 2001) were the consequence of poor corporate performance. These cases highlighted numerous governance failures to implement legislative guidelines by public officials, or in some cases were a result of misconceived compliance with legislation. More pertinent to ethical governance in local government is the example of the recent failings that resulted in postal vote irregularities by councillors prior to two local council elections in Birmingham.[3] But it has proved more difficult for the Commission to identify at an early stage the underlying factors and behaviours which could lead to corporate and/or service failure, if they are not addressed.

This is despite confirmation from analysis of the Commission's corporate governance inspection reports that there are indicators for poor governance. The Commission has conducted 17 corporate governance inspections in local government. These rare inspections are designed to diagnose the root causes of poor organizational performance. The areas of weakness common to poorly governed local authorities are poor working relationships; low levels of internal accountability; a 'closed' culture that does not accept external challenge and scrutiny; poor strategic risk management; lack of clarity about objectives, roles and responsibilities; poor information for decision makers; and poor leadership. Sadly, however, it is easier to see these in hindsight than to predict there may be trouble ahead.

## EXTRACTS FROM CORPORATE GOVERNANCE INSPECTION REPORTS

> Some members are seen to be antagonistic towards other organizations. The Council does not treat its partners with respect in all circumstances and the Leader has been cited by some partners as behaving in an unprofessional manner.

> Partners told us that there was a lack of consensus amongst the politicians and the bitterness which has developed between politicians presents itself to partners as a culture of internal feuding rather than external community leadership.

> It was not always possible to be clear about how and why decisions were taken . . . members need high quality information from officers if they are to make informed decisions. The quality of information provided to members at times was observed as poor.

> Progress in the past has been impeded by ineffective and sometimes abrasive relationships between councillors and officers. These relationships are now undoubtedly much improved, but there remains some way to go.

It is important, however, to distinguish between malpractice or mismanagement in poor governance and poor ethical standards. As noted earlier, incidents of misbehaviour and corruption are isolated. But despite the low numbers of public interest reports, it should be remembered that when the public believes that governance standards have slipped, this can reduce its confidence in public services. Research carried out by MORI for the Commission in 2003 found that 64 per cent of the public said their confidence in public bodies was reduced by major corporate failures (Audit Commission, 2003b).

As required under the Code of Audit Practice (Audit Commission, 2004), auditors routinely assess the structures and processes underpinning organizational performance. As part of this, they will assess the risks to public bodies of failing to establish the structures and processes to support ethical standards. A number of PIRs have highlighted what happens if standards are not taken into account. For example, a PIR on a Borough Council in 2003 showed that

> in the absence of a standards committee, there had been serious failings in the governance of the Council and in the conduct of the Leader of the Council and some senior officers. There was a breakdown in the corporate controls and systems of decision-making. The prevailing culture of the Council was one of fear and blame, and as a result, there had been no challenge to inappropriate conduct by senior officers and members.

The Commission has reviewed all PIRs against the Nolan seven principles of public life. This review highlighted standards and behaviours common to all which can be associated with failing services and/or fraudulent and corrupt practices. It found that, in 21 PIRs, there were breaches of the ethical code of conduct by members and protocols by officers, often caused by the lack of an open culture and trust. Poor relations between executives and non-executives were apparent, exemplified by intimidation and bullying. This finding echoes those from a national taskforce set up to look at the worrying problem of bullying within local government, which found that 27 per cent of female and 19 per cent of male chief executives reported being bullied or harassed by members (Whitehead, 2002). Table 8.1 highlights a number of common characteristics of poor behaviour found across 21 PIRs and maps them against the Nolan principles.

However, it is the case that these behaviours and standards can also be found in otherwise well-run organizations. For example, Westminster City Council was considered a high performing organization at the time it was pursuing an illegal policy of 'homes for votes' in order to advance the prospects of the then ruling Conservative party at the 1990 elections. Several recent PIRs highlight issues of poor standards of behaviour and conduct in authorities that have been given Fair, Good and Excellent CPA scores by the Commission in the period 2002 to 2004. Similarly, the ethical governance reviews highlighted areas of weakness at authorities scored as 'Good' by the then current CPA process. This is due in part to the fact that, until recently, the 'key lines of enquiry' (KLOE) followed by assessment teams in corporate assessments did not set out specifically to assess performance against standards of behaviour. Their focus was on good management practice in producing high performance and good service and other outcomes for the public. The revised approach to CPA from 2005 does address ethical standards in more detail (see Appendix 8.1).

*Table 8.1    Common standards and behaviours drawn from 21 public interest reports*

| Principles | Common findings |
|---|---|
| **Selflessness**<br>Holders of public office should act solely in terms of the public interest. They should not do so in order to gain financial or other benefits for themselves, their family or friends | • Arrogance<br>• Full of self importance<br>• Autocratic, dominant and dictatorial |
| **Integrity**<br>Holders of public office should not place themselves under any financial or other obligation to outside individuals or organizations that may seek to influence them in the performance of their official duties | • Unofficial deals to get own way |
| **Objectivity**<br>In carrying out public business, including making public appointments, awarding contracts, or recommending individuals for rewards and benefits, holders of public office should make choices on merit | • Grants prejudicial benefits to individuals or groups because of their own intolerance or discriminatory views<br>• Threatens to influence the action of others against the common good |
| **Accountability**<br>Holders of public office are accountable for their decisions and actions to the public and must submit themselves to whatever scrutiny is appropriate to their office | • Manipulative<br>• Lack of working partnerships<br>• Denies external challenge |
| **Openness**<br>Holders of public office should be as open as possible about all decisions and actions that they take. They should give reasons for their decisions and restrict information only when the wider public interest clearly demands it | • Evasive or provides excessively complicated answers to questions<br>• Reluctant to delegate<br>• Prone to secrecy<br>• Lack of transparency in decision making |
| **Honesty**<br>Holders of public office have a duty to declare any private interests relating to their public duties and to take steps to resolve any conflicts arising in a way that protects the public interest | • Grants prejudicial benefits to individuals or groups<br>• Makes decisions for their own personal gain |

*Table 8.1    (continued)*

| Principles | Common findings |
|---|---|
| **Leadership**<br>Holders of public office should promote and support these principles by leadership and example | • Driven<br>• Obsessed by performance standards<br>• Engenders blame or fear<br>• Intimidates or bullies<br>• Workaholic<br>• Interferes in low level operational matters |

*Source:*    Audit Commission – *There may be trouble ahead* (2004).

Further research is needed to build up a greater understanding of how and at what stage poor standards of conduct and behaviour can begin to have a negative impact on the delivery of public services. In particular, it is important to know more about whether poor ethical governance will eventually adversely affect performance: if so, it would be useful to know more about the degree of governance problems likely to trigger service failures and the timescales involved. For example, can performance only be maintained in the short term, where some of the above attributes are displayed?

Public sector audit has traditionally focused on compliance and risk. One charge has been that this leads to a 'tick box' approach that rewards the existence rather than the application of structures, systems and processes. The Commission recognizes this danger, and has developed audit tools within its Changing Organizational Cultures (COC) toolkit that test the operation of ethical standards and facilitate internal benchmarking. The Commission regularly conducts workshops where practitioners (officers and elected members) can self-assess their councils against the standards and criteria contained in the COC toolkit.

The toolkit assesses members' and officers' understanding of the code of conduct. It focuses upon the positive promotion of ethical standards and helps those in authority to explore the cultural norms and standards of behaviour that may place the organization at risk.

The implementation of the toolkit is at an early stage. As it is used more widely by local authorities, the Commission will build up a national picture of ethical standards operating across local governments. An analysis of ethical audit reviews carried out at 38 local authorities in 2004 highlighted a range of common issues resulting from the implementation of the ethical framework. These are listed in Table 8.2.

The Commission's findings highlight considerable variability in the way the ethical framework is being implemented across the authorities surveyed.

Table 8.2    *Analysis of 38 governance local authority reviews – common findings*

---

Failure to monitor registers of gifts and hospitality

Members unclear whether or not they have signed a code of conduct

Unclear as to whether their authorities had a whistleblowing policy

No corporate drive to establish a set of positive values and behaviours across an authority

Lack of pro-activeness of standards committees to address ethical issues

Little engagement with partners

Variability in views regarding whether or not ethical standards were making a difference

Lack of resources to support ethical framework at a local level for the monitoring officer and standards committee

Lack of integration of codes of conduct into other policies

Lack of further awareness raising about the negative impact of inappropriate behaviour

Lack of communication regarding the code of conduct to external stakeholders

---

*Source:*    Audit Commission ethical governance reviews (2004).

In part this has resulted from both a lack of resources and pro-active guidance for authorities in areas such as how to develop an effective standards committee and engage more effectively with partners. The Commission is working with the Standards Board for England and the Improvement and Development Agency to bridge this gap.

It is not certain whether or not the problems identified by these audits will lead to service failure or poor quality services. The Commission's 2003 report on corporate governance in the public sector (Audit Commission, 2003b) stated that

> no one participating in this study suggested high service quality could be achieved and maintained without a strong governance foundation in areas like risk management, financial control and codes of behaviour. Nonetheless, not all believe that these or others are necessarily the determinant of quality and some felt that they might not even be the major factor in driving up service quality, or failing to protect the organization from failure.

## WHAT'S DIFFERENT ABOUT REGULATING FOR ETHICAL GOVERNANCE?

The traditional skills for auditing governance and financial management require auditors to have a good understanding of professional codes and

technical rules. These skills are usually acquired through professional training routes in the accountancy or other specialist professions. Although the
skills provide a good basis for auditors to assess compliance with regulations and financial instruments, they do not necessarily equip them with the
ability to reach sound judgements about organizational culture and ethical
behaviour.

The complexities of auditing for ethical governance have led the
Commission to recruit people who are skilled in this area and to invest in
training to deliver ethical audits effectively. As well as specific knowledge
about regulatory provisions such as Codes of Conduct, auditors involved
in ethical audits need to have and apply some skills more frequently than
those required for traditional audits. Good communication skills are a
necessary attribute for all audit work, but ethical audits involve a greater
emphasis on personal contact and the ability to discuss potentially difficult
organizational and personal issues with care and rigour. The different
emphases in ethical audits compared with traditional audits are summarized in Table 8.3.

The Commission has also had to refine its approach to reporting as
experience has shown that local authorities are not always receptive to
reports on these topics. For example, it can be particularly difficult to
engender understanding in local authorities as to why changes might need
to be made in the 'softer' aspects of organizational culture, and to explain

*Table 8.3    Comparison of traditional audit skills against those skills
              required to carry out an ethical audit*

| The skills emphasized in traditional audits | The skills emphasized in ethical audits |
| --- | --- |
| Co-ordination skills | Local knowledge of an authority's issues and organizational culture |
| Technical skills in accountancy and corporate governance | Ability to work at a corporate level with chief executives, senior management and members |
| Planning and supervision of work | Strong interpersonal and facilitation skills |
| Building effective relationships at operational and senior management levels | Record of maintaining credibility in a politically sensitive environment |
| Quality assurance skills | Project management skills |

*Source:*    Audit Commission Ethical Audit Guide and Competency framework for auditors
(2005).

that these can be important contributory factors to organizational success. These 'softer' factors include the appropriate leadership style for the organization's current and likely future performance; a degree of openness and honesty in acknowledging poor performance or standards of behaviour; a willingness to learn from mistakes; and being willing to accept external challenge.

As well as providing a traditional audit report which is time-bound and focuses on 'hard' issues, the Commission has found that long-term improvement can follow a more facilitative approach to working with chief executives and elected leaders. The Commission must be careful to ensure that its independence and objectivity are not jeopardized through this activity. But such an approach can lead to organizational change: in one 'Fair' council, for example, the audit involved working alongside the chief executive, the chair of the standards committee and the monitoring officer to improve their understanding of how standards of conduct affected public confidence. As a result, the council adopted a new priority of promoting public confidence through better and more professional conduct of the chief executive, leader and standards committee, and by managing elected members' behaviour.

## THE IMPACT OF ETHICAL CHANGE

Despite the clear focus on ethical standards in recent years, it remains unclear what effect this has had on the overall quality of standards of conduct in local government. There is no evidence that public interest reports are either more or less likely to be issued than hitherto. There is no indication yet that corporate assessments in CPA are finding evidence of changes in this area and while overall performance is increasing, as measured through CPA, there is no evidence that this is primarily or in part driven by higher standards of conduct.

Higher performance in service and managerial terms has, however, to be set in the context of declining public satisfaction with councils as a whole (as measured by the Best Value Performance Indicator 3).[4] Whether this is a function of ethical standards per se is not clear; there are many possible variables affecting public satisfaction as the ODPM is currently investigating. It suggests, however, that at least any improvement in ethical standards, if it exists, is not translating into higher public esteem.

There is some evidence from the results of the self-assessments undertaken as part of the Changing Organizational Cultures toolkit. By March 2005, 1726 middle and senior managers from 38 local authorities had completed the COC exercise. These results show that, within this sample, local government managers are generally positive about their councils' commitment to combating fraud and corruption (Figure 8.1).

Of those who are positive about their council's commitment, the vast majority believe this commitment is translated into positive outcomes (Figure 8.2).

These data are not drawn from a representative sample of English local authorities, however, so caution is needed; the Commission does not draw

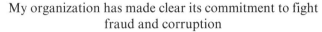

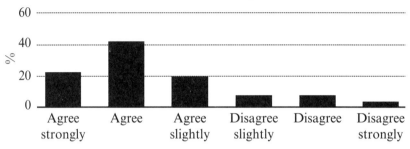

*Note:*   Base = 1726 managers in local government in England – March 2005.

*Source:*   The Audit Commission.

*Figure 8.1     Officers' perceptions of organizational commitment to fighting fraud and corruption*

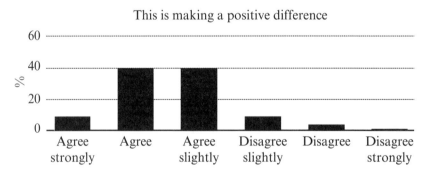

*Note:*   Base = 1356 managers in local government in England who agree that their organization has made clear its commitment to fight fraud and corruption – March 2005.

*Source:*   The Audit Commission.

*Figure 8.2:   Officers' perceptions of the impact this commitment is having on reducing fraud and corruption*

wider conclusions at this stage. A number of smaller, local workshops have sometimes produced more negative findings. There is still some way to go to assess with accuracy whether the introduction of a number of codes of practice and anti-fraud and corruption initiatives in the last ten years has manifested itself in an ethical culture. Further research is required to measure the extent to which local government in England is close to fulfilling the requirement of the tenth report by the Committee on Standards in Public Life that 'embedding the right culture as well as the right processes is key to achieving long-lasting improvements in the governance of public services' (Committee on Standards in Public Life, 2005).

Further evidence on ethics, and in particular on the impact of the New Council Constitutions introduced in the 2000 Local Government Act, will be available from research sponsored by the Department of Communities and Local Government (CLG), previously the Office of the Deputy Prime Minister (ODPM). The CLG has sponsored a major research programme evaluating the different initiatives within the Local Government Modernisation Agenda (LGMA), brought in by the 2000 Act, of which New Council Constitutions and the Ethical Framework is one.[5] Progress reports from the long-term evaluation of the LGMA initiatives show that it is too early to say what affect this and other measures have had on ethical conduct in local government, or on public trust and confidence.[6]

Indications from CPA judgements for District Councils are that corporate assessment teams are recording more strengths than weaknesses in the areas of leadership and standards of behaviour. This could itself be a function of the fact that the assessment framework addresses standards of behaviour, on the basis that 'what gets measured gets done'. Alternatively, it could reflect the impact of other initiatives in this area. Councils that score well in corporate assessment reports in this area demonstrate the professional and sometimes non-partisan conduct of standards committee and other meetings. They also indicate the perhaps indirect ways in which effective ethical governance can affect service quality, as this extract from a corporate assessment for an 'Excellent' council shows:

> Decisions, challenge and robust debate are conducted in a non-political atmosphere of trust and respect. For example, the leadership team challenged the current customer service performance in August 2003. As a result, there is now council-wide customer care training, a corporate complaint monitoring system, a £40 000 new budget to fund future customer services, and an overall improved quality of service (Colchester Borough Council, 2004).

There will always be problems in ascribing cause and effect to specific initiatives, particularly when the final outcome is itself notoriously difficult to quantify. Corporate assessment judgements show that some councils score well on monitoring elected members' compliance with ethical codes, but nonetheless do not achieve the highest performance ratings under CPA. Nor is there yet any evidence that the ethical framework has had any effect on improving public trust in local government, one of its key aims (House of Commons ODPM, 2005).

## CONCLUSIONS

It is encouraging that the overall incidence of major fraud and corruption in English local government remains low. It is true that there are relatively frequent instances of poor or inappropriate conduct that are dealt with by local authority standards committees, and reported on occasion to the Standards Board for England, but few such referrals result in serious consequences. The Commission's early evidence that local government officers believe their councils are committed to preventing fraud and corruption, and that such action is having a beneficial effect, is also encouraging.

But the issues of public trust and accountability show no signs of diminishing in importance in debates about public services. There is evidence to suggest that inappropriate behaviour can damage public confidence. It is less clear precisely what the relationship is between ethical standards and service quality. High performing councils – as measured through CPA – can display poor ethical standards, and some poorly performing councils have high ethical standards. A revised approach to CPA 2005 that addresses ethical governance in more detail may shed more light on this relationship. As things stand, the Commission has a growing body of evidence that shows that poor behaviour and relationships between officers and elected members are often a component of poor organizational and service performance. Whether they are a result or a cause is not always clear: that they have to improve for the organization to recover is usually not in doubt.

Accordingly, the Commission's revised approach to audit and inspection focuses more clearly on standards of behaviour. For auditors in particular, this requires a different emphasis from traditional audit. They need to assess the risks involved in culture and individual behaviour, as well as those more traditionally associated with structures, systems and processes. Part of the problem in investigating this topic is the personal and subjective nature of what constitutes good or poor ethical standards. Fraud and malpractice are clear wrongdoing, but 'strong' management and/or leadership might be seen as bullying or harassment by some. The Commission will support further research into this important topic.

It will also play its own part in influencing a changing ethical agenda. The increased use of contracting and attention to meeting targets may mean that local public bodies will be distracted from proper controls and processes, leading to greater opportunities for fraud and mismanagement. At the same time, regulators like the Commission will have to adapt their approaches to audit and inspection to take account of 'cultural' characteristics such as leadership as well as systems and controls, and the ways in which these affect service and other outcomes for the public.

## NOTES

1.  Section 8 of the Audit Commission Act 1998 requires auditors to consider:

    *(a) whether, in the public interest, he should make a report on any matter coming to his notice in the course of the audit, in order for it to be considered by the body concerned or brought to the attention of the public, and*
    (b) whether the public interest requires any such matter to be made the subject of an immediate report rather than of a report to be made at the conclusion of the audit.

2.  In 1994, Hansard (the Official Report of the proceedings in both Houses of Parliament) included this statement: 'Ethical governance is concerned about the standards of conduct of all holders of public office, including arrangements in relation to financial and commercial activities.'

3.  In 2005, Election Commissioner Richard Mawrey QC upheld allegations of postal fraud relating to six seats won by Labour in Birmingham in the local elections held in June 2004. Six Labour councillors were convicted of postal votes fraud and the polls in two wards were required to be rerun.

4.  Best Value Performance Indicators (BVPIs) are measures of performance set by departments in central government. A 'Best Value' authority as defined in the Local Government Act 1999 is one that must: 'make arrangements to secure continuous improvement in the way in which its functions are exercised, having regard to a combination of economy, efficiency and effectiveness' (Section 3). Prior to best value, the Audit Commission set similar measures of performance. BVPI 3 measures the percentage of citizens satisfied with the overall service provided by their authority, based on a sample survey of residents.

5.  The published reports from this strand of the LGMA evaluation are available at the website of the CLG: http://www.communities.gov.uk/index.asp?id=1137115.

6.  At the time of writing, the CLG was in the process of publishing five progress reports from the long-term evaluation of the Local Government Modernisation Agenda, on: Service Improvement; Accountability; Community Leadership; Stakeholder Engagement; and Public Confidence. For further details on the LGMA evaluations, see the CLG website at http://www.communities.gov.uk/index.asp?id=1137781.

## REFERENCES

Audit Commission (2003a), *Corporate Governance: Improvement and Trust in Public Services*, London: Audit Commission.
Audit Commission (2003b), *Trust in Public Services*, London: Audit Commission.
Audit Commission (2004), *Code of Audit Practice 2004*, London: Audit Commission.
Audit Commission (2005a), *Codes of Audit Practice*, London: Audit Commission.
Audit Commission (2005b), *CPA – the Harder Test*, London, Audit Commission.

Bristol Royal Infirmary Inquiry (2001), *Learning from Bristol: The Report of the Public Inquiry into Children's Heart Surgery at the Bristol Royal Infirmary 1984–95*, London: HMSO.

Cadbury Committee (1992), *Committee on the Financial Aspects of Corporate Governance*, London: Gee Publishing.

Colchester Borough Council (2004), *Corporate Assessment Report*,

Committee on Standards in Public Life (2005), *Tenth Report: Getting the Balance Right – Implementing Standards of Conduct in Public Life*, London: HMSO.

Duffy, Bobby, Philip Browning and Gidean Skinner (2003), *Trust in public institutions*, London: MORI.

House of Commons Office of the Deputy Prime Minister, Housing, Planning, Local Government and the Regions Committee (2005), *The Role and Effectiveness of the Standards Board for England*, London: HMSO.

Independent Commission on Good Governance for Public Services (2004), *Good Governance Standard for Public Service, OPM and CIPFA*, London: CIPFA.

Kelly, Gavin and Stephen Muesrs (2002), *Creating Public Value: An Analytical Framework for Public Service Reform*, Londen: Cabinet Office.

Laming, Lord (2003), *The Victoria Climbie Inquiry: Report of an Inquiry by Lord Laming*, London: HMSO.

Nolan Committee (1995), *First Report of the Committee on Standards in Public Life*, London: HMSO.

Redfern, Michael (2000), *The Royal Liverpool Children's Inquiry*, London: HMSO.

Wheatley, Margaret (2001), *Leadership and the New Science: Discovering a New Order in a Chaotic World*, 2nd edn, San Francisco, CA: Berrett-Koehler.

Whitehead, Alan (2002), *Room at the Top?*, Bristol: University of West England.

# APPENDIX 8.1     APPROACHES TO ASSESSING AND INSPECTING ETHICAL STANDARDS

## Comprehensive Performance Assessment (CPA)

The CPA framework for local government in England was created in 2002. It originally comprised a complex mix of service and corporate performance information, brought together to reach a single assessment of overall council performance: Excellent, Good, Fair, Weak or Poor. The information was drawn from a corporate assessment, performance indicators, auditor judgements on financial management, performance management and the financial aspects of corporate governance, and service inspection judgements, including judgements from the Audit Commission, Ofsted (the schools and local education authority inspectorate), the Commission for Social Care Inspection and the Benefit Fraud Inspectorate. The final assessment category was reached using a combination of points and rules.

CPA was revised in 2005 (*CPA – the harder test*, Audit Commission, 2005b) and further revised in 2006 to reflect important changes in local government (including, for example, the shared priority objectives between local and central government in the corporate assessment inspection framework). The Commission also strengthened its approach to assessing a council's 'Use of Resources', to reflect a new focus on value for money in public services and a stronger assessment of probity and stewardship of public funds. The previous performance categories have now been replaced with a 'star' rating, where four stars indicates the highest performance possible and no stars indicates a poorly performing council. The revised framework is shown in Figure 8.4.

For more information about CPA, and the Commission's proposed new Comprehensive Area Assessment from 2008, please visit the Audit Commission's website at: http://www.audit-commission.gov.uk/cpa/index. asp?page=index.asp&area=hpcpa.

For ethical governance, the revised CPA framework focuses on the application and achievement of ethical governance standards, rather than simply the existence of structures and processes to promote them. In the corporate assessment key line of enquiry 3.1 – Is there clear accountability and decision making to support service delivery and improvement? – in particular, assessment teams address relationships between elected members and officers. This key question, among other things, requires assessment teams to address how well councillors and officers work within the ethical framework.

A council that is performing well will meet the following standard on the ethical framework: The standards committee and monitoring officer

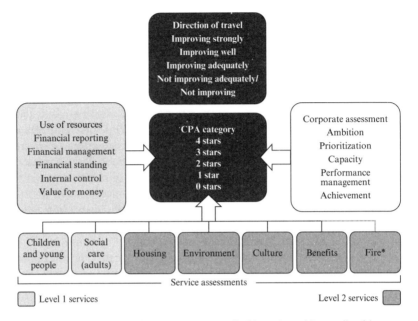

*Note:* *Fire and Rescue Service assessment – applicable to those 16 councils with responsibility for fire and rescue.

*Source:* The Audit Commission.

*Figure 8.A1    The comprehensive performance assessment framework from 2006*

promote and maintain high ethical standards, and have a high profile within the council. An independent member chairs the committee. The council is seen as upholding high standards of ethics and probity, efficiency and integrity. Documents relating to standards and conduct are easily accessible to members of the public and other stakeholders. The council has integrated the code of conduct into its diversity policies and its duties under the Disability Discrimination and Race Relations Acts. Linkages have been made between the Human Rights Act, the Freedom of Information Act, the Sex Discrimination Act and the code of conduct. The leader, chief executive, standards committee and monitoring officer actively promote the importance of the ethical agenda.

**Corporate Governance Inspections**

A corporate governance inspection (CGI) is different from a corporate assessment in both objectives and process. Whereas corporate assessment seeks to assess performance and identify improvement and good practice, CGI takes as its premise that serious problem areas are likely to exist. The objective of CGI is not to assess a council's performance relative to its peers, but to provide an opportunity, through recommendations, for the council to address and rectify the identified problems. In the more serious cases, a CGI can be used to obtain up-to-date evidence in order to establish whether there are grounds for referral to the Secretary of State (SoS) under section 13 of the Local Government Act 1999. A referral is a recommendation by the Commission that the SoS gives a direction under section 15 of the Local Government Act, which may include, for example, a direction that the authority takes any action considered necessary, or that a function of the authority be taken over by another body.

The CGI methodology has also recently been revised. From 2006 the inspection framework comprises four modular themes:

- community focus – addressing access, communications and partnerships;
- structures and processes – addressing democratic accountability, decision-making and planning;
- risk management and internal control – addressing financial, performance and risk management; and
- leadership, culture and standards of conduct – addressing community, political and managerial leadership, member-officer relationships, ethical standards and behaviour.

Using this modular assessment framework, inspection teams reach judgement on two key questions:

1. How good are the council's corporate governance arrangements?
2. What are the prospects for improvement in the council's corporate governance arrangements?

Further information about the methodology can be found on the Commission's website.

## APPENDIX 8.2    EXTRACT FROM THE AUDIT COMMISSION CODE OF AUDIT PRACTICE (2005)

It is the responsibility of the audited body to put in place proper arrangements to secure economy, efficiency and effectiveness in its use of resources and to ensure proper stewardship and governance, and regularly to review the adequacy and effectiveness of them. Such corporate performance management and financial management arrangements form a key part of the system of internal control and comprise the arrangements for:

- establishing strategic and operational objectives;
- determining policy and making decisions;
- ensuring that services meet the needs of users and taxpayers and for engaging with the wider community;
- ensuring compliance with established policies, procedures, laws and regulations;
- identifying, evaluating and managing operational and financial risks and opportunities, including those arising from involvement in partnerships and joint working;
- ensuring compliance with the general duty of best value, where applicable;
- Code of Audit Practice 2005 | For local government bodies 13
- managing its financial and other resources, including arrangements to safeguard the financial standing of the audited body;
- monitoring and reviewing performance, including arrangements to ensure data quality; and
- ensuring that the audited body's affairs are managed in accordance with proper
- standards of conduct, and to prevent and detect fraud and corruption.

(Paragraph 19)

# 9. A paradigmatic shift in ethics and integrity management within the Dutch public sector? Beyond compliance – a practitioners' view

**Alain Hoekstra, Alex Belling and Eli van der Heide**

## INTRODUCTION

The chapter focuses on the development of ethics and integrity management within the Dutch public sector. In the next section we describe, from a practitioners' point of view, how integrity became an important issue in the Netherlands in the early 1990s and its subsequent development. The following section presents a policy analysis and a theoretical framework, which brings us to the conclusion that Dutch integrity policy has mainly been dominated by what is known as the compliance-based approach. This approach is based on the prevention of fraud and corruption by formulating rules and regulations, whereby monitoring and punishing wrongdoers encourages compliance with standards. Possible factors that contribute to the predominance of that specific approach are identified. The next section describes which developments and trends emphasize the necessity to move beyond compliance towards a more values-based approach, focused on stimulating civil servants to act according to collectively defined organizational core values, strengthening (moral) competence, and creating a culture of shared responsibilities. The following section describes the first steps that have been taken regarding this challenging task in the Netherlands. The last section addresses the relationship between integrity and Human Resource Management via the concepts of good employeeship and good employership. The chapter does not pretend to provide clear-cut answers as to how organizations can arrive at a viable (more) values-based ethics program. Rather, it illustrates the need for change and the complexities involved in implementing such changes.

## DEVELOPMENTS IN ETHICS AND INTEGRITY POLICY WITHIN THE DUTCH PUBLIC SECTOR

Before delving into developments that have occurred within the integrity policy, a brief outline of the institutional setting and the specific role the Ministry of the Interior and Kingdom Relations plays regarding integrity policy is presented.

The Netherlands is a decentralized unitary state. As such, governmental bodies – within the context of formal legislation as well as integrity policy – possess a large degree of autonomy. This means that individual governing bodies are themselves primarily responsible for formulating, implementing and enforcing integrity policy within their organizations. The Minister of the Interior and Kingdom Relations, however, retains a coordinating responsibility for the overall public sector integrity policy, encompassing both a steering and a stimulating role. By including specific provisions in the Civil Servants Act, integrity-related aspects are made mandatory for all public servants (steering). At the same time the minister fulfills a stimulating role by developing and providing practical and ready-to-use instruments that are directive but not binding and allow for individual applications of such models, tools and guidelines that assist government organizations in formulating their policies.

### Developments in Dutch Integrity Policy: A Bird's Eye Perspective

Before the 1990s, Dutch public administration can mainly be characterized by a technical orientation. The main questions were framed in terms of the aims, means, instruments, planning and effects of governance. There was far more attention paid to the techniques than toward the ethics of governance (Huberts, 2005). This is not a situation unique to the Dutch, as Adams and Balfour have described the same scientific and technical mind-set in public administration that drives out ethical considerations in the USA (Adams and Balfour, 1998). Although integrity was not a completely unknown concept in the Dutch public sector before the 1990s, it was by no means a hot topic placed high on the political and administrative agendas. Certain events, however, increased the importance attached to integrity in the early 1990s and it has remained an agenda item ever since. This is evident given the growing number of questions raised in the Dutch parliament in relation to the topic. An historic distinction can be made between roughly three periods in the development of integrity policy.

**Awareness and agenda setting (1990–1995)**

Concerns regarding integrity emerged in the early 1990s with the growth of organized crime and its potential linkages with government. There were also signals that criminal organizations tried to bribe civil servants and attempted to infiltrate in key governmental positions, in order to corrupt vital parts of the machinery of government from within. At the same time a raft of larger integrity breaches occurred within several southern municipalities. As a result, the then Minister of the Interior, Mrs Dales, made the theme of public sector integrity an explicit part of the political and administrative agenda at the end of 1992. Mrs Dales stressed that a government of high integrity is an absolute prerequisite for the existence of democracy. If the state or government is corrupt or acts immorally, this will negatively affect the trust, support and the cooperation of citizens. This could lead, as Thoreau pointed out, to civil disobedience and in the end possibly even to the collapse of the democratic state (Thoreau, 1849). Shortly thereafter, the Ministry of the Interior published its first policy document on integrity.

Despite all this, one cannot speak of a substantial improvement of integrity awareness and policy implementation within the Dutch government. It is difficult to explain why nothing much changed during this period, despite Mrs Dales' *cri de coeur*. A possible explanation, though, may be found at the end of her own argument in which she stated that politicians and administrators are inclined to try to reduce integrity breaches to incidents, and that people may simply look the other way in embarrassment. After all, acknowledging that government integrity may be subjected to structural damage does not correspond to the image of the government as a bearer of the democratic constitutional state (Dales, 1992). Scholars in the field of public sector ethics and integrity, too, observed that Dutch politicians and administrators tended to downplay the seriousness of the problem (Van Hulten, 2002; De Haan and Van den Heuvel, 2003).

**Legislation and instruments (1995–2003)**

The period from 1995 to 2003 was characterized by the development of rules and instruments, and several provisions aimed at promoting integrity were formally legislated. The Civil Servants Act (1997) included an obligation to declare outside activities that relate to the function of the official concerned; the registration of activities that are permitted; and the prohibition of certain activities that could pose a risk to the proper functioning of the public service. Other provisions were added later (2003), such as the disclosure of registered outside activities; an obligation to declare financial interests and stock exchange transactions; an obligation for government bodies to draw up reporting procedures for suspected integrity breaches; and a provision for protecting those who have reported any wrongdoing in accordance with the procedure and in good faith.

In addition to an integrity hotline (General Intelligence and Security Service), a number of instruments and guidelines were developed for assessing integrity risks and guidelines for carrying out integrity audits. Although the Ministry of the Interior and Kingdom and Relations frequently referred to the importance of enhancing awareness amongst staff and the role of organizational culture, it was still unclear how to provide clear structure and substance to this initiative. Specific instruments and support were not yet available in this area. Nevertheless, first steps were taken at a local level (see p. 153).

### Increased attention and beyond compliance (2003 to date)
In 2003 the Parliamentary Inquiry Committee for the Building Industry published its findings on large-scale fraud within the building industry, that subsequently had an intensifying effect on the importance of public sector integrity. It also fuelled new policy intentions and most recently it led to an amendment of the Civil Servants Act (2006). This act obliges government bodies to pursue integrity policy that must become a permanent component of personnel policy. Moreover, all governmental bodies are required to draw up a code of conduct for civil servants. Once a year, these aspects are to be accounted for at the relevant democratically representative body. All new civil servants will also have to take the oath of office. And last but not least, the competent government body and the civil servant will be obliged to act as a good employer and a good civil servant.

But the most important contribution of the findings of the Parliamentary Inquiry Committee for the Building Industry was that it made painfully clear that the main problem is the way staff perceives, understands, and acts according to integrity policy. This led to the conclusion that more effort should be put into improving integrity awareness and internalization of the values. Yet prior to 2003 there was hardly any experience with such a cultural and values-oriented integrity approach. Specific support in this particular area was simply not available. This led to a change beginning in 2004 that in the view of the coordinating Minister for Integrity, policy should no longer focus solely on rules and control-oriented instruments. Although these are crucial instruments that can be used as a basis for integrity policy, it became apparent that more attention should be paid to support policy that goes beyond compliance alone. The establishment of the National Office for Promoting Ethics and Integrity in the Public Sector was viewed as an important step toward achieving this challenging task and encompasses an expansion from a basically legal and structural approach to a more pedagogic, integrity-based approach (see p. 153).

## International Perspective and Domestic Research and Debate

In 2005 an international comparative study conducted by Transparency International pointed out that the Netherlands dropped three places on the Corruption Perceptions Index (Transparency International, 2005). Although this indicates that the Netherlands is still perceived as relatively incorrupt, it marked a substantial deterioration.

Recently GRECO, the Group of States against corruption, a working party of the Council of Europe, adopted an Evaluation Report on the Netherlands in its 25th plenary meeting. The report mentioned that both Dutch public authorities and civil society believe that corruption is not a major problem. This fairly positive self-image reflects with what we stated on p. 145. The report also states that the image of the Dutch public administration has deteriorated because of some past cases of illegal and dishonest activities within the public administration and that the authorities of the Netherlands remain, despite the traditionally low corruption rates, aware of the potential dangers of corruption (GRECO, 2005).

In addition to the impact of the building fraud and additional legislation which increased the attention paid to integrity, furtherance of the issue is understandable in light of the rather disappointing outcomes of national research on public sector integrity policy. Two governmental inventories, along with research from Huberts and Nelen, illustrate that integrity policy within the Dutch government still needs to be improved. The lower tiers of government in particular lack the capacity and specific knowledge for formulating effective integrity policy. There is considerable room for improvement at the central level, too, as revealed by Huberts and Nelen in their seminal research in the field of corruption and integrity within the Netherlands. They conclude that most government organizations in the Netherlands are rather naïve and put insufficient effort in trying to detect corruption and other integrity breaches (Huberts, 2004; Huberts and Nelen, 2005). They demonstrated that the problem is bigger than we wish to think. Other scholars seem to disagree with this and argue that problems with corruption and integrity are negligible and that we already pay too much attention to it, which is costly, unnecessary, and provokes a negative and distrustful image of the public sector. The debate is ongoing, but for now Huberts *cum suis* seem to possess the stronger empirical evidence and arguments.

# ANALYSIS OF THE DEVELOPMENT OF ETHICS AND INTEGRITY POLICY

The preceding section outlined the development of Dutch integrity policy over the past 15 years. From the outset it was clear that an effective integrity policy ought to be a combination of a structure and rules orientation on the one hand, and a cultural and awareness orientation on the other. It was also observed that the first period was mainly characterized by placing integrity on the political and administrative agenda. Most of the efforts during the second period centered on formulating rules and improving the organizational structure against violations of integrity. The phase in which Dutch integrity policy currently finds itself can be characterized as the search for a more balanced ethics program, which implies more attention for the values approach in addition to compliance approach.

   This section will analyse the aforementioned development in greater detail. The next subsection presents a theoretical framework that clarifies the distinction between a compliance-based and a values-based approach. The following subsection offers a number of possible explanations for the predominance of the compliance-based approach, which has characterized the second period.

## Theoretical Framework: Compliance-based Versus Values-based Approach

Paine introduced a theoretical framework that is based on the compliance-integrity continuum (Paine, 1994). The compliance-based approach is based on a narrow definition of integrity and focuses on the prevention of fraud and corruption. The focus lies on the formulation of rules, guidelines and procedures, whereby punishing wrongdoers encourages compliance with standards. The emphasis is placed on external controls on the behavior of civil servants, and expanding checks and monitoring. Paine called the other part of the continuum the integrity-based approach, also known as the values-based approach, which we prefer to use. This second approach is based on a broader definition of integrity and focuses on promoting the principle of acting as a good employer and civil servant. The related measures are characterized by reinforcing (moral) competence and stimulating a culture of responsibility. The emphasis is placed on internal self-control of individual civil servants, and encouraging them to take the responsibilities associated with their position seriously and with care. Table 9.1 provides a brief description of the governing principles of both approaches.

*Table 9.1   Compliance-based versus values-based approach*

| Compliance-based | Values-based |
|---|---|
| **Rules and procedures**<br>Emphasis on rules, procedures, provisions, commands and prohibitions | **Values and aspirations**<br>Emphasis on the creation of guiding values and aspirations and an environment that stimulates ethical behavior |
| **Unilateral imposition**<br>The unilateral imposition of rules and guidelines by government bodies | **Multilateral formulation**<br>The joint formulation and internalization of values. Joint responsibility for honest behavior with management playing the role of an initiator |
| **Prevent wrongdoing**<br>The threat associated with checks, monitoring and punishment must dissuade staff from acting in a dishonest manner | **Promoting good conduct**<br>Trust of staff promotes moral and responsible behavior |
| **Negative perception of people's motivations**<br>The assumption is that people are lazy and cannot be trusted. They must be guided by rewarding good conduct and punishing undesirable conduct. The disadvantage is that staff start behaving according to the assumption | **Positive perception of people's motivations**<br>The assumption is that people are in search of job satisfaction and wish to be responsible. Responds to human impulses to act in a morally correct manner and invites staff to strive towards good conduct |
| **Narrow**<br>Formalistic and minimal moral-based on the 'if it's legal it's ethical' principle | **Broad**<br>Compliance with rules is no guarantee for ethical conduct. People must also be able to handle situations that are not (yet) governed by rules |
| **Rigid**<br>Laws and regulations are rigid and inflexible. Circumstances are usually too complex and variable to be laid down in laws and regulations | **Flexible**<br>Values and aspirations are broader and provide a more robust system that is better geared to changes |
| **Traditional**<br>Based on the traditional form of government management: hierarchical, directive, focused on rules and procedures | **Modern**<br>Dovetails with new developments in government management such as decentralization, privatization and increased complexity and policy discretion |

### Explanations for the Predominance of the Compliance-based Approach

As mentioned before the focus during the second period was centered on the formulation of rules, guidelines and procedures as well as strengthening the organizational structure's defenses against violations of integrity. The line of approach during this period therefore primarily featured a legal and structural nature. Legal as well as structural integrity instruments are necessary elements of an integrity policy and can be seen as exponents of the compliance-based approach. The appeal of this approach lies in the fact that through the unilateral and directive imposition of rules, and through the focus on procedures and provisions relatively quick integrity wins can be achieved. The process of jointly identifying values, creating a culture of shared responsibilities and stimulating staff to act (morally) properly is a more time consuming process and is perceived as 'fuzzy' and unmanageable by some public managers.

There are several other explanations for the relative predominance of the compliance-based approach. We assume that historical, managerial, political and practical arguments and the occupational background of staff play a role in this as well. Table 9.2 provides an overview of factors that influence the compliance-based character of Dutch integrity policy (Karssing and Hoekstra, 2004).

First of all, bureaucracy is strongly rooted in rules, checks, compliance and the limitation of policy discretion for civil servants. Second, policy-making officials in the Netherlands who are responsible for shaping integrity policy often have a legal background that contributes to the predominance of the compliance-based approach. Occupational groups with a different mindset such as psychologists, educators and philosophers are under-represented in this field. Third, the government traditionally has considerable experience with legislative and regulative instruments. We live in a society where tremendous value is attached to rules as a steering mechanism. This leads to the almost natural reflex that integrity breaches mostly lead to more of the same tried and trusted legal instruments. Fourth, the New Public Management (NPM) philosophy is basically focused on making policy measurable by translating it into quantifiable objectives and products and by monitoring results. Values-based initiatives are more difficult to operationalize in these terms. They are culture-oriented and are perceived as 'intangible issues of culture, values, human relations – matters that many managers regard as fuzzy and unmanageable' (Rainey, 1991: 251). The issuance of rules, the establishment of procedures, the imposition of sanctions and counting integrity violations appear to fit in this context. Moreover we live in an era in which monitoring, control and repression prevail.

*Table 9.2   Explanations for the predominance of the compliance-based approach*

| Factors | Features |
| --- | --- |
| Bureaucracy | Hierarchical structure<br>Clear definition of tasks, powers and responsibilities<br>Subjected to rigid, uniform discipline and control<br>Obedience/subordination toward management of the department<br>Classic political-civil servant relationships (decision-makers vs. executors) |
| Occupational background | Strong legal-technical background of the civil servants<br>Under-representation of occupational groups that focus on the stimulation strategy |
| Practical experience | Familiarity with the application of the legislative and regulative instruments<br>Tendency to use tried and tested instruments<br>Social trust in regulations<br>Issuing rules is an easy political approach to a problem |
| NPM | Focus on hard, clear and quantifiable output indicators<br>Averse to soft values that are difficult to measure<br>Rules, procedures, sanctions and numbers of reports of integrity violations are more tangible than the stimulation strategy that is perceived as 'soft' and vague |
| Control and enforcement | New magic words: monitoring, checks and enforcement<br>Contemporary spirit of the age aimed at prohibition, control and penalizing non-complying conduct<br>Politicians can score points as 'hardliners' |

## DEVELOPMENTS AND TRENDS: THE NECESSITY TO MOVE BEYOND COMPLIANCE

The predominance of the compliance-based approach in the Netherlands doesn't seem to be unique. An effective integrity policy, however, is characterized by a balanced combination of instruments from both approaches. In the Netherlands the tide seems to be turning and it seems that the integrity policy is moving beyond compliance. A number of developments contributed to the need for this broadening.

In the first place integrity violations still occur within the Dutch government despite countless rules, procedures, more stringent monitoring and increased attention to the theme of integrity. The greater the number of rules that are introduced, the more apparent it becomes that this alone cannot suffice. The findings of the Parliamentary Inquiry Committee for the Building Industry make it clear that integrity policy must fully be understood, applied and become ingrained in staff. What is required is the internalization of the values and standards of being a good civil servant. And this corresponds better to the values-based approach.

In the second place the need for a more balanced integrity policy is fueled by the worldwide New Public Management (NPM) trend (Osborne and Gaebler, 1993). That trend also took place in the Netherlands NPM. One of the consequences is that policy discretion for civil servants has increased. This implies that civil servants have to be trained to handle such discretionary privilege in a responsible and professional manner, especially in new and complex situations for which rules and regulations simply do not exist. Managing integrity via a strong rule and procedure-oriented system is insufficient in such situations. What it really entails is that the civil servant is able to act independently according to the spirit of the values and standards of government. In this context the OECD states that: 'a country's ethics management regime should be consistent with its approach to public management in general . . . it would be inconsistent to marry a strict centralized compliance-based ethics infrastructure with devolved results-based management systems' (OECD, 1996: 7).

In the third place rules and regulations are not the calibrated instrument for restoring integrity. There are drawbacks to overly relying on legislation in an ethics infrastructure: 'It tends to encourage minimum compliance. The enforcement of sanctions, while necessary, is designed to discourage undesirable behavior rather than promote desired behavior. Because of its conceptual reliance on absolutes and objectivity, the law can be an inflexible tool for the day-to-day management of workplace ethical problems' (OECD, 1996: 31). Merely focusing on the development of stringent guidelines and procedures can therefore be regarded as counterproductive. All the more so since working with rules and checks provokes the impression of distrust: 'Designing "institutions for knaves" risks making knaves of potentially more honorable actors, whereas a more trusting model embodying a more direct appeal to moral principles might actually do a better job of evoking high minded motives for action and of supressing low minded ones' (Goodin, 1996). A study by Anechiarico and Jacobs criticizes excessive reliance on the compliance approach as well. They point out negative consequences such as delayed decision making, excessive centralization, poor morale, and defensive management (Anechiarico and Jacobs, 1996).

# FIRST STEPS

Although there is no established protocol to transform the integrity system from compliance to values in the Netherlands, it is widely acknowledged that more attention needs to be given to the values-based approach. This is underscored in several policy documents of the Ministry of the Interior. The establishment of the National Office for Promoting Ethics and Integrity in the Public Sector in 2006 will support this challenging task by developing values-based integrity policy and instruments. The focus is on themes including improving ethical leadership and moral judgment, designing multimedia dilemma training instruments, organizing moral consultation and training management to discuss ethics and integrity in a positive way. The office also organizes integrity platforms where all types of governmental organizations jointly search for new instruments and exchange best practices in this field. From this point of view one could say that a bottom up strategy is followed.

Another trend worth mentioning is the pursuit of more coherence in integrity policy. Integrity policy within Dutch government organizations often has a fragmented character. For the most part, a cohesive integrity policy does not exist. This can be explained by the fact that integrity-related measures and instruments are managed by various disciplines and departments within the organization. The focus nowadays is placed on improving internal coordination between various actors involved with integrity policy. Therefore, government administrators are advised to appoint an integrity coordinator to handle the internal coordination between these different actors. These coordinators will also have an overview of the integrity policies and instruments that provide them with an agenda for addressing the imbalance often witnessed between the compliance- and the values-based approach.

The paradigmatic policy shift is already evident in some Dutch government agencies; the city of Amsterdam is probably the best example. The Amsterdam Bureau of Integrity employs some 15 people who are responsible for a wide range of integrity instruments and policies. In addition to using traditional compliance-based instruments such as risk assessments, investigations into reports of (possible) integrity violations and the registration of integrity breaches, the Amsterdam Bureau also places a strong focus on improving the moral competence of the cities' public officials. The approach used in which officials are trained by philosophers to analyse and judge complex ethical questions can be qualified as both a unique and promising way to stimulate civil servants' ethical behavior. In the Netherlands the Amsterdam Bureau is a good example of giving substance to the values-based approach.

# INTEGRITY AND HUMAN RESOURCE MANAGEMENT (HRM)

Integrity management and HRM are closely related. First, integrity instruments can be incorporated into HRM, which enables the promotion of good employeeship. Second, good working conditions, fair salaries, an open and motivating working atmosphere, well functioning and active communications at all levels, and model role playing by political and administrative leaders (Bossaert and Demmke, 2005) are all HRM instruments which should be used in a fair manner, both because it is the right thing to do and because it reduces breaches of integrity by employees. We will explain that this is all part of good employership (p. 155).

### The Application of Specific Integrity Instruments Within the Context of HRM to Stimulate Good Employeeship

By now the link between good employeeship and HRM has been established. In integrity literature the central issue is how the employee relates to the organization, its resources, colleagues and citizens in a decent, respectful and fair manner. Via the application of specific HR integrity instruments, management can try to influence employee behavior. This involves the use of specific HR instruments to place integrity under the constant focus of staff and members of management and to promote ethical conduct. This use of HRM is aimed primarily at protecting the organization, but also at protecting civil servants from integrity risks and temptations. It should be clear that an employee should act in a fair manner in addition to being efficient and effective. For this reason, the task of management is to adequately equip the employee to act in a fair way. From an HRM point of view this can be done in several ways. HRM can ensure that the employee relates to the organization, resources, colleagues and citizens in a decent, respectful and fair manner. The compliance-based approach involves applicable HR instruments that relate to the formulation of rules, guidelines, and procedures. The values-based approach focuses on HR instruments that stimulate civil servants to take the responsibilities associated with their position seriously. Three of these – each with a strong values-based focus – are mentioned below.

First, the HR function can ensure that the integrity of applicants becomes a major focal point during the recruitment and introduction procedure. In addition to aspects with a compliance-based nature such as pre-employment screening, checking résumés, certificates and references and confidentiality statements, this procedure should also comprise important values-based aspects focused on raising awareness such as mentioning in the job advertisement that integrity is a job prerequisite, including integrity in the competence profile, informing the applicant about integrity-related aspects in the new job, allowing integrity-related issues to be a part of assessment procedure, let civil servants take the oath of office, paying attention to integrity in the introduction training for new members and having discussions about the code of conduct.

Second, the HR function can stimulate every management member within the organization to discuss integrity during structural contact moments between management and staff. This includes work meetings, job appraisals and exit interviews. This is not always the case in practice, and if it is, it is not always done effectively. The HR function has a role in highlighting this obligation and explaining how integrity should be discussed in a positive way during these meetings between management and the employee.

Third, the HR function can ensure that management as well as staff take training courses. Dilemma training can be useful for staff as well as management (Karssing, 2000). During these training sessions civil servants learn to analyse morally complex situations and to make sound ethical decisions. Participants can also be informed and discuss the integrity policy of the organization and the applicable frameworks, for example a code of conduct.

HR literature containing chapters on the use of integrity instruments is scarce. For the above mentioned integration of integrity instruments in HRM, further HR research is needed to ascertain the extent to which integrity instruments have a place within traditional HRM.

## Fair HRM for Good Employership

In the Netherlands the perspective of good employership is less commonly used in relation with integrity. The central question is how the organization, or more specifically management, relates to the employee in a decent, respectful and fair manner. This is not only necessary from a moral perspective in that it is good to pursue a fair HR policy, but also because this strongly influences the employee's ethical behavior. Research carried out by Trevino and Weaver reveals that if staff perceive the organization as being 'unjust', attempts to discourage unethical behavior become less effective. Furthermore, the willingness of staff to facilitate integrity policy, for example by reporting violations, also appears to decrease. Trevino and Weaver conclude that organizations that implement an integrity policy must focus on the fairness in which staff is treated (Trevino and Weaver, 2001). This entails, among other things, that not only the use of general HR instruments such as remuneration, recruitment and selection, appraisal,

*Table 9.3   Moral reflection with regard to recruitment and selection*

---

- The selection of new employees is made based on objective and functional criteria without discrimination;
- The applicant is treated with respect;
- Recruitment and selection policy proceeds along professional lines;
- Interviewers/selectors are trained to conduct interviews. Often it is not the process itself but the incompetence of the interviewer that is the cause of criticism about the application process;
- Interviews are conducted as consistently as possible. This means that the same interviewer must interview the candidates and the style of interviewing must be as similar as possible. This also entails interviewers must be aware of the way in which they act towards applicants

---

exit policy, but also reorganizations, mergers and cutback operations must be applied in a fair manner. Within the context of HRM, the (moral) standards and values of society must serve as criteria during the formulation and application of HR policy, and each HR instrument must be used in a fair manner (Paauwe, 1994). This offers protection for the employee in particular as well as the organization, for the temptation to (re)act in a unfair way appears to arise quicker if staff perceives unfair treatment is taking place. Table 9.3 gives an idea of possible results based on moral reflection with regard to recruitment and selection (Spence, 2000). Such exercises can be carried out for all HR instruments and they contribute to the integration of standards and values within HR instruments (Wistanley and Woodall, 2000).

Further moral reflection on HR theory and HR instruments is necessary to flesh out the concept of good employership. But first of all, research should focus on the question as to what extent a paradox might exist between the focus of HRM on productivity, effectiveness and efficiency and the fair use of HR instruments.

## CONCLUSIONS

The chapter describes the development of ethics and integrity management within the Dutch public sector during the last 15 years. Three subsequent phases can be distinguished with regard to this development. After the phase of agenda setting in the early 1990s, the basis of integrity policy was designed from a compliance point of view from the mid-1990s, and seems to move toward a more balanced integrity approach by searching for a viable values orientation in the new millennium. Although it was clear from the beginning that value aspects such as integrity awareness and organizational culture were important, it was still unclear how to give substance to this and consequently remain *terra incognita* for the most part. Factors that contributed to the predominance of the compliance-based approach in the Netherlands are identified. This approach is based on the prevention of fraud and corruption by formulating rules and regulations, whereby monitoring and punishing wrongdoers encourage compliance with standards. The results of the Parliamentary Inquiry Committee for the Building Industry in 2003, however, led to important changes, and can be seen as an impetus for a paradigmatic shift toward a more values-based approach. This approach is based on stimulating civil servants to act according to collectively defined organizational core values, strengthening (moral) competence and creating a culture of shared responsibilities. Other contributing factors to this change include ongoing integrity breaches, the increasing policy discretion of civil servants, the inflexibility and the counter productiveness of rules and regulations, as well as the growing attention to the relation between integrity and HRM concepts of good employeeship and good employership.

# REFERENCES

Adams, Guy B. and Danny L. Balfour (1998), *Unmasking Administrative Evil*, Thousand Oaks, CA: Sage.

Anechiarico, Frank and James B. Jacobs (1996), *The Pursuit of Absolute Integrity: How Corruption Control Makes Government Ineffective*, Chicago, IL: The University of Chicago Press.

Bossaert, D. and C. Demmke (2005), *Main Challenges in the Field of Ethics and Integrity in the EU Member States*, prepared in cooperation with the Irish and Dutch Presidencies of the European Union, Maastricht: European Institute of Public Administration (EIPA), p. 108.

Dales, I. (1992), 'Om de integriteit van het openbaar bestuur', speech made to the annual meeting of the Vereniging van Nederlandse Gemeenten.

De Haan, J. and J.H.J. Van den Heuvel (2003), 'Corruptie en fraude in het openbaar bestuur. Op zoek naar patronen in het verleden', *Openbaar Bestuur*, (October), 24–9.

European Union (2004), *Main Features of an Ethics Framework for the Public Sector*, proposal by the Dutch Presidency and adopted by the Directors General responsible for Public Administration in the Member States and the institutions of the European Union in their 43rd Meeting in Maastricht, November 2004.

Goodin, Robert E. (1996), 'Institutions and their design', in Robert E. Goodin (ed.), *The Theory of Institutional Design*, Cambridge: Cambridge University Press.

GRECO (2005), *Second Round Evaluation Report on the Netherlands*, Strasbourg.

Huberts, L.W.J.C. (2004), *Nederland fraude- en corruptieland. De omvang, achtergronden en afwikkeling van corruptie- en fraudeonderzoeken in Nederlandse gemeenten in 1991 en 2003*, Onderzoeksgroep Integriteit van Bestuur, Afdeling bestuur en organisatie, Faculteit der Sociale Wetenschappen, Vrije Universiteit Amsterdam.

Huberts, L.W.J.C. (2005), *Integriteit en integritisme in bestuur en samenleving*, Rede uitgesproken bij de aanvaarding van het ambt van hoogleraar Bestuurskunde in het bijzonder integriteit van bestuur, bij de Faculteit der Sociale Wetenschappen van de Vrije Universiteit Amsterdam op 23 februari 2005.

Huberts, L.W.J.C. and J. Nelen (2005), *Corruptie in het Nederlandse openbaar bestuur, Omvang, aard en afdoening*, Utrecht: Lemma BV.

Karssing, Edgar D. (2000), *Morele competentie in organisaties*, Assen, Netherlands: Koninklijke van Gorcum.

Karssing, E.D. and A. Hoekstra (2004), 'Integriteitsbeleid als evenwichtskunst', *Bestuurswetenschappen*, **3**, pp. 167–92.

Legge, K. (1995), *Human Resource Management: Rhetoric and Realities*, Basingstoke: Macmillan.

Niessen, R. (2004), 'Professional integrity in the Dutch civil service', in *Dutch Civil Service*, Ministry of the Interior and Kingdom Relations, pp. 49–61.

Organisation for Economic Co-operation and Development (OECD) (1996), *Ethics in the Public Sector, Current Issues and Practice*, Paris: OECD.

Osborne, David and Ted Gaebler (1993), *Reinventing Government: How the Entrepreneurial Spirit is Transforming the Public Sector*, New York: Plume.

Paauwe, J. (2002), in J. Paauwe and P. Boselie, 'Challenging (strategic) human resource management theory: integration of resource-based approaches and new institutionalism', research paper prepared for the Erasmus Research Institute of Management (ERIM) at RSM Erasmus University, Rotterdam, accessed at http://ideas.repec.org/p/dgr/evreri/2002194.html.

Paine, L.S. (1994), 'Managing for organizational integrity', *Harvard Business Review*, **72** (2), 106–17.

Rainey, Hal G. (1991), *Understanding and Managing Public Organizations*, San Francisco, CA: Jossey-Bass.

Spence, L. (2000), 'What ethics in the employment interview?', in D. Wistanley and J. Woodall (eds), *Ethical Issues in Contemporary Human Resource Management*, Basingstoke: Macmillan.

Thoreau, Henry D. (1849), *Civil Disobedience*, reprinted in Henry D. Thoreau (1986), *Walden and Civil Disobedience*, New York: Penguin Classics.

Transparency International (2005), 'Corruption perceptions index'.

Trevino, L.K. and G.R Weaver (2001), 'Organisational justice and ethics program "follow-through": influences on employees' harmful and helpful behaviour', *Business Ethics Quarterly*, **11** (4), 651–71.

Van Hulten, M. (2002), *Corruptie, Onbekend, onbemind, alomtegenwoordig*, Amsterdam: Boom.

Weaver, G.R. (2001), 'The role of human resources in ethics/compliance management: a fairness perspective', *Human Resource Management Review*, **11**, 113–34.

Wistanley, D. and J. Woodall (eds) (2000), *Ethical Issues in Contemporary Human Resource Management*, Basingstoke: Macmillan.

# 10. How to encourage ethical behavior: the impact of police leadership on police officers taking gratuities

**Terry Lamboo, Karin Lasthuizen and Leo W.J.C. Huberts**

## INTRODUCTION

The police are responsible for upholding the law and as a result are held to a high personal standard. Behavior that is condoned in citizens, business or other public offices, can lead to scandal if committed by police officers (Elliston, 1985; Presidents Commission, 1967), such as the public's reaction to police officers receiving and asking for gratuities. Gifts and discounts can be questionable or can appear to be questionable because they might influence the decisions of police officers. As a consequence, many police organizations formulated policies on gratuities in order to protect the integrity of police officers, their organization and their profession. The International Association of Chiefs of Police (1995), for example, took a zero tolerance stance towards gratuities. Her Majesty's Inspectorate of Constabulary (HMIC, 1999), however, simply advised that police leadership in the United Kingdom should make clear under which conditions gifts or gratuities could be accepted. Little is yet known of the effectiveness of efforts of police associations, police forces and police management to influence the practice of taking gratuities.

Empirical research on the Dutch situation can shed some light on this issue. Gratuities construed as examples of corruption are not unfamiliar occurrences to the Dutch police and contributed to a major scandal involving the Amsterdam police in the late 1970s (Van Laere and Geerts, 1984; Punch, 1985; Koring, 2000), leading eventually to reforms within the Amsterdam police force (Zwart, 1999). After this scandal, Dutch police officers nonetheless continued to view discounts and small perks as a customary part of the job. This changed in the mid-1990s when integrity became a more important topic in Dutch politics and policing. On a number of integrity issues, the opinions as well as the behavior of police officers changed (Naeyé *et al.*, 2004), and acceptability of gratuities was among those issues. Lamboo (2005) reported the results of an extensive study regarding how the integrity policies of Dutch police forces developed, and what the consequences were for the views and behavior of police officers. Here, those results are framed within the literature on behavior of management, identifying key variables influencing the ethics and integrity of employees (Ciulla, 1998; Dickson *et al.*, 2001; Fulmer, 2004; Lewis, 1991; Trevino and Nelson, 1999; Trevino *et al.*, 2000).

## THEORY AND CONCEPTS

### Gratuities

The concept of gratuities is rarely defined, with the exception of Cohen and Feldberg: 'any goods or services which are given to law enforcement officers because they are law enforcement officers, which are not part of their regular remuneration' (cited in Feldberg, 1985: 267). More generally, gratuities are described using terms such as discounts, presents, gifts, perks, services, and with specific examples such as a free cup of coffee, discounted meals, holiday gifts, discounted goods from stores and business, and presents from citizens.

Thus, gratuities can take a variety of forms as detailed by the well-known Knapp Commission (1972) report on the New York Police Department or by the Royal Commission into the New South Wales Police Service (1997). It includes the occasional unasked-for gift from citizens, the regularly received discounts from frequented businesses or the extortion of goods and services from clubs and premises where police have to enforce vice, gaming, licensing and drug laws.

Gratuities are a hotly debated issue within police ethics. Do gratuities involve a violation of accepted norms and can they be seen as a form of corruption (Feldberg, 1985; Cohen and Feldberg, 1991; Kania, 1995; Prenzler and Mackay, 1995; Kleinig, 1996; Jones, 1999)? Corruption is often defined as 'behavior which deviates from the formal duties of a public role because of private-regarding (personal, close family, private clique) pecuniary or status gains; or violates rules against the exercise of certain types of private-regarding influence' (Nye, 1967, p. 419; Caiden, 2001; Gardiner, 2002). Taking gratuities can be seen as the use of police authority for private benefit and can influence the performance of police duties; either refraining from upholding the law or giving inequitable police protection. On the other hand, small gratuities can also be seen as the result of maintaining good community relations (Feldberg, 1985;

Cohen and Feldberg, 1991; Kania, 1995; Prenzler and Mackay, 1995; Kleinig, 1996; Jones, 1999).

The discussion about the relationship between gratuities (or gifts) and corruption (or bribes) is an interesting one. It is a central aspect of the literature on the economics of corruption with a focus on the relationship between giver and recipient, the strategic choices to either give or accept a gift or bribe depending on the expected outcomes (benefits and costs) (Klitgaard, 1991). Additionally, research on gifts and bribes in an international context often focuses upon whether gifts and favors are an important element of the moral obligations of more traditional societies (Williams and Theobald, 2000). However, the relationship between gratuities and bribery in different cultures is not the topic of this chapter. The focus is rather on the moral ambiguity of gratuities and how leadership might be able to influence the opinions and behavior of employees on an integrity issue.

## Leadership

Although a number of relevant aspects of leadership influencing the ethics and integrity of employees can be identified, we explore only three of the most often cited qualities of ethical leadership in relation to integrity violations of employees: 1. role modelling of managers by setting a good example for employees; 2. strictness of managers in applying clear norms and sanctioning misbehavior of employees; and 3. openness of managers to discussing integrity problems and dilemmas. According to Trevino *et al.* (2000: 131, 134–6) these three aspects are necessary to develop a reputation for ethical leadership; together they constitute the 'pillar' of the moral manager.

Managers act as role models for employees (Bass and Steidlmeier, 1999; Ciulla, 1999; Dickson *et al.*, 2001; Ford and Richardson, 1994; Fulmer, 2004; Lewis, 1991; Price, 2003) and lead by the example they set. Based on a case study they conducted, Sims and Brinkman (2002) assert that the moral tone and example set by managers is the most important element of an ethical organization. Their behavior reflects the norms of the organization and conveys how things are really done. Subordinates are likely to imitate supervisors since these individuals are significant others in the organizational lives of employees.

The second aspect relates to the expectation that employees are more likely to do what is rewarded, and avoid doing what is punished (Paine, 1994; Butterfield *et al.*, 1996). According to Trevino (1992), employees will refrain from committing ethical violations if they can expect that such behavior would be punished and that the level of punishment would outweigh any potential reward. Furthermore 'discipline for rule violators serves an important symbolic role in organizations – it reinforces standards, upholds the value of conformity to shared norms and maintains the perception that the organization is a just place where wrongdoers are held accountable for their actions' (Trevino *et al.*, 1999: 139). Managers should therefore be clear on what is right and what is wrong, what is permitted and what is forbidden (Bovens, 1998).

Openness in an organization is associated with a decreased likelihood of employee misconduct (Trevino *et al.*, 1999; Mason, 2004). In an open organization, employees can be honest about mistakes, ask for advice when confronted with issues related to integrity, discuss integrity dilemmas and report deviant behavior. In a closed organization criticism is not tolerated, delivering bad news is not appreciated, employees are not called to account for their misbehavior, and employees are encouraged to keep quiet, close their ears and avert their eyes (Bird, 1996; Trevino and Nelson, 1999; Kaptein and Wempe, 2002). Managers should therefore take an open stance and be willing to discuss integrity issues with their employees.

These three aspects give rise to the question: which of the three leadership characteristics is most important in curbing integrity violations? In the literature on this subject a distinction is made between a compliance-based approach which focuses primarily on rules and sanctions, and an integrity or value-based approach which concentrates on instilling values that promote a commitment to ethical conduct (Paine, 1994; Anechiarico and Jacobs, 1996; Anechiarico, 2002). The leadership characteristics 'openness' and 'role modelling' seem to coincide more with an integrity-based approach, while 'strictness' is more consistent with a compliance-based approach; the integrity approach is perceived as the more effective (Paine, 1994; Anechiarico and Jacobs, 1996; Anechiarico, 2002). However research by Lasthuizen *et al.* (2005) showed that setting a good example, strictness, and to a lesser extent openness, were correlated with a lower perception of the number of integrity violations within the organization. Nonetheless, little is yet known about how this relationship takes shape in the daily practice of organizations. The aim of this chapter is to provide insights on the roles of management and integrity policies, and the reactions to these by police officers.

## MINISTRY OF THE INTERIOR AND INTEGRITY

Following World War II integrity became a silent issue within Dutch government (Vriends, 1999) until the late Minister of Interior, Ms Dales, rekindled the subject with two speeches in 1992. This reinvigorated focus on integrity resulted from a major corruption scandal in Italy, a Dutch scandal concerning corrupt relations between construction companies and municipal government (see Dohmen and Langenberg, 1994), and general worries about the rise of organized crime and its potential corruptive influence (Vriends, 1999).

Since 1992 a body of policies, regulations and laws relating to integrity has been developed by the ministry of the Interior. At the same time, Ms Dales and subsequent ministers have stressed that they have no reason to doubt the overall integrity of Dutch government, including the police. This is confirmed by the yearly Transparency International Corruption Index, which places the Netherlands among the top ten of least corrupt countries (Transparency International, 2005). Being thus, integrity policies developed by the Ministry are preventive in nature (Anechiarico, 1998) and are targeted to different layers of government, including the police. The minister, after consultation with the Council of Police Chiefs, formulated several measures that the police forces were required to implement, such as a bureau for internal investigations, information campaigns and human resource management (education, selection procedures and performance evaluations) (TK 1994-1995, 23900 VII nr. 32 1995). Regulations regarding gratuities were not an issue in this initial policy document.

In 1997 administrative law relating to sideline activities was changed and at the same time extended with an article relating to gratuities: 'Public servants are forbidden, except with the approval of proper authorities, to accept or solicit money, gifts, services or discounts in relation to his official capacity' (Barp article 66a, 1997), indicating there is no absolute ban on taking gratuities. The law refers to the role of proper authorities, maintaining integrity relating to gratuities was seen as a responsibility of the organization and not just of individuals.

Since 1997 the police have had a national code of conduct which includes the two following references to gratuities in relation to the value of independence of the police: 1. A police official should show restraint in accepting gifts and 'fixes' within his official duties; and 2. no private-discounts on the delivery of services or goods should be accepted. The code makes a distinction between discounts, which are always unacceptable, and gifts which may be acceptable.

## METHODOLOGY

At the Vrije Universiteit of Amsterdam several research projects have focused on the integrity of the police (for an overview see Huberts and Naeyé, 2005), of which the study reported here is one. This chapter

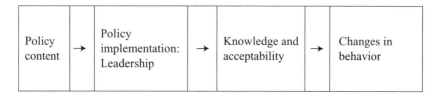

*Figure 10.1    Research model effectiveness of integrity policies*

addresses the effect of leadership on gratuities and will primarily employ
the findings from a broad study by Lamboo (2005) on the integrity policies
of Dutch police and how their success or failure could be explained.
Intensive case studies were conducted which focused not only on the
content of seven specific integrity policies and measures (only one of them
on gratuities), but also on the implementation of these policies by leadership, and the effect on police officers in terms of their knowledge and
acceptability of these policies as this is seen as a prerequisite for changes in
behavior (see Figure 10.1).

**The Case Studies**

In the Netherlands, a country with approximately 16 million inhabitants,
the police force totals more than 50 000 including officers and other personnel. In 1994, a major institutional reform took place, re-organizing the
Dutch police into 25 regional forces and one central force. The forces have
their own powers and policies, but the Minister of Interior bears an overall
responsibility for the quality of public administration, including the police.
Decisions and rulings relating to recruitment, training, salaries, uniforms,
and a large share of the equipment are made on a national basis. Also, the
national Council of Police Chiefs plays a role in developing national policies for the police forces, including policies on integrity.

   For the study, three police forces were selected so that a diverse perspective of how integrity and integrity policies take shape in the daily practices
of the 25 regional police organizations could be assembled. The main selection criterion was whether formal integrity policies were implemented and
running for at least three years, in order to be able to investigate its
effectiveness. The case selection is therefore an example of 'criterion sampling' (Patton, 1987: 56). The Amsterdam-Amstelland police region was
included as it is generally considered to be a forerunner in integrity policies
and thus is a 'critical case' (Patton, 1987: 54). Additional criteria for selection were size of the organization, urbanization (number of citizens per
km²), and location within the country. Based upon these criteria, the three

police forces selected for this study were the regional police force Amsterdam-Amstelland (5207 fte, in the western part of the country); Fryslân (1443 fte, in the north); and Limburg-Noord (1147 fte, in the south). Within each police force the police chief is responsible for operational matters; he shares this authority with one or more directors and together they form the police force management. The police forces are comprised of districts and divisions. Within each of the three selected police forces, three basic units (neighborhood teams) were sampled, located in different districts.

The policies that were developed within the selected police forces over the period 1995 (when institution of national integrity policies began) to 2001 (when this study was conducted) were documented. The content of the integrity policies was reconstructed based on documentation and information regarding implementation gleaned through interviews with functionaries responsible for integrity policies, such as the head of the bureau of internal investigators, as well as the chief of the police force, chiefs of the three districts and the three basic units within each district. Most interviews were conducted within the basic units with sworn officers who were selected by the researcher. In total 82 interviews were completed.

The interviews were conducted using a semi-structured questionnaire and were recorded on tape. Although some allowances for socially desirable answers must always be made, honest responses were encouraged by emphasizing that integrity policies were the central focus of the interviews, not the respondents' own or their colleagues' misconduct. In addition, strict confidentiality was guaranteed. Each respondent received a transcript of the interview and was given the opportunity to make (factual) adjustments if needed. Overall, respondents of all ranks talked openly about the integrity policies and about the changes in attitudes and behavior that resulted. This is less surprising as one considers that the topics – such as gratuities, discounts, side line activities and (sexual) harassment – turned out to be seen as relatively minor types of violations and that the officers had experienced positive changes in relation to them.

## CHANGES IN ACCEPTING GRATUITIES

In all three police forces it was not uncommon that shops and restaurants would offer discounts or free goods. Stores traditionally provided the local police station with 'oliebollen' (a kind of donut) on New Year's Eve and in earlier years with liquor and salads. There were restaurants and pubs where police officers could eat the leftovers after closing time or paid with a 10 guilder note and received change in two fivers. Some restaurants located by a highway had a formal policy to give discounts to all uniformed guests, benefiting in this way from the perceived extra security. In the more rural police forces of Fryslân and Limburg-Noord it used to be common for police officers to come home with bicycle bags filled with vegetables, potatoes and meat from farmers. As a senior constable commented, 'Let's be honest. I think that in the old days, certainly in the smaller municipalities, police officers, but also the local general practitioners, had a lot of benefits'.

Police officers from Amsterdam-Amstelland were the most open about discounts. Every respondent of the Amsterdam-Amstelland regional police force was familiar with the concept of 'dalven', the term refers to asking for and receiving discounts from businesses and shops. This was a widespread practice in the police force and management took part in it. Every basic unit had its own places to eat where it could get discounts, with a preference for Chinese restaurants and shoarma. At McDonalds police officers received a discount of 50 percent which was supposed to be restricted to employees. These discounts were not limited to the police, but also included such municipal services as the local health service and the fire department. According to the police officers, accepting discounts had not influenced their behavior and they attempted to avoid situations where a reciprocal favor could be expected (the complicating factor here, of course is that when discounts are so widespread it is nearly inevitable that occasionally a favor was expected or given in return).

According to the officers, discounts and requests for gratuities diminished in the mid-1990s (a finding echoed in Naeyé *et al.*, 2004: 231–5, but with the exception that some older police officers in Limburg-Noord and Fryslân were still known for shopping in uniform), and they gave several accounts for this change. At the level of society, police officers pointed at the distance that has grown between authorities, including the police and citizens, and that society looks more critically at the police. Also the economic welfare of police officers has improved since 'the old days'. At the level of the police organizations and police work, it was stated that gratuities used to be habit, officers were brought up with that behavior, and considered it normal. Furthermore little attention was paid by police management to these practices, and it was not unusual for lower management to participate in these practices. Only later did police officers start to realize that these practices were unethical and reflected back as to why it was initially acceptable. An inspector from Amsterdam-Amstelland states:

Police officers automatically received a discount at McDonalds. But when a citizen standing behind me said 'give me the same for the same price', then I did feel uncomfortable. Of course one could say that we did nothing, that we're just ordering four hamburgers and pay with 10 guilders, and that it is the responsibility of the cashier how much change she gives. That is one way to reason. But then citizens began to state 'I'm a police officer' in order to get a discount. At a certain moment I dissociated myself from it and said 'I no longer want to do that'. Just like everybody else I've had my discounts, but it started to give me an uncomfortable feeling.

## FORMAL POLICIES

The three police forces studied here had limited written rules regarding the accepting of gratuities by police officers and those appeared only within the context of regulating sideline activities, wherein a brief reference was made to article 66a of the administrative law. The Amsterdam-Amstelland police force extended this notation to include that in most cases the basic unit supervisor would be able to decide whether specific gratuities were admissible. But the lack of rules doesn't necessarily imply a lack of (informal) policy, as Amsterdam-Amstelland and Limburg-Noord demonstrate.

According to the Amsterdam-Amstelland police force, it had deliberately forgone a formal written policy about gratuities. The police force management stood for the principle that gratuities were not acceptable, but at the same time the police force had to avoid being 'allergic to society' because the police are in service to society. The police force stated: 'When in contact with the police citizens give their judgments, sometimes critical, but often positive and thankful. They show their gratitude in letters, flowers or cake. These are not registered, but for the police officers involved such gratuities are unforgettable.' This means that gifts from citizens as a true kind of gratuity are acceptable.

The police chief of Limburg-Noord took a different stance in the book *A Hazardous Profession* (1995), which was developed with two other police regions, and which discussed several integrity-related subjects. The stance towards gratuities was one of zero tolerance. The book proposed that gratuities could be accepted only to be transferred to, for example, an elderly home. The same year, at the request of the management team, an inventory was made of discount arrangements resulting in a diverse range of shops and businesses offering discounts to the police, such as passes for free swimming in the Centre Parcs holiday center, passes for a retail supermarket, discounts at cafeterias, bakeries and several shops. In response to this inventory the policy document 'Discounts' was formulated in 1996, but was not approved. The police chief thought a guideline was not necessary and could lead to calculated behavior.

# ROLE OF MANAGEMENT

### Strictness of the Manager

In the mid-1990s, in all three police forces, the norms about gratuities were tightened. In Limburg-Noord norms became stricter directly following a major reorganization in 1995. In the perception of the police officers this change was made overnight by the police management who declared that no gratuities were accepted, including gifts from citizens. The previous year the Amsterdam-Amstelland police management stated very specifically which practices it no longer tolerated. These included free copies of the newspaper *de Telegraaf* that could be picked up early in the morning at the company's main office in Amsterdam, discounted meals, and fraudulent expenses claims. In a basic unit, management stated that police officers were not allowed to have a night out within their working area (an entertainment district), not allowed to frequent certain bars, and could not shop during lunch breaks. Certain shops were announced to be prohibited areas because police officers had received (unsolicited) discounts. Some managers even went to these shops to report this new policy. These new norms were enforced and violations resulted in internal investigations, which frightened the police officers into changing their perspective. An inspector reported: 'You don't risk your job for 100 guilders [50 euros]. It is not worth it. At several basic units three, four or even six police officers were suspended. And when you hear why, then that does bring about a shock effect.' Formulating the norms and applying them went hand in hand.

The new strictness included gifts from citizens in all three forces and caused resentment from police officers. They thought the new policy went 'too far', that police management was so tight that it became 'silly' and 'childish'. They could not understand why being ethical meant taking such a straight line to the extent that the cake or flowers from a grateful citizen had to be refused. According to these officers, managers didn't understand the notion that refusing such gifts can be very upsetting, insulting the giver. Several police officers had experienced that leadership had them refuse the gift that thankful citizens brought to the local police station. Some did refuse, or left it to the group supervisor to make the refusal. Police officers were not always sure whether the zero tolerance strictness was intended by police management. In spite of their criticism, police officers thought a positive side effect of the strict norms was that management was on top of the issue.

The initial strictness that extended to gifts from citizens dissipated and that witnessed at the time of the interviews (around 2001–2) varied amongst the leadership. This was not out of line with the formal policies of the police forces. Amsterdam-Amstelland had for example explicitly stated that the basic unit supervisor should decide on which gratuities were acceptable. Specifically in Amsterdam-Amstelland the rules at the basic units depended for a great part on the reputation of the district chief. The stricter district chiefs would place greater emphasis on the issue in instructing their basic unit supervisors. The basic unit supervisors were supposed to ensure that all the inspectors within the unit took one and the same position. Even if this did not succeed entirely, police officers did know at large what was, and what wasn't allowable.

In Limburg-Noord most respondents thought that the police chief took a zero tolerance position and that the police chief did appear as if he was strict. Other respondents thought that the police chief used to be strict, but had become more balanced. According to the police chief himself the zero tolerance position was outside the social order: 'I have one golden rule: police officers should report all gratuities to their superior. It is the superior that decides. It is important that personnel don't decide for themselves, but involve another person.'

Within the police force at Fryslân the new strictness had not resulted in clear norms. Not only police officers, but also the supervisors and lower management had little knowledge of the opinion of the police management about gratuities. Some thought that the police chief would take a black-white stance: no single gratuity would be allowed. This expectation was not based on concrete announcements of the police chief on this subject.

**Openness of the Manager**

One can assume that discussions developed around the new strictness on gratuities. The respondents remembered a lot of discussion around gifts from citizens, as the temporary zero-tolerance policy had resulted in conflict. There was almost no reference to discussions about discounts and other types of gratuities. Apparently it was understood and accepted by police officers that these were not allowable, even if not everyone (had) adhered to this norm.

Police officers thought the stricter norms had a positive side effect as the subject became debatable and resulted in a dialogue about what was acceptable. Gratuities became a subject of conversation more often, while this was rarely the case before 1995. Openness was also part of the new norms as gifts had to be reported: 'That it gets reported is progress. I think that before, it would have been taken and eaten.' Whether a gift was acceptable or not was judged on the extent to which it could be brought out in the open, or as they say 'whether it could be published in the newspaper your mother reads'.

As gifts from citizens were usually delivered to the station, management generally used these instances for an informal discussion about the norms, such as during holidays when management would address the situation with recipients of unsolicited Christmas boxes. Basic unit supervisors noticed a change following these interventions regarding how police officers dealt with gratuities. Police officers began approaching them with questions about the acceptability of certain gifts, and one police officer reported to his supervisor that he was offered a discount at a Chinese restaurant after which the supervisor went to the restaurant to prevent it from happening again. However, when it was felt that the strictness had gone too far, and was foreign to their own norms, there were instances where police officers sought their own way. For example they wouldn't tell where the cake came from until it was shared with the team. This example illustrates how strictness can also lead to a lack of openness.

The case of Fryslân shows that a lack of clear norms can also result in a lack of communication. Police officers felt that the group supervisor or the district management should facilitate a discussion about gratuities. At the same time a member of the district management admitted that he avoided discussion with his own officers on the subject, because he didn't know which norms he had to espouse:

> The district management team doesn't speak about the subject. One reason is maybe that I myself don't have a clear notion of the subject and that the subject only leads to huge discussions. So I just assume that the group supervisors know where to put the line. That's why there should be an outline, because that would facilitate discussion. Even though rules and regulations wouldn't cover all situations, it would provide some certainty.

Discussion without clear norms led to feelings of uncertainty and distrust. A sergeant referred to training on integrity by the bureau of internal investigations and the following discussion that developed about gratuities:

> They don't say what is and isn't allowed, but in the meanwhile one gets the impression that it is not allowed. They say that you know for yourself what's right and wrong. But what if that doesn't correspond with their norms? Then the result is that there is something wrong with your norms and values, while the organization just never dared to provide clear rules.

This suggests that police officers are open to discussion, but within some kind of notion of the position of the organization.

The discussions were seen in a twofold manner by police. They were seen as an indication of the changes that had occurred, and at the same time as a cause of (further) change.

### The Manager as Role Model

The officers of the three police forces gave almost no examples of exemplary behavior on the part of their supervisors and managers, although a few managers gave examples of how they set a good example for employees. One chief of neighborhood policing from Fryslân said that he had discussed with his group supervisors a gift he'd received. A district chief from Amsterdam-Amstelland:

> There is this image that I am stricter than the Pope. [. . .] I am constantly aware of the question whether certain behavior is acceptable for a manager. For example, I don't shop within my own district because I don't want to give the impression that I am shopping during working hours. Also in my former district [containing an entertainment district], I would not have a drink at a terrace within the district.

Another district chief from Amsterdam-Amstelland that was known for his more informal manners stated:

> It is a subject that cannot be strictly regulated. Some say that even a free cup of coffee is not allowed. I think that it is allowable [gives an example]. What do you do in a situation like that? I don't want to hurt someone's feelings. [. . .] You have to resolve such issues in such a way that everyone can keep his dignity.

These examples demonstrate that managers can be role models in different ways.

## CONCLUSIONS AND IMPLICATIONS

Integrity is an important subject for the police. One of the subjects belonging to the ethics and integrity of daily police work is the acceptance of gratuities by police officers. The acceptance of gifts and favors by citizens and businesses can threaten independence and impartiality, and thus the incorruptibility of police functionaries and the police organization. In the Netherlands, accepting gratuities has become a subject of occasional fierce discussions within the police. This study showed that the actual behavior of police officers has changed during recent decades.

Members of the three police forces acknowledged that receiving and asking for gratuities used to be common practice and were unanimous in their opinion that this practice has now almost disappeared. What caused the changes?

The research showed that none of the three Dutch police forces had a formal written policy regarding gratuities. According to the forces a formal policy would only lead to calculated behavior from the police officers. Instead the police forces relied on management. They had to enforce the national rules that discounts were unacceptable while gifts from citizens could be acceptable, at the discretion of management and police officers.

Management mainly used strictness to curb the widespread practice of accepting gratuities. A clear definition of the norms was most effective as shown by the knowledge of police officers of the norms and policies of their organization and of their management. The research also demonstrated that punishing employees is a strong means to communicate new norms. The interviews did not indicate that rewarding employees was used as an instrument. Strictness, or more specific clarity of the norms, was combined with openness. Management had a strong view on openness: they generally encouraged discussion of the subject and were open to police officers for advice. Openness was also part of the norms: police officers had to report gifts from citizens and other gratuities.

A side effect of these strict norms was tension between management and executive officers. Zero tolerance was not accepted by police officers. Refusal of a cake or flowers from citizens was perceived as alien to maintaining good contact with the public. As such there has been a lack of acceptance of some parts of the new norms. Over time the norms became less strict concerning small gifts from citizens, although there are still stricter and more lenient managers.

Additionally, the research showed that the police commissioner played a central role. When the 'boss' is clear, this top-down clarity influences the whole organization. In two of the three police forces' lower management had no clear view of the police commissioner's position and was therefore uncertain about the rules they had to enforce. Because of this uncertainty they were also less open, as they did not know which norms to discuss with their officers. The uncertainty also created resentment and unease between the hierarchical levels, which inhibited the effectiveness of the organizational integrity policy on gratuities. Change is by definition a period of moral uncertainty. Police officers did experience it as such and looked at management for advice and for a clear stance on the subject.

Police leadership influenced police officers taking gratuities but the positive changes respondents experienced in their police force cannot be attributed to leadership alone. Some other factors seem to be important, too. Internal reorganizations were pointed out by the respondents as they provided a 'window of opportunity' for change. It was also felt that it has to do with more general changes in police culture (resulting from the growing numbers of female police officers). Other explanations laid beyond the scope of police forces, such as social changes – improving economical circumstances and fewer close relationships between authorities and citizens in smaller communities, and national developments within policing and government – especially the major reorganization of the police in 1994 and the growing national attention on integrity since 1992.

**Discussion**

Although we should be careful not to over exaggerate the importance of our findings, it is useful to note some implications.

First the results add new insights to the literature about police culture (Crank, 1998; Skolnick, 2002). The literature is rather pessimistic about the possibilities for cultural change within police forces as a type of organization that very much relies on professional freedom as well as loyalty towards colleagues and the organization. Our study showed that change in values and behavior did occur within the Dutch police, justifying some optimism about the possibility for change.

Second, there are possible consequences for existing knowledge about the strategies to protect the ethics and integrity of an organization and its members. It has been supposed that the integrity of organizations can best be improved by leadership that uses openness and role modeling, whereas strictness might be less effective. However, the results of this study suggested that the changes in behavior and values were primarily brought about by strict norms. As such a compliance approach seems to be more effective than an integrity approach, which counters the current dominant discourse.

Moreover this research focused on how the three aspects of leadership take shape in the daily practice of organizations. It was shown that strictness does not exclude openness and role modeling. Rather, they not only reinforce each other, but are mutually dependable. It was shown that openness without clear norms to discuss only led to uncertainty. As such the relevance of openness should not be exaggerated to the expense of the contribution of strictness. Even introducing norms that are too strict in the eyes of employees might be stimulating for the process of rethinking standard practices, although it may lead to conflict. When this strictness is only temporary, it might have the benefit of discussion without leaving lasting resentment between officers and management.

The main new hypothesis is that for management to influence the integrity of their employees, strictness is a first prerequisite, but that it needs to be reinforced by openness and role modeling. Part of role modeling is that management is open about their actions and dares to discuss them with employees. This hierarchy between the three aspects of leadership is depicted in Figure 10.2.

Of course, such a hypothesis will have to be tested in further research, especially in organizations other than police organizations. This can be done by qualitative as well as quantitative research and should also involve other types of integrity violations and views. Our findings are based on the studies of gratuities that were not only widespread, but also readily

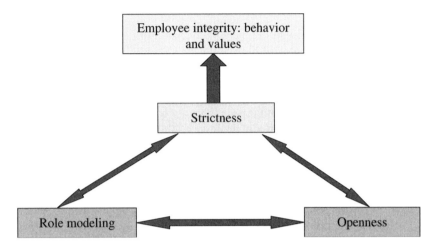

*Figure 10.2    The relationship between aspects of leadership and employee integrity*

acknowledged by police officers as they involve a less serious kind of integrity violation. Therefore other direct and indirect relationships might be found for other violations such as bribery, sexual harassment and private time misconduct.

## REFERENCES

Anechiarico, F. (1998), 'Administrative culture and civil society', *Administration & Soceity*, **30** (1), 13–34.

Anechiarico, F. (2002), 'Law enforcement or a community-oriented strategy toward corruption control', in C. Fijnaut and L. Huberts (eds), *Corruption, Integrity and Law Enforcement*, Dordrecht: Kluwer Law International, pp. 293–306.

Anechiarico, F. and J.B. Jacobs (1996), *The Pursuit of Absolute Integrity: How Corruption Control Makes Government Ineffective*, Chicago, IL: University of Chicago Press.

Bass, B. and P. Steidlmeier (1999), 'Ethics, character, and authentic transformational leadership behaviour', *The Leadership Quarterly*, **10**, 181–217.

Bird, F.B. (1996), *The Muted Conscience: Moral Silence and the Practice of Business Ethics*, Westport, CT: Quorum Books.

Bovens, M. (1998), *The Quest for Responsibility: Accountability and Citizenship in Complex Organizations*, Cambridge: Cambridge University Press.

Butterfield, K.D., L.K. Trevino and G.A. Ball (1996), 'Punishment from the managers' perspective: a grounded investigation and inductive model', *Academy of Management Journal*, **39**, 1479–512.

Caiden, G.E. (2001), 'Corruption and governance', in E. Caiden, O.P. Dwivedi and J. Jabbra (ed.), *Where Corruption Lives*, Bloomfield, CT: Kumarian Press, pp. 15–37.

Ciulla, J.B. (ed.) (1998), *Ethics: The Heart of Leadership*, Westport, CT: Praeger.

Cohen, H.S. and M. Feldberg (1991), *Power and Restraint: The Moral Dimension of Police Work*, New York: Praeger.

Coleman, S. (2003), 'When police should say "NO!" to gratuities', Centre for Applied Philosophy and Public Ethics (CAPPE) working paper 2003/6, Australia, accessed at www.philosophy.unimelb.edu.au/cappe/working_papers/Coleman2.pdf.

Crank, J.P. (1998), *Understanding Police Culture*, Cincinnati, OH: Anderson.

Dickson, M.W., D.B. Smith, M.W. Grojean and M. Ehrhart (2001), 'An organizational climate regarding ethics: the outcome of leader values and the practices that reflect them', *The Leadership Quarterly*, **12**, 197–217.

Dohmen, J. and H. Langenberg (1994), 'Corruptie en fraude: lessen uit Limburg?', in L.W.J.C. Huberts (ed.), *Machtsbederf ter discussie. Bijdragen aan het debat over bestuurlijke integriteit*, Amsterdam: VU Uitgeverij, pp. 19–28.

Elliston, F.A. (1985), 'Police, privacy, and the double-standard', in F.A. Elliston and M. Feldberg (eds), *Moral Issues in Police Work*, Totowa, NJ: Rowman & Allanheld, pp. 277–88.

Feldberg, M. (1985), 'Gratuities, corruption, and the democratic ethos of policing: the case of the free cup of coffee', in F.A. Elliston and M. Feldberg (eds), *Moral Issues in Police Work*, Totowa, NJ: Rowman and Allanheld, pp. 267–76.

Ford, R.C. and W.D. Richardson (1994), 'Ethical decision-making: a review of the empirical literature', *Journal of Business Ethics*, **13**, 205–21.

Fulmer, R.M. (2004), 'The challenge of ethical leadership', *Organizational Dynamics*, **33** (3), 307–17.

Gardiner, J.A. (2002), 'Defining corruption', in A.J. Heidenheimer and M. Johnston (eds), *Political Corruption: Concepts & Contexts*, New Brunswick, NJ and London: Transaction Publishers, pp. 25–40.

Her Majesty's Inspectorate of Constabulary (HMIC) (1999), *Police Integrity England, Wales and Northern Ireland: Securing and Maintaining Public Confidence*, Her Majesty's Inspectorate of Constabulary.

Huberts, L.W.J.C., M.E.D. Lamboo and M. Punch (2003), 'Police integrity in the Netherlands and the United States: awareness and alertness', *Police Practice and Research: An International Journal*, **4** (3), 217–32.

International Association of Chiefs of Police (1995), 'Canons of police ethics', in D. Close and N. Meier (eds), *Morality in Criminal Justice: An Introduction to Ethics*, Belmont: Wadsworth, pp. 61–2.

Jones, M. (1999), 'Religion, race and public opinion about police officer gratuities', *Journal of Contemporary Criminal Justice*, **15** (2), 191–204.

Kania, R.R.E. (1995), 'Should we tell the police to say "yes" to gratuities?' in: D. Close and N. Meier (eds), *Morality in Criminal Justice: An Introduction to Ethics*, Belmont, CA: Wadsworth, pp. 327–39.

Kaptein, M. and J. Wempe (2002), *The Balanced Company: A Theory of Corporate Integrity*, Oxford: Oxford University Press.

Kleinig, J. (1996), *The Ethics of Policing*, New York: Cambridge University Press.

Klitgaard, R. (1993), 'Gifts and bribes', in R. Zeckhauser (ed.), *Strategy and Choice*, 2nd edn, Cambridge, MA: MIT Press, pp. 211–39.

Knapp Commission (1972), *The Knapp Commission Report on Police Corruption*, New York: Commission to Investigate Allegations of Police Corruption, Braziller.

Koring, C. (2000), *Bureau Warmoesstraat*, 's Gravenhage: Bzztôh.

Lamboo, M.E.D. (2005), *Integriteitsbeleid van de Nederlandse politie*, Delft: Eburon.

Lasthuizen, K., L.W.J.C. Huberts and M. Kaptein (2003), *Politiële integriteit. Integriteitsopvattingen bij de Nederlandse politie nader onderzocht*, Amsterdam: Vrije Universiteit.

Lasthuizen, K., L.W.J.C. Huberts and M. Kaptein (2005), 'Analyse van integriteitsopvattingen', in L.W.J.C. Huberts and J. Naeyé (eds), *Integriteit van de politie. Wat we weten op basis van Nederlands onderzoek*, Zeist: Kerckebosch, Apeldoorn: Politie en Wetenschap, pp. 69–93.

Lewis, C.W. (1991), *The Ethics Challenge in Public Service: A Problem-solving Guide*, San Francisco, CA: Jossey-Bass.

Mason, R.O. (2004), 'Lessons in organizational ethics from the Columbia disaster: can a culture be lethal?', *Organizational Dynamics*, **33** (2), 128–42.

de Minister van Binnenlandse Zaken en Koninkrijksrelaties (1999), *Circulaire aanvaarden van geschenken door rijksambtenaren*, AD1999/U75958, 14 juli.

Naeyé, J., L.W.J.C. Huberts, C. van Zweden, V. Busato and B. Berger (2004), *Integriteit in het dagelijks politiewerk: Meningen en ervaringen van politiemensen*, Politiewetenschap nr.13, Apeldoorn: Kerckebosch.

Newburn, T. (1999), *Understanding and Preventing Police Corruption: Lessons from the Literature*, police research series paper 110, London: Home Office Policing and Reducing Crime Unit.

Nye, J.S. (1967), 'Corruption and political development: a cost-benefit analysis', *The American Political Science Review*, **61** (2), 417–27.

Paine, L.S. (1994), 'Managing for organizational integrity', *Harvard Business Review*, **72**, 107–17.

Paine, L.S. (2003), *Values Shift*, New York: Prentice-Hall.

Patton, M.Q. (1987), *How to Use Qualitative Methods in Evaluation*, London: Sage.

Politie Brabant Zuid-Oost, Politie Limburg-Noord and Politie Limburg-Zuid (1995), *Een beroep met risico's* [*A Hazardous Profession*], Phaedon: Culemborg.

Prenzler, T. and P. Mackay (1995), 'Police gratuities: what the public think', *Criminal Justice Ethics*, **14** (1), 15–25.

President's Commission (1967), *Task Force Report: The Police*, Washington, DC: The President's Commission on Law Enforcement and Administration of Justice.

Price, T.L. (2003), 'The ethics of authentic transformational leadership', *The Leadership Quarterly*, **14**, 67–81.

Punch, M. (1985), *Conduct Unbecoming: The Social Construction of Police Deviance and Control*, London: Tavistock.

Punch, M., L.W.J.C. Huberts and M.E.D. Lamboo (2004), 'Integrity perceptions and investigations: The Netherlands', in C.B. Klockars, S.K. Ivkovic and M. Haberfeld (eds), *The Contours of Police Integrity*, London, New Dehli and Thousand Oaks, CA: Sage, pp. 161–74.

Royal Commission into the New South Wales Police Service (1997), *Final Report. Volume I: Corruption*, The Government of the State of New South Wales.

Skolnick, J.H. (2002), 'Corruption and the Blue Code of Silence', *Police Practice and Research: An International Journal*, **3** (1), 7–19.

Sims, R.R. and J. Brinkman (2002), 'Leaders as moral role models: the case of John Gutfreund at Salomon Brothers', *Journal of Business Ethics*, **35**, 327–39.

Transparency International (2001), *Crossing the Thin Blue Line. An International Annual Review of Anti-corruption Strategies in the Police*, Prague: Center for Police Studies.

Transparency International (2005), 'Transparency International corruption perceptions index 2005', accessed at www.transparency.org.

Trevino, L.K. (1992), 'Moral reasoning and business ethics: implications for research, education, and management', *Journal of Business Ethics*, **11** (5,6), 445–59.

Trevino, L.K. and Nelson K.A. (1999), *Managing Business Ethics: Straight Talk About How to do it Right*, New York: John Wiley & Sons.

Trevino, L.K., L.P. Hartman and M. Brown (2000), 'Moral person and moral manager: how executives develop a reputation for ethical leadership', *California Management Review*, **42** (4), 128–42.

Trevino, L.K., G.R. Weaver, D.G. Gibson and B.L. Toffler (1999), 'Managing ethics and legal compliance: what works and what hurts?', *California Management Review*, **41** (2), 637–47.

Tweede Kamer (1995), *Vaststelling van de begroting van de uitgaven en de ontvangsten van het Ministerie van Binnenlandse Zaken (VII) voor het jaar 1995*, TK 1994-1995, 23900 VII, nr. 32, 17 maart 1995.

Van Laere, E.M.P. and R.W.M. Geerts (1984), *Wetshandhaver of wetsontduiker: een onderzoek naar ontoelaatbaar gedrag in een politie-organisatie*, Den Haag: Ministerie van Binnenlandse Zaken, Directie Politie, Afd. Onderzoek.

Vriends, E.A.I.M. (1999), *Niet van nature: Bestuurlijke integriteit op de politieke agenda*, Politicologie en Bestuurskunde, Amsterdam: Vrije Universiteit.

Williams, R. and T. Robin (eds) (2000), *Corruption in the Developing World*, Cheltenham, UK and Northampton, MA, USA: Edward Elgar.

Zwart, C. (1999), *Diender in Amsterdam: de beproevingen van een politiekorps 1966–1999*, Amsterdam: Uitgeverij Balans.

# PART IV

# Ethics and integrity and the politics of governance

# 11. Removing employee protections: a 'see no evil' approach to civil service reform

## James S. Bowman and Jonathan P. West

## INTRODUCTION

Ethics in public service is influenced by two norms – political exchange and civic culture – that co-exist in varying degrees and at different times in many Western democratic societies. The first is premised on contracts, favors and jobs in exchange for political support; it is susceptible to corruption because it feeds an environment of cronyism, sycophancy, favoritism and waste. In contrast, a civic culture is one in which the commonweal is the central value; it is based on universally applicable rules, equal treatment, professional ethics and stewardship of public resources. Promoting the public good, not personal gain, is the objective (adapted from Rosenbloom, 1998: 536–8; also see Schlesinger, 1986).

Civil service systems, reflecting such tensions, confront competing demands for political responsiveness and professional competence. In the last generation, the emphasis between these two traditions has shifted in most democracies from a public service imbued by civic culture norms toward one of political exchange. The New Public Management (NPM) movement (Hood, 1991; Pollitt, 1990; Pollitt and Bouckaert, 2004) challenged the long-standing merit system model, characterized by non-partisan public servants, as inflexible and unresponsive to contemporary needs.

To improve effectiveness, reduce expenditures and enhance accountability, reform deregulated personnel systems, defunded agencies, downsized staff, privatized services, augmented managerial discretion, empowered citizens and strengthened political control. Such actions often included reforms in financial management (emphasizing results and performance), civil service (relaxing rigidities), organizational structures (mandating decentralization) and service delivery (seeking competition in the name of higher quality and less cost). For administrators tasked to fulfill these expectations, reforms frequently meant increased job insecurity, the need to learn new skills and greater workloads.

In the process, the character of the employee relationship with government has undergone a metamorphosis: the transfer of many of the risks of management decisions and market fluctuations, previously borne by the organization, to employees (Stone, 2004). In particular, the long-standing public employee-employer covenant – modest pay in exchange for job security – is being eroded by removing safeguards against partisan influence. The most sweeping measure is the use of at-will employment (and its equivalents) to eliminate the defining component of merit systems: job protection from political intrigue.

Because the quality of the public service is central to the field of ethics and integrity of governance, this chapter focuses on the contemporary debate over civil service reform.[1] It begins by examining the origin and nature of the at-will employment doctrine. An analysis of its use in government follows, first in the United States and then in the United Kingdom, two nations that differ in interesting ways, but are part of the 'core NPM group' (Pollitt and Bouckaert, 2004: 98).[2] The discussion closes with conclusions about the future of public service in democracy. The management of human capital reflects societal norms and clashing values. It is at the core of governance. As such, the integrity of civil service systems is a matter of profound importance for citizens, scholars and public officials alike. If these systems do not work, then neither does government. As Franklin D. Roosevelt stated so clearly, 'A government without good management is a house built on sand.'

## EMPLOYMENT AT-WILL

Early American labor-management law was based on British master-servant law which assumed employment would last one year. However, consistent with laissez-faire capitalism of the Industrial Revolution, the English approach was abandoned for the American Rule near the end of the nineteenth century. Under this rule, employees work for an unspecified period of time at the will of the employer (www.workforce.com/Hugh; also see Hogler, 2004; Werhane *et al.*, 2004; for an interpretation emphasizing legal, not economic, developments, see Morriss, 1994). The relationship would be defined by the freedom to contract where neither party was compelled to create the affiliation and either party could terminate it at will. The discipline of the free market would ensure the societal efficiency of these individual voluntary agreements as both parties would have incentives to recover their investments in each other (Epstein and Rosen, 1984).

In concept, the absolute right of the employer to discharge a worker coincided with the sovereignty doctrine in the public sector. Because employment was a privilege, not a right, it was subject to terms specified by government. Government is sovereign; it is inappropriate to dilute its management rights (for example, no person has a right to a public job). Indeed for much of the nineteenth century – the last time that at-will employment was used in US public service – the spoils system dominated personnel policy. Citizens sought a position not on the basis of character or competence but on political connections, and they could be terminated on the same basis. Public office was perverted into a private fiefdom as arrogance, greed, and opportunism prevailed over honor, openness and prudence.

Favoritism, cronyism, intimidation, corruption, waste, scandals and rampant dismissals were widespread in that squalid era. Rather than emphasizing good government and policy, the system encouraged mediocre governance; its highest priority was to reward its friends, to grant favors for favors given. To protect the legitimacy of the state from private interests and to cleanse public service of partisan interference, English merit principles (including entrance examinations, job tenure, career service political neutrality) were adopted in the 1883 Pendleton Act (and state 'mini-Pendleton' laws) as well as the 1912 Lloyd-LaFollette Act. A merit-based civil service – as a moral guardian of democracy – would shield employees from politically inspired employment actions. Public servants would be loyal to the system of government, not to a particular political party. They would only give free and candid advice if their positions were safeguarded. In fact, job security facilitated government responsiveness by ensuring efficient and uninterrupted service delivery. Clean government would mean effective government. Competence would be the foundation of moral public management; government would be run like a business when organized by administrative principles, led by an executive, and staffed by nonpartisan employees protected from unscrupulous politicians.

Although the US merit system was created to 'clean up government' by eradicating spoils, it is not surprising that with the passage of time the past would be forgotten. Toward the end of the twentieth century, a simpler, private sector-inspired employment system gained favor. New Public Management, while not always clearly defined in the literature, is identified by four models according to Ferlie *et al.* (1996): the drive for efficiency, 'downsizing and decentralization', the search for excellence, and a public service orientation. Variously called 'managerialism', 'market-based public administration', or 'entrepreneurial government', the emphasis was on 'letting managers manage' by increasing their discretion and using private sector management styles to ensure improved performance and results (Pollitt, 1990; Lan and Rosenbloom, 1992; Osborne and Gaebler, 1992).

Relaxing traditional job protections for civil servants has been seen as a key method to accomplish these objectives. Indeed, at-will employment is now seen as solving, instead of causing, public management problems, as there seems to be little appreciation of the ethical context of the merit system.

Proponents of change support the removal of controls over organizational processes and elimination of employee safeguards in order to enhance political responsiveness. Given the history of the American civil service reform as one of battling partisan corruption (Ingraham, 1995), expanding the number of personnel susceptible to unfettered administrative discretion raises concerns – apprehensions that have been greeted with indifference or incredulity, and largely dismissed by ideologically driven reformers with anti-government views. Running government like a business and giving priority to increasing efficiency, reducing waste, adding flexibility, and conserving resources may, as Hood (1991) suggests, come at the expense of other values such as 'honesty and fair dealing and the avoidance of bias'. Indeed, 'marketizers' and 'anti-state minimizers' favor substituting permanent government employees with their hard-won job protections for contract workers who are obliged to provide specific outputs with few, if any, job guarantees (Pollitt and Bouckaert, 2004; Sulieman, 2003). These developments, together with the emergence of contingent and part-time workers as a large, growing proportion of the nation's workforce, suggest that employees are increasingly seen as disposable commodities.

## CONTEMPORARY REFORM IN THE UNITED STATES

Fueled by entrepreneurial strategies, budget cutbacks and devolution, the contemporary reform movement (Condrey and Maranto, 2001) has gained exceptions from merit systems across the nation by expanding management prerogatives and restricting employee rights (Kellough and Nigro, 2006). In recent years, a variety of federal departments received full or partial waivers from Title 5 of the US Code which defines the merit system. Further, in the wake of the 11 September 2001 attacks, the Transportation Security Agency established at-will employment for its personnel. Subsequently the departments of Homeland Security and Defense were authorized, in the name of the 'war on terror', to create new human resource management systems that generally strengthen administrative discretion and diminish employee protections. Today, reformers are seeking to use these untested approaches as templates for government-wide change.

At the state level, major reform examples exist: Texas nullified its merit system in 1985, making all state employees at-will; a 1996 Georgia law mandated that all new civil servants be hired on an at-will basis; and in 2001 Florida eliminated job tenure for most incumbent middle managers (Walters, 2002). South Carolina and Arkansas recently abolished their merit systems; less dramatically, many states (for example, Indiana, Delaware, Kansas) are reclassifying career service positions to unclassified ones as a consequence of reorganizations, reductions-in-force, and/or attrition. Such strategies are often mutually reinforcing in a manner that promotes the on-going deterioration of career public service; the effect is that the status and role of the public employee today is not too different than that found in business (Hays and Sowa, 2006).

More broadly, and as a result of reform, the concept of merit today is increasingly associated with corporate-style performance pay plans in lieu of public interest values and civil service responsibilities. Unfortunately, there is little evidence that these monetary incentive programs have resulted in desired outcomes in either business or government (Lane *et al.*, 2003: 138; also see Berman *et al.*, 2005, chapter 6). In the private sphere the systems are so problematic that they are the subject of a recent Harvard University Press book entitled *Pay Without Performance* (Bebchuk and Fried, 2004).

In the public sphere, 'the jury is still out on how the [federal] government's 7100 senior executives have fared under a performance-based pay system that took effect last year,' according to one labor leader. 'To administer [it] . . . is not easy. If you can't do it for this small of a population, it does not bode well for doing it well for the entire workforce' (Carol Bonosaro, quoted in Kaufman, 2005, 25 July, 6). With respect to pending changes affecting the rest of the federal workforce, one employee said:

[C]ivil service employees are somewhat 'buffered' from politically motivated actions of top management. Employees can openly disagree with the policies and proposed actions of their agencies (within limits, of course) . . . With 'pay for performance' I wonder if I should just please my boss rather than fight for what I believe is right . . . I will need to balance feeding my family against fighting for the public interest (quoted in Barr, 2005c, p. B2).

It would be especially useful to learn why numerous past performance initiatives, including pay for performance, failed (Milkovich and Wigdor, 1991; US Office of Personnel Management, 1992). Echoing scholarly studies on performance pay, a union spokesman pointed out reformers, 'have no data whatsoever to indicate that this (change) will improve organization performance' (Brian DeWyngaert, quoted in Lee, 2005, p. A2).

The linchpin of civil service reform, according to Office of Personnel Management Director Linda Springer, is a 'rigorous' personnel appraisal system as managers will be asked to 'do the right thing' and not inflate evaluations (Rutzick, 2005a or b). One employee asked, 'Who believes that performance ratings will be realistic and avoid grade inflation?' (quoted in Barr, 2000b, p. B2). In brief, because the conditions for success for these programs – the nature of output produced, the type of personnel who do the work, and the kinds of organizations where it is done – are usually not met in the world of industry or government (Bohnet and Eaton, 2003: 241), predicting success is hazardous. One suspects that the root problem is not technique or system, but rather aspects of human nature such as risk aversion and cognitive limitations (Berman *et al.*, 2006, chapter 9).

Perhaps in recognition of these concerns, the president's top advisor on management policy expressed doubt about pay for performance because 'it sounds like we are on a commission basis here. We're not. It suggests that the entire raise is going to be based on performance. It's not' (Clay Johnson II, quoted in Barr, 2005a, p. B2). Indeed, the US Government Accountability Office has had performance pay for years and confronts not only 'evaluation inflation', but also budget constraints, both of which undermine pay for performance (Rutzick, 2005a or b). The Bush Administration maintained that a large part of raises under civil service reform will not be based on performance, but rather on market rates (Kaufman, 2005b, p. 1).[3]

To summarize, changes reducing or abolishing job security (and otherwise altering basic merit system tenets) have occurred across the country. While little evidence exists on the benefits of these programs, the most prominent vestige of merit today is found in pay-for-performance plans. Available research demonstrates that these plans are often more efficacious in the abstract than in practice. Hollowed out of the meaning and content of merit, reformers have attempted to use the symbols of merit to legitimate change. As Joel D. Aberbach (2003) observes, difficulties arise, 'in part because the very features that make the US political system resemble a market make it difficult to apply many of the features of NPM . . . and in part because of problems with some of the NPM ideas themselves' (p. 57). Globalization trends suggest, however, the confluence of organizational policies across boundaries. Although the United States has been an outlier, the rest of the developed world uses International Labor Organization standards which, for example, forbid unjust dismissal. Yet to the extent that American-style capitalism is emulated in other countries, management practices like employment at-will and performance pay may also be adopted elsewhere.

# REFORM IN EUROPE: THE UNITED KINGDOM CASE

The penchant toward a business-oriented approach to public administration (namely, 'managerialism' with its emphasis on regionalization, decentralization, marketization, restructuring and modernizing to enhance management rights and reduce government size) is evident not only in the United States, but in Europe as well. While generalizing about the nature of civil service reform is difficult given the differing legal frameworks and practices in each country, some converging organizational structures and guiding principles can be identified. An initial distinction between an employment system and a career system found in northern and southern Western Europe is a useful starting point.[4]

An employment system is modeled in the private sector where those with special skills are hired for specific posts and lack job security. A career system, in contrast, is composed of those who spend their entire working life in the civil service and have stable employment and job protection. While most countries are hybrids or mixed systems of these pure forms, the distinction can be useful for classification purposes. The employment system in northern countries (for example, the United Kingdom, Switzerland, Denmark, France, Sweden and the Netherlands) is favored whereby public employees generally lack job protections beyond those personally or collectively negotiated. The career system is predominant in southern nations (for example, Italy, Spain, Portugal and Greece) with greater civil servant rights, protective mechanisms and guarantees (Committee on Economic Affairs and Development (CEAD), 2003). The risks of civil service politicization are greater in predominantly employment systems where loyalty to the government in power receives more emphasis than in a career system.

To varying degrees, countries throughout Europe are experiencing reforms promoting greater flexibility and modernizing human resource management. The New Public Management reform that took place during the 1980s and 1990s, was modeled on corporate management with its emphasis on competition, efficiency, privatization, contracting, assessment and results. These changes are especially evident in England under the governments of Prime Ministers Margaret Thatcher, John Major and Tony Blair.

Thatcher era reforms of the 1980s reflected the NPM concentration on eliminating waste, reigning back bureaucracy and introducing market forces. This was part of a wider consideration of industrial relations and a commitment to reduce trade union power, especially in the government sector. It was also propelled by a desire to save public monies and improve efficiency by introducing private sector practices and attitudes. Initially using unflattering slogans ('deprivilege the civil service', 'rolling back the frontiers of the state', 'jam the bureaucracy' and characterizing unions as the 'enemy within') to propel her 'Next Steps' reforms, advocates later toned down their rhetoric and focused on the nuts and bolts of organizational change. Their diagnosis: the problem was with systems, not with civil servants; their solution: reduce civil service numbers and powers, provide 'value for money', cultivate a managerial culture and increase political control. Distinctions were drawn between 'political' tasks (those in the minister's purview) and 'managerial' tasks (day-to-day administration), with a 'framework document' outlining the responsibilities, objectives, budget and evaluation criteria of 'executive' agencies. In other words, 'steering' was decoupled from 'rowing', flexibility was enhanced, job security was compromised, authority was decentralized and devolved, and results were emphasized (CEAD, 2003; Coyle-Shapiro and Kessler, 2003; Dillman, 2005; Pilkington, 1999; Osborne and Plastrik, 1997; Toonen and Raadschelders, 1997).

Agencies were audited, evaluated and 'market tested' on a regular basis to determine whether they were to continue or to be partially or fully privatized. In the process, civil service tenure was denied for chief executives, budgets and staffs were cut and efficiencies were scrutinized. In 1988, local public services, organized under the employment system, were required to compete with private companies under a controversial Compulsory Competitive Tendering (CCT) system. While a certain amount of contracting had been used previously, local governments and health authorities were obliged to contract out services and minimal service levels were established by the central government. The main attraction of CCT and market testing was cost-cutting based on cheaper labor. Often the same workers did the same tasks as before, but under less favorable conditions. In some cases pay was reduced, but frequently it was other employee benefits that were cut.

NPM tools were used to prompt changes: contracts, public/private competition, performance-related pay, customer surveys, total quality management and process engineering. Between 1988 and 1996 the civil service was reduced by 15 percent (Osborne and Plastrik, 1997), and it is no surprise that opinion polls in the mid-1990s showed a significant decline in the morale of public servants and growing skepticism regarding the reforms (Pilkington, 1999: 97). Unfair dismissals accounted for the largest number of complaints regarding employment rights (Newmark and O'Brien, 2000).

Privatization initiatives continued as John Major succeeded Thatcher, by ending tenure for civil servants and making them at-will. Job security was now dependent on delivering results negotiated with ministers. His government stressed the quality of services, establishing customer service standards and authorizing compliant agencies to display the 'Charter Mark' as a sign of their accomplishments (this initiative was seen as a publicity stunt and was later dropped). The Labor government of Tony Blair did not reverse most of the NPM initiatives (for example, market testing, contracting out, customer focus), however it did cease CCT extension. Indeed, in a key 2004 report titled, *Delivery and Values*, there was an emphasis on the need to shift away from 'the traditional concept of a career for life' toward officials possessing 'the abilities needed by the business' and who could 'stay ahead of a changing environment' (cited in Dillman, 2005: 12).

Civil service reform is not without it critics. Vernon Bogdanor (2001), in particular, lamented the absence of public inquiry, analysis and legislative involvement preceding reforms. He observed, 'The agenda for Civil Service reform has been set by politicians, businessmen and management consultants, and much of it has been implemented by non-legislative means after discussions in closed arenas' (299). His criticisms focused on the substance of reforms as well as the process by which they were adopted. Bogdanor contended that the civil service became the 'scapegoat for perceived economic underperformance' and that reform is premised 'upon a view of the corporate world which is quite inaccurate' (p. 299). He worried that the infusion of outsiders makes it difficult to ensure both that standards are maintained and that the civil service does not become politicized. The efforts to decentralize and 'incentivize' employees via pay for performance to achieve the reformers' goal of agency and individual responsibility, in Bogdanor's view, work against fundamental notions of holistic government, interdependence and shared responsibility. Finally, he questioned whether a persuasive case was made warranting a change in the traditional contract whereby 'civil servants are offered job security in exchange for levels of pay generally lower than they could command elsewhere' (298).

In the initial rush to reform, European NPM advocates extolled the virtues of managerialism, but seemingly turned a blind eye to the unintended consequences of proposed changes. In more recent years, the temptations of politics and money, the increased risks of politicization, the erosion of a public service ethic, and the altered relations between the public and private sectors as well as between public servants and politicians led both to scandals and to increased reports of conflict of interest and corruption in civil service systems (CEAD, 2003; Ridley and Doig, 1995; Doig and Wilson, 1995). Instances of illegal, unethical and inappropriate behavior have highlighted the need for preventive mechanisms and ethics management strategies.

Such responses have taken different forms in various places. In those countries lacking a statutory framework that protects employee rights and specifies duties, a code of conduct for civil servants was often adopted similar to the one approved in the United Kingdom in 1996 (Dillman, 2005). In other countries, the necessary legal protections (constitutional, legislative, regulatory, case law) render adoption of a code of ethics less essential. Nonetheless, nations are using multiple techniques to ensure ethical behavior, including legal requirements (for example, disclosure requirements, conflict of interest restrictions), professional socialization activities (seminars, training, publications), and efforts to create an ethical organizational environment (grievance procedures, whistle-blowing protection) (Shim, 2001; Lawton, 1998).

To summarize, civil service reforms and reductions in job security are found in Europe as well as the United States. The appeal of managerialism has spread, although making comparisons of developments across countries is difficult because the state and administrative traditions are very different (Toonen and Raadschelders, 1997). While restrictions on individual rights are more limited in Europe than in the United States, the quest for employer flexibility has resulted in fewer employee protections. Variations in labor laws and practices among countries make harmonization unlikely in the near term. However, the 'just cause' standard for terminations is more likely to be upheld on the European Continent than in American and English settings. Nonetheless, with diminished job protections, the decline in career employees and decentralized authority, public servants are more vulnerable to political machinations and erosion of a public service ethos – a problem which points to the need for ethics management mechanisms to prevent undesirable forms of behavior.

## CONCLUSION

The nature of public service is changing, and in many ways and in selected places it already has changed. Since the rise of merit systems more than 100 years ago, personnel practices recognized the signal import of professional competence. In recent years, however, those demanding accountability have been successful in bringing about change. The delicate balance between the norms of civic culture and political exchange in democratic governance is shifting from the former to the latter. The crucial concern, as Green *et al.* (2006) note, is how much politicization is desirable.

Reformers demand that officials have the 'freedom to manage', resulting in the deterioration of the traditional employer-employee relationship as well as personnel safeguards from partisan pressures. Whether through ignorance or arrogance, seldom are the ramifications of these changes considered as advocates seem blind to abuse brought on by a mix of power, aspiration and sycophancy. Politically connected special interests or politically protected appointees can intimidate career staff, alter checks and balances, dismiss whistleblowers and create a modern-day spoils system. New personnel policies, usually without the benefit of evidence from demonstration projects, promote management myths (such as the impossibility of employee termination) and impose heavy-handed solutions (notably, tenure elimination and performance pay) and the management by fear that they engender.

Such initiatives needlessly endanger non-partisan public service, a priceless asset in democracy. For example, NPM-style management 'flexibility' in the US to capriciously hire, reassign and fire employees has emboldened commercial interests to 'inappropriately induce reversal or withdrawal of scientific conclusions' through political intervention (Smith, 2005). It is no surprise, then, that personnel at the Defense Department believe that reforms 'give managers too much authority to adjust salaries and change work assignments, strip workers of basic rights and protections, and will destroy morale' (Kauffman, 2005a: 11). Not unexpectedly, there has been an increase in blatant retaliation against military officers, Medicare experts, climate change scientists, procurement professionals, public health physicians, and other administrators who question the suppression or manipulation of public information (*New York Times*, 1 September 2005).

Officials already face difficult circumstances in determining what might be appropriate behavior in today's public service. The civil service reform movement adds to these challenges by emphasizing managerialism at the expense of employee protections. Corporate monetary incentives like pay-for-performance, for example, can easily be used to reward political loyalty. Radical reform, writes George Frederickson, 'will almost certainly result in less ethical government' (1997: 194). Over time, the public service ethos – the ideal of a politically neutral, expert, permanently staffed civil service devoted to the greater good – will surely wane. The blurring of boundaries, which produces many different types of public servants in various sectors of the economy, has been corrosive to such an ethos. More and more employees, 'seeing no evil', will not 'speak truth to power' when witnessing pernicious activities that put the public interest at risk (Roehling, 2003).

Meaningful work supports the dignity of human beings as moral agents (Bowie, 1998) through management that strengthens – not weakens – rational capacities and moral development. An organization that imposes unilateral, autocratic work practices like unjust dismissals that lack accountability is inconsistent with democratic norms. Indeed, the doctrine is reminiscent of the Soviet management command-and-control system that compelled obedience and suppressed participation (Radin and

Werhane, 1996). As civil service reformers and their ideal of a corporate-run state spreads, the human resource management problems in demo-cracies will intensify. The idea seems to be, writes Jonathan Walters (2001), 'that if you can fire people with impunity, and reward or punish them with pay, then public servants will be whipped into shape just like employees at all those corporations that have been mired in corruption and/or lost market share in recent years'.

The controversy over civil service reform is not about better services for citizens at less cost; changes such as terminating tenure have less to do with their validity than with the political power of the dominant party that establishes them. Since there is little evidence of a business case for reform, advocates seldom consider the dysfunctional impacts of change or include evaluative mechanisms in reform. What seems to be more important is that simplistic changes are politically popular and divert citizen attention from substantive issues.

Using heroic assumptions about the transformatory character of public management, Pollitt and Bouckaert point out NPM proponents have sought to redefine policy weakness as managerial failure (2004: 157). The irony is that political officials may claim that the problem is the adminis-trative system, but the citizenry believes that it is the political system, and holds elected representatives responsible. In fact, voters seem to care less about management and more about the failure of leaders to uphold ethical standards. If so, the authors continue, reforms – absent any effort to enhance the recruitment, training and integrity of politicians – are unlikely to contribute much to public confidence in government. And, given the difficulty in evaluating NPM reforms, it is doubtful that the benefits gained in selected new administrative procedures can be expanded to sweeping assertions of better government overall. Indeed, not only may management changes fall short of hoped-for benefits, but they may produce effects that render processes worse than before (Pollitt and Bouckaert, 2004, Chapter 1).

The real questions, then, that the civil service reform debate raises are, 'which bureaucracy, operated in whose interests, with what capacity, and held accountable to democratic values in what way?' (Durant, 2001: 6). The decisions made in response to these concerns will be critical for the quality of the world's democracies in the years ahead. Reforms such as removing job security and instituting performance pay encourage raw political decis-ions at the expense of neutral competence in public service. The United Nations Convention Against Corruption requires that the public service be based on merit and equity. If the critique of civil service reform in these pages is correct, then at some distant point in the future, a new movement will emerge to restore ethics and integrity in government.

## ACKNOWLEDGMENTS

The authors would like to thank Mark Jeffery, Universitat de Catalunya Barcelona, Spain, for helpful suggestions on selected parts of the paper, portions of which are incorporated here, and Herman Siebens, Flemish Network for Business Ethics, for comments on the overall manuscript. Our gratitude does not imply that they endorse the interpretations here. Appreciation is also expressed to Shreya Agrawal for her assistance.

## NOTES

1. As Green *et al.* (2006) point out, there are few systematic data on ethics and civil service reform. Little attention is devoted to the topic in Cooper's (2001) authoritative examination of administrative ethics. Menzel's (2005) literature review of ethics and integrity in governance also found that the subject is seldom addressed in public affairs journals. In the civil service reform literature, ethics is not a central concern in the United States (Kellough and Nigro, 2006) or Europe (Lawton and Doig, 2006).
2. The book contains 12 descriptive country profiles in an appendix that forms the basis for the analysis in the body of the work.
3. In any case, overall pay levels would have to change if a public employer does not offer job protection against arbitrary dismissal (for example, 'Someone might as well work for business for more money as there is no security in government,' according to an anonymous Florida state agency supervisor; personal communication, February, 2005). Yet, increasing remuneration appears to be an unrealistic expectation because most American jurisdictions have historically used a below-market compensation strategy. 'Let's not be naïve,' a union official stated, 'They (the reformers) are not going to use pay-for-performance to increase federal pay' (Kauffman and Sullivan, 2005: 6).
4. An analysis of selected reforms on the Continent is available from the authors. NPM-type reforms are evident as well in Australia, Canada and New Zealand (Committee on Economic Affairs and Development (CEAD), 2003). It also should be noted that while the American at-will doctrine is not often explicitly referred to in the European literature, the trends described in the text are consistent with the spirit of the doctrine. On dismissal policies in Europe see for example, Baker and McKenzie, 2000.

## REFERENCES

Aberbach, J. (2003), 'Protecting liberty and benefiting society: can market-based administrative reforms and market-based political institutions effectively co-exist in the US?', in T. Butcher and A. Massey (eds), *Modernizing Civil Services*, Cheltenham, UK and Northampton, MA, USA: Edward Edgar, pp. 59–73.

Baker & McKenzie (eds) (2000), *Worldwide Guide to Termination, Employment Discrimination, and Workplace Harassment Laws*, Chicago, IL: CCH Inc.

Barr, S. (2005a), 'Name that civil service proposal: if its not "pay for performance", what is it?', *Washington Post*, 13 June, p. B2.

Barr, S. (2005b), 'Workers speculate on challenges of performance-based pay', *Washington Post*, 25 July, p. B2.

Barr, S. (2005c), 'On pay for performance, rank and file workers speak out anonymously', *Washington Post*, 9 August, p. B2.

Bebchuk, L. and J. Fried (2004), *Pay Without Performance*, Cambridge, MA: Harvard University Press.

Berman, E., J. Bowman, J. West and M. Van Wart (2005), *Human Resource Management in Public Service: Paradoxes, Problems, and Processes*, 2nd edn, Thousand Oaks, CA: Sage.

Bogdanor, V. (2001), 'Civil service reform: a critique', *The Political Quarterly*, **73** (3), 291–9.

Bohnet, I. and S. Eaton (2003), 'Does performance pay perform? Conditions for success in the public sector', in J. Donahue and J. Nye, Jr. (eds), *For the People: Can We Fix the Public Service?*, Washington, DC: Brookings, pp. 238–54.

Bowie, N. (1998), 'A Kantian theory of meaningful work', *Journal of Business Ethics*, **17**, 1083–92.

Committee on Economic Affairs and Development (CEAD) (2003), 'Civil service reform in Europe', report of the Committee on Economic Affairs and Development, Council of Europe, Parliamentary Assembly document 9711, 19 February, retrieved 28 February 2005, accessed at http://assembly.coe.int/Documents/Workingdocs/doc03/EDOC9711.htm.

Condrey, S. and R. Maranto (eds) (2001), *Radical Reform of the Civil Service*, New York: Lexington Books.

Cooper, T. (2001), *Handbook of Administrative Ethics*, 2nd edn, New York: Dekker.

Coyle-Shapiro, J. and I. Kessler (2003), 'The employment relationship in the UK public sector: a psychological contract perspective', *Journal of Public Administration Research and Theory*, **13** (2), 213–30.

Dillman, D. (2005), 'Deconstructing boundaries: the journey from next steps to delivery and values in the senior civil service', paper presented at the Ethics and Integrity of Governance Conference, 2–5 June, Leuven, Belgium.

Doig, A. and J. Wilson (1995), 'Untangling the threads', in F. Ridley, and A. Doig (eds), *Sleaze: Politicians, Private Interests and Public Reaction*, Oxford: Oxford University Press, pp. 14–30.

Durant, R. (2001), 'Politics, paradox, and the "ecology" of public administration: challenges, choices, and opportunities for a new century', in T. Liou (ed.), *Handbook of Public Management Practice and Reform*, New York: Marcel Dekker, pp. 1–31.

Epstein, R. and S. Rosen (1984), 'In defense of contract at will', *University of Chicago Law Review*, **51** (4), 947–88.

Ferlie, E., L. Ashburner and A. Petrigrew (1996), *The New Public Management in Action*, Oxford: Oxford University Press.

Frederickson, G. (1997), *The Spirit of Public Administration*, San Francisco, CA: Jossey-Bass.

Green, R., A. Golden, R. Forbis, S. Nelson and J. Robinson (2006), 'On the ethics of at-will employment relations in the public sector', *Public Integrity*, **8** (4), 305–28.

Hays, S. and J. Sowa (2006), 'A broader look at the "accountability" movement: some grim realities in state civil service systems', *Review of Public Personnel Administration*, **26** (2), 102–17.

Hogler, R. (2004), *Employment Relations in the United States*, Thousand Oaks, CA: Sage.

Hood, C. (1991), 'A public management for all seasons', *Public Administration*, **69** (1), 3–19.

Ingraham, P. (1995), *The Foundation of Merit: Public Service in American Democracy*, Baltimore, MD: Johns Hopkins University Press.

Kauffman, T. (2005a), 'Employees blast proposed personnel policy changes', *Federal Times*, 16 May, 11.

Kauffman, T. (2005b), 'New spin on reform: OMB backs off on union curbs, stresses market pay', *Federal Times*, 25 July, 1.

Kauffman, T. and E. Sullivan (2005), 'The future of civil service reform', *Federal Times*, 31 January, 1, 6, 7.

Kellough, J. and L. Nigro (eds) (2006), *Civil Service Reform in the States*, Albany, NY: SUNY Press.

Lan, Z. and D. Rosenbloom (1992), 'Editorial', *Public Administration Review*, **52** (6) 535–7.

Lane, L., J. Wolf and C. Woodard (2003), 'Reassessing the human resource crisis in the public service', *American Review of Public Administration*, **33** (2), 123–45.

Lawton, A. (1998), *Ethical Management for the Public Services*, Buckingham: Open University Press.

Lawton, A. and A. Doig (2006), 'Research ethics for public sector organizations: the view from Europe', *Public Integrity*, **8** (1), 11–34.

Lee, C. (2005), 'Bush aims to expand system of merit pay', *Washington Post*, 19 July, A2.

Menzel, D. (2005), 'Research on ethics and integrity in governance: a review and assessment', *Public Integrity*, **7** (2)(Spring), 147–68.

Milkovich, C. and A. Wigdor (1991), *Pay for Performance: Evaluating Performance Appraisal and Merit Pay*, Washington, DC: National Academy Press.

Morriss, A. (1994), 'Exploding myths: an empirical and economic reassessment of the rise of employment at-will', *Missouri Law Review*, **59**, 679–773.

Newmark, S. and C. O'Brien (2000), 'United Kingdom', in Baker & McKenzie (eds), *Worldwide Guide to Termination, Employment Discrimination, and Workplace Harassment Laws*, Chicago, IL: CCH Inc., pp. 291–301.

*New York Times* (2005), 'Banished whistleblowers', 1 September, accessed 1 December from www.whistleblowers.org/Banished_Whistle-Blowers_-_New_York_Times.htm.

Osborne, D. and T. Gaebler (1992), *Reinventing Government: How the Entrepreneurial Spirit is Transforming the Public Sector*, Reading, MA: Addison-Wesley.

Osborne, D. and P. Plastrik (1997), *Banishing Bureaucracy*, Reading, MA: Addison-Wesley.

Pilkington, C. (1999), *The Civil Service in Britain Today*, Manchester: University of Manchester Press.

Pollitt, C. (1990), *Managerialism and the Public Service*, Cambridge: Basil Blackwell.

Pollitt, C. and G. Bouckaert (2004), *Public Management Reform: A Comparative Analysis*, 2nd edn, Oxford: Oxford University Press.

Radin, T. and P. Werhane (1996), 'The public/private distinction and the political status of employment', *American Business Law Journal*, **43** (2), 245–60.

Roehling, M. (2003), The employment at-will doctrine: second level ethical issues and analysis, *Journal of Business Ethics*, **47** (2), 115–24.

Ridley, F. and A. Doig (eds) (1995), *Sleaze: Politicians, Private Interests and Public Reaction*, Oxford: Oxford University Press.

Rosenbloom, D. (1998), *Public Administration: Understanding Management, Politics and Law in the Public Sector*, New York: McGraw-Hill.

Rutzick, K. (2005a), 'OPM chief advises agencies to prepare well for personnel reforms', GovExe.com Daily Briefing, 26 July, accessed 26 July at www.govexe.com/.

Rutzick, K. (2005b), 'Report outline lessons of GAO personnel reform', GovExe.com Daily Briefing, 2 August, accessed 2 August at www.govexe.com/.

Schlesinger, A. (1986), *Cycles of American History*, Boston, MA: Houghton-Mifflin.

Schultz, D. and R. Maranto (1998), *Politics of Civil Service Reform*, New York: Lang.

Shim, D. (2001), 'Recent human resources developments in OECD member countries', *Public Personnel Management*, **30** (3), 323–47.

Smith, D. (2005), 'Political science', *New York Times Sunday Magazine*, 4 September, accessed 4 September from www.nytimes.com.

Stone, K. (2004), 'Change at work: implications for labor law', *Cornell Journal of Law and Public Policy*, **13** (3) (Summer), 563–80.

Suleiman, E. (2003), *Dismantling Democratic States*, Princeton, NJ: Princeton University Press.

Toonen, A.J. and J.C. Raadschelders (1997), *Public Sector Reform in Western Europe*, accessed at www.indiana.edu/~csrc/toonen1.html.

United States Office of Personnel Management (1992), *Final Report of the Joint Labor-Management Committee on Pay for Performance*, Washington, DC: The Office of Personnel Management.

Walters, J. (2001), 'Civil disservice', 17 May, accessed 17 February 2005 at www.Governing.com.

Walters, J. (2002), *Life After Civil Service Reform: The Texas, Georgia, and Florida Experiences*, Arlington, VA: IBM Endowment for the Business of Government.

Werhane, P., T. Radin and N. Bowie (2004), *Employment and Employee Rights*, Malden, MA: Blackwell Publishing.

# 12. In defence of politicking: private, personal and public interests

**Robert P. Kaye**

## INTRODUCTION

In the 1990s the British political system experienced profound ethical change. Prompted by concerns about the behavior of backbench MPs, political appointments to quangos, and the revolving door between government and private industry, the Government appointed a specialist Committee on Standards in Public Life (CSPL), initially under Lord Nolan, which set about examining – and reforming – areas of government that gave rise to concerns over public integrity. Nolan was not an attempt to start from first principles. Its reforms were designed to work within the framework of institutional opinion. Nonetheless the ensuing reforms were not immune to an 'ethics backlash'. Just as writers such as Anechiarico and Jacobs (1996) and Mackenzie and Hafken (2002) have pointed to ways in which ethics measures can act antithetically to good government and stymie public administration, so in the last three to four years post-Nolan reforms[1] have been criticized as excessive, burdensome, disproportionate, outmoded, irrelevant – a critique that has resulted in a rolling back of the ethics regime for Members of Parliament and a CSPL report on 'getting the balance right' in the rules for local councillors and public appointments.

This chapter uses examples from the new ethics regimes in British local government and the House of Commons in an attempt to provide a more theoretical understanding of the limits of public integrity policies. By concentrating on institutions with legislative functions, the cases bring into sharp focus the potential clash between public integrity and democratic representation; between independence and neutrality; and between public administration and politics.

In particular, it suggests that a neat distinction between private and public interests is singularly unhelpful. Ethics regulation needs to recognize that the 'unencumbered official' is illusory, that interests may cohere as well as conflict, that there is no single 'public interest' but different 'publics', and hence a variety of 'public interests' which must compete within a political system.

I start by examining the idea of 'encumbrance', arguing that elected officials will inevitably possess a variety of 'interests' (broadly defined) that are unique to them as individuals; some will be relatively personal to the individual, some will be widely shared. Some will be relatively selfish, others broadly altruistic. Since these 'interests' fall along a continuum, it is not even theoretically possible to conceive of the 'unencumbered legislator'. Furthermore, I argue, this continuum highlights the absence of a clear 'public interest'. I then highlight some cases where 'public interests' have been treated as encumbrances and examine the extent to which to do so involves intolerable intrusions into democratic accountability. I suggest that the answer is to avoid a 'compliance-based' approach which seeks to distinguish between permissible and impermissible conflicts and activities, and instead to adopt a system of regulation in which interests are pro-actively managed using a range of tools, strategies and regimes.

## CORRUPTION, CONFLICT OF INTEREST AND THE MYTH OF THE UNENCUMBERED LEGISLATOR

I assume for the purpose of this chapter that 'ethics measures' are imposed in order to counter a number of potential problems that arise from what is loosely termed 'conflict of interest':

1.  Outright corruption in which a public office is abused for personal profit (although in truth simple ethics regulation can do little against the most egregious forms of corruption).
2.  'Gray' forms of corruption (Heidenheimer, 1978) in which officials subvert the official duties out of personal interest or other 'private-regarding' considerations (Nye, 1967).[2]
3.  Unconscious but nonetheless impermissible influence on the actions of legislators and officials caused by conflicts of interest (Stark, 2000: 36–59; Thompson, 1987: 111–16).

At the same time, it should be recognized that there is an empirical problem in ascertaining whether an official has been motivated by an improper interest; we have no way of observing how the official would have behaved absent that interest. For this reason it is usually considered legitimate to control both conflict of interest and the appearance of impropriety, regardless of whether that interest actually does exercise an impermissible influence over the official. Philp (2001: 358-9) defines political corruption as follows:

> *Core* cases of corruption [emphasis added] involve four key components:
> – an official (A), who, acting for personal gain,
> – violates the norms of public office, and
> – harms the interests of the public (B)
> – to benefit a third party (C) who rewards A for access to goods or services which C would not otherwise obtain.

This is essentially bribery. But corruption may occur in a variety of ways. Although Philp's definition would include both regular bribes proffered, and extortive bribes (or 'facilitation payments') demanded by officials, it would not include some other situations in which public office was abused for personal gain, what Key (1936) refers to as graft. For instance, some corruption scenarios, such as misappropriation or abuse of confidential information to make a profit do not require a third party.

More satisfactory may be Johnston's (1997: 62) definition of corruption as 'the abuse of public roles or resources or the use of illegitimate forms of political influence by public or private parties'. Johnston acknowledges that the word, 'abuse', 'illegitimate', 'public' and 'private' all need unpacking.

However, when unpacked the idea of 'private' interests (or influences) is an elastic concept. Nye (1967) points out that 'private-regarding' considerations might include the interests of one's own family or small cliques. The operation of government in the interests of a particular sector, group, sector or tribe might constitute corruption. At one extreme, one can argue that 'pork-barrelling', subverting the wider national interest to parochial concerns is a form of institutionalized corruption. But with each stage, we move further from direct private benefit; and with each it becomes more arguable that the official was acting for 'the public'. An element of self-interest never goes away, but likewise only the most maladjusted of politicians will act without any regard to the position of others.

One could think, therefore, of a series of 'interests' radiating outwards from an official:

(a)   private, personal gratification;
(b)   dependent family (spouse, dependent children, siblings or parents);
(c)   other family;
(d)   friends;
(e)   social groups and societies;
(f )   political parties;
(g)   community and supported interest groups;

(h)	constituency; and
(i)	'causes'.

All of these might have a bearing on the actions of an official. Where exactly, is the line to be drawn between legitimate and illegitimate sources of influence?

This dilemma becomes more profound if it is accepted that there is no single 'public interest'. The Third Report of the CSPL (on local government) talks of membership of lobbying groups as public interests (plural).

A councillor may also be involved with a particular interest group, or may be concerned with a particular cause. A councillor may well take a particular standpoint on an issue that divides the community . . .

In such situations, even though the councillor has direct contacts with organizations, the interest is a public interest, not a private one.

That is to say, Nolan draws the public/private distinction somewhere above (h) in the list at the beginning of this section. Implicitly, he rejects the idea of a single 'public interest'. If we do so, it seems that the public interest must be recast as the product of a well-functioning political process; not as the aim of it.

With the notions of public and private interest blurred, there is scope for much greater disagreement and uncertainty as to the conditions in which an action might be said to be improper. Consider the following scenarios:

### 'Westminster Homes for Votes'

Porter was the Conservative party leader of Westminster council. Along with a group of Conservative colleagues, she formulated a strategy of shoring up political support for the party by targeting the forced sale of council houses at marginal constituencies. These homes were sold at a considerable (and legitimate) discount. In 1996 the District Auditor concluded that the policy was illegal and that Porter and five other councillors were liable for the resulting losses – £27 million. The issue with which the appeal courts had to grapple was this: is a political decision unlawful because it is pursued for party advantage; does it, in fact, legitimate a political decision that those involved believed it would reap political advantage; or does the truth lie somewhere in between?

### The Skateboard Park

A councillor took part in decisions relating to proposals to build a new skateboard park. His mother led the campaign against the skateboard park. However, she did so as a 'public-spirited campaigner' and had no personal, private interest in the proposal. The Standards Board, which investigated local government behavior, held that the son had broken the Code of Conduct by not withdrawing. The issue for the adjudicating tribunal was whether the mother's involvement amounted to an interest on the part of the councillor, and if so, whether it was 'prejudicial' and, thus, requiring the councillor to withdraw.

**The McConnell Case**

In 2002, the Parliamentary Commissioner for Standards, who investigates complaints about the ethical conduct of Members of Parliament, received a complaint from a Labour MP, John McConnell. McConnell said:

> Since 1999 I have opposed . . . the City of London (Ward Elections) Bill . . . [T]he promoter of the Bill in the Commons invited me to meet him and representatives from the City Corporation to discuss amendments to the Bill . . .
> [The promoter] stated that if I dropped my opposition to the . . . Bill it would enable him to obtain for me a place on the [Northern Ireland] Committee.[3]

Although the Commissioner found the facts as alleged unproven, he would otherwise have had to come to a conclusion on whether this amounted to the offer of an improper advantage to a member.

None of these cases, however, rests on a clash between the politician's representative duties and direct, private, personal, pecuniary advantage. The situation was far more complicated, involving questions of mixed motivation, procedural propriety and conflicting public or quasi-public interests. In the following sections I want to discuss the difficulties of trying to incorporate three potential sources of influence as 'interests' within an integrity regime: 'electoral' and constituency 'interests'; tradable political positions; and causes, preferences and other 'biases'.

# ELECTORAL 'INTERESTS'

Electing officials is not a neutral act with regard to circumstances involving conflict of interest. On the one hand, electing officials may help resolve or reduce the potential for officials to be influenced by private interests. Some writers have suggested that a communion of interests is necessary for effective representative government (Madison, 2006 [1788]; Burke, 1792). Some also take this as an argument for an official having private personal interests which reflect those of their constituency or constituents. However, electing, and in particular re-electing, officials obviates the need for this. Ideally, election creates a communion of interests between officials and their constituents. Realistically, this relationship is blurred by factors such as the electoral system, the cultivation of swing voters, and so on. The electoral system may not perfectly aggregate voters' interests. But it is likely to do so at least as well as hoping for an advocacy representative.

However, depending on the normative basis of the political system, considerations such as electoral advantage and the interests of one's constituents might be considered as improper influences. Degenerate forms of legitimate concern might include clientelism and pork-barrelling.

In the UK, the balance between national and constituency interests is left undefined. The Code of Conduct for MPs recognizes the Members' 'special duty to their constituents'. Presumably these various constituency interests can be aggregated at the collective level. As one Speaker of the House of Commons put it, 'this place is all about interests'; while Reeve and Ware (1991) note that geographical constituency boundaries have often been drawn specifically in order to represent particular sectoral interests. However, when a House of Commons committee considers private legislation, usually relating to a specific organization or promulgated on behalf of a particular authority, MPs are required to declare that neither they nor their constituents have any special interest in the legislation.

For the most part, the House of Commons however allows an exemption for constituency interests from conflict of interest rules:

> Irrespective of any relevant interest which the Member is required to register or declare, he or she may pursue any constituency interest in any proceeding of the House or any approach to a Minister or servant of the Crown, except that: where the Member has a financial relationship with a company in the Member's constituency the [usual rules applying to companies] shall apply.[4]

The 'flip-side' of seeing election as creating a communion of interests between representative and constituents is that local interests become personal interests. This creates a tension between democratic pressures for representation of local interests and public integrity pressures for disinterested decision-making. As Thompson (1987: 113) puts it, 'representation does not readily accommodate autonomy'. This tension is also evident in the words of Nick Grenier, cited by Philp (1997: 437), who was acquitted of corruption offenses in Australia after apparently appointing an MP to a public office as an act of patronage:

> Under the English common law very serious obligations to act in the public interest are placed on those elected to public office, and yet our highest public officials are at the same time, part of a political system which is about what is in many ways a largely private interest in terms of winning or holding a seat.

The 'integrity' position involved, here, however needs unpacking. It has become detached from concerns about conflict of interest, and instead attached to a more general concern with 'neutrality'. It certainly cannot be based on the notion of conflict of interest, because the public and private interests in question are the same. This is not a mere coincidence: it is not just a shared interest between representative and constituency; it is a common interest. (One possible analogy might be to think of the difference between two people who own shares in a company, and a married couple owning property jointly.)

The *Westminster Homes for Votes* case is illustrative here because it seemed at times to be suggested that it was improper for councillors to allow electoral considerations to play a part in their decision-making. This was something of a red herring, but seemed to occupy an amount of the judges' attention as the case first went to the Divisional Court, which upheld the auditor's conclusions, was overturned in the Court of Appeal, and was finally reinstated in the House of Lords.[5] Kennedy J for instance, argued:

> Some of the submissions advanced on behalf of the auditor have been framed in such a way as to suggest that any councillor who allows the possibility of electoral advantage even to cross his mind before he decides upon a course of action is guilty of misconduct. That seems to me to be unreal. In . . . politics many if not most decisions carry an electoral price tag, and all politicians are aware of it.[6]

Schiemann LJ was somewhat more on target:

> It is legitimate for councillors to desire that their party should win the next election. Our political system works on the basis that they desire that because they think that the policies to which their party is wedded are in the public interest . . . There is nothing disgraceful or unlawful in councillors having that desire . . . [T]o hold otherwise would depart from our theory of democracy and current reality.[7]

For Schiemann, electoral considerations merely reflect valid local considerations. The Court of Appeal therefore concluded that the Homes for Votes policy was not unlawful.

The House of Lords, however, disagreed with the Court of Appeal's approach. For instance, Lord Bingham, said:

> Elected politicians of course wish to act in a manner which will commend them and their party . . . to the electorate. Such an ambition is the life blood of democracy and a potent spur to responsible decision-taking and administration. Councillors do not act improperly or unlawfully if, exercising public powers for a public purpose for which such powers were conferred, they hope that such

exercise will earn the gratitude and support of the electorate and thus strengthen their electoral position. The law would indeed part company with the realities of party politics if it were to hold otherwise. But a public power is not exercised lawfully if it is exercised not for a public purpose for which the power was conferred but in order to promote the electoral advantage of a political party.[8]

Bingham appears to be arguing for a ranking of motivations: electoral advantage can be a subordinate but not a primary motivation.

For Lord Scott meanwhile,

there is all the difference in the world between a policy adopted for naked political advantage but spuriously justified by reference to a purpose which, had it been the true purpose, would have been legitimate, and a policy adopted for a legitimate purpose and seen to carry with it significant political advantage.[9]

Hard cases, it is said, make bad law. In this case, while paying lip service to the idea that there is nothing wrong with courting approval, the courts seemed too content to conclude that local authorities were, ultimately, officials rather than representatives. What both the Appeal Court and the House of Lords failed to grapple with was that a key consideration in the Westminster case was the nature of the impact of electoral politics. Porter, *et al.* were not pursuing the policy because they thought it would be popular, would reap votes, would therefore keep them in power and able to pursue the Conservative policies that they thought were good for Westminster. They were trying to change the composition of the electorate for electoral gain to undermine and to supplant, not to benefit, the existing electorate. Electoral considerations could not be used to justify the councillors' actions given the essentially anti-democratic nature of their policy. Porter, *et al.* realized that the interests of the constituents and the Conservative party were categorically not the same – that was precisely why they were trying to change the composition of the constituencies! They were acting as agents of the Conservative party, whose interests conflicted with those of the relevant public, thus constituting what Scott LJ rightly described as 'corruption'. But it was what Thompson (1995) described as 'institutionalized corruption' where the benefits were political, not personal. And it was what Thompson (1993) and Johnston (1996) describe as 'mediated corruption' – the 'short-circuiting [of] an open, accountable democratic process' (Johnston, 1996: 332).

At the same time, however, one assumes that Porter's motivation for retaining Tory control of Westminster was not entirely selfish; that she thought it in Westminster's interests (regardless of what Westminster residents may have thought). One could even argue she was following Burke's injunction, 'Your representative owes you . . . his judgement . . . and he betrays [you] if he sacrifices it to your opinion' Burke (1854) [1774].

Unfortunately, by allowing the issue to be turned into one of conflict versus communion of interest, the courts established judgments which seemed to imply that one could have regard to party considerations, so long as they weren't paramount (theoretically questionable), when the real issue was whether party interests were – in a particular case – really an illegitimate sectoral interest, or a legitimate means of divining a public interest.

## HORSE-TRADING, MIXED MOTIVATIONS AND THE AGGREGATION OF INTERESTS

A further difficulty in the Westminster case, however, was what Thompson (1987: 11–69) calls the problem of many hands. Legislatures are collective bodies, composed of individuals with varied motivations. In Westminster, some of those who initiated the policy, and knew its partisan motivation, were not on the committee that formally implemented it, and most of those who were on that committee did not know of its origin. As Lord Scott observed.

> There were twelve members of the housing committee. Seven of them voted in favour . . . Five voted against. Of the seven, two . . . were found guilty of misconduct by the auditor . . . As for the other five . . . who voted in favour of the resolution, they so voted because the resolution was Conservative party policy. They did not know that the purpose of the resolution was to obtain electoral advantage in the eight key wards.[10]

Scott LJ went on to describe the votes of the five as 'valid' – overturning previous findings which had viewed them as tainted by the partisan considerations contributing to their becoming party policy.[11] Likewise Schiemann LJ noted:

> A vast number of decisions come before local authorities at each meeting and it is simply not practicable for each councillor to have examined the merits of each decision. In practice the immediate motivation of the councillors voting for it will often be that the proposal has the support of members of their party some of whom will have carefully considered the merits of the proposal in the light of general values which a particular councillor member of that party will broadly share.[12]

This problem of mixed motivations is not just theoretical. It is a real consideration because there comes a point where it might be difficult to disentangle legitimate aggregation of interests from improper pressures. Politicians inevitably have mixed motivations: on a particular issue, some will likely be considering the issue in isolation, some will be following a party line, some will be accepting some form of political compromise or deal – and most will be aggregating a number of these considerations. This mixed model of representation means that a single model of legislative ethics is not possible.

The issue of 'horse-trading' came to the attention of the Courts in the *Westminster* case, where it was given tacit acceptance. The quote from Schiemann above continues:

> [C]ouncillor A will frequently vote for the sewage scheme proposed by his party or by councillor B because councillor A wishes to persuade his party and councillor B to vote for councillor A's education proposal.[13]

A theoretical model of legislative ethics which blindly assumes every official takes every decision 'on the merits' (see Bauer, 1996, for a discussion of 'the merits') in isolation from all other decisions and extraneous considerations is frankly unrealistic. Political decisions invariably have wider consequences, for example, vote for the sewage scheme, and there will be less in the budget for the education policy. Political interaction, compromise and trading are necessary components of the aggregation of interests. Thompson (1987: 113) acknowledges that 'legislators could still trade votes on legislation they think less important in order to win passage of legislation they think more important – but only if such logrolling did not prevent consideration of the more important measures on their merits'.

The danger is that such horse-trading becomes log-rolling and pork-barrelling: the type of activity Thompson has in his sights in *Ethics in Congress* (Thompson, 1995) and legitimate behavior will fall into institutional corruption. Thompson argues, similar to the judges in the *Westminster* case, that a necessary component in identifying institutional corruption is procedural impropriety. The difficulty is that it is not always clear what constitutes legitimate versus illegitimate considerations and, consequently, determining what may be legitimately traded?

This issue was played out in the *McConnell* case. As noted, the Parliamentary Commissioner for Standards found McConnell's allegations unproven. Assume, however, that the Chairman of the Select Committee had made an offer of a committee position explicitly conditional on McConnell dropping his opposition to the Chairman's bill. The Commissioner chose to approach the case under a 'catch-all' provision of the Code of Conduct requiring that MPs do nothing that would bring the House into disrepute. But he also noted that 'as the Code in addition provides that Members shall not accept any reward in connection with the promotion of, or opposition to, any Bill, it might also be argued that no Member should offer another Member such a consideration'.[14]

The offer is fascinatingly ambiguous. To begin with, it demonstrates the difficulty of disentangling personal and political considerations. Was the inducement the private, personal advantage of a seat on the committee in question? If the offer of a position on the Northern Ireland Committee is taken as a purely personal inducement to the MP then it might be seen as corrupt. But as the quotation from the MP makes clear, the value for the MP was the political value that lay in being able to influence Northern Irish affairs. Unless an MP is politically interested in a matter, committee membership is often thought of as a chore. 'Horse trading' therefore falls into a morally ambiguous gray area in which legitimate, public policy trade offs segue into self-serving inducements.

But even if the inducement was political, was it wrong for the bill's promoter to link the two issues? There was, on the face of it, no reason why the membership of the Northern Ireland committee had any bearing on elections to the Corporation of London. From an administrative point of view, Northern Ireland had no relevance to the City of London Elections bill, and therefore to mix the two involved irrelevant considerations, illegitimate reasons and hence a decision 'not on the merits'. However, from a political point of view, such horse-trading is simply the stuff of politics, without which a parliament cannot perform its essential function of aggregating interests. The practice may be somewhat unedifying and slightly distasteful, but it might also be argued that a legislature cannot operate without it. British politics sees nothing wrong with party managers using patronage as a tool of political loyalty. Indeed, the Ministerial Code – which governs the ethical behavior of ministers – compels a minister to resign if s/he votes against the Government's policy. Had the Commissioner upheld the McConnell complaint, it could have been argued that the Government was constantly in contempt of parliament.

Crucial to an understanding of the case, is to realize that had the proposal been agreed upon, McConnell would have been able to pursue his interests on the Northern Ireland Committee, which presumably he would have considered more important than blocking the bill, while the other MP would have gotten his bill through, which presumably he considered more important than blocking McConnell. To all concerned it would, in public policy terms, have been a more optimal position. These various interests would have been aggregated, one of the core functions of a legislature.

## PREJUDGMENT AS BIAS

Perhaps the most tangible threat to representative forces from avowedly ethical measures comes from Common Law rules against bias applicable to local councillors. These precede the new ethical environment.

In British administrative law, bias can involve not only cases of actual or apparent bias arising from personal gain, but also from prejudgment. Subsumed within the leading authority on bias, '*Locabail*',[15] was *Timmins v Gormley*[16] in which the defendant of a claim for negligence successfully argued that the judge in that case should have disqualified himself because he had published articles in which he had consistently supported claimants in personal injury cases, and written in trenchant terms against defendants and their insurers.

Similar constraints apply in local government – and they are especially problematic when applied to councillors who are involved in political lobbying groups. The difficulty arises from two conflicting principles. As the Standards Board for England (2004, pp. 2–3) acknowledges, 'It would be wholly unreasonable to expect [councillors] to be devoid of general views about a range of local issues. In fact, [they] may well have been elected because of [their] views on those issues'. At the same time it advises councillors, 'your statements and activities should not create the impression that your views on a matter are fixed, and that you will not fairly consider the evidence or arguments presented to you when you are making a decision' (ibid., p. 3).

Here, one should turn to the Third Nolan Report which prompted the creation of the new ethics regime in local government. As noted previously, Nolan refers to lobbying organizations, and so on, as public interests – that is to say, he draws the public/private distinction somewhere above (h), referring to the list on p. 199.

> A councillor may also be involved with a particular interest group, or may be concerned with a particular cause. A councillor may well take a particular standpoint on an issue that divides the community . . .
> 　　In such situations, even though the councillor has direct contacts with organizations, the interest is *a public interest* [emphasis added], not a private one. The important principle is that everyone concerned should know that the councillor approaches the matter from a particular standpoint, so that his involvement with discussions and decisions can be weighed by colleagues, the press and the public, against that background.

It is argued here that Nolan's approach is more realistic than that of the courts. Different conceptions of the public interest exist and the place for those interests to compete is at the ballot box. Such attitudes are not 'private interests' opposed to the public interest, rather, they reflect the individual politician's conception of the public interest. That is, they are 'constitutive of his subjective capacity for political judgment, not [. . .] an encumbrance' (Stark, 2000: 253).

Guidance from the Standards Board highlights the problems that impartiality requirements place on politicians.

Campaigning about a particular issue does not, in our view, indicate a possibility that you will not fairly consider the evidence and arguments presented. Simply approaching the issue from a particular point of view does not make an interest prejudicial. This is particularly relevant to budget issues and matters of broad policy . . . [I]t is highly unlikely that campaigning on issues of this kind will amount to a prejudicial interest. One may need to consider policy decisions and their implementation more carefully. Here, specific decisions are being made about specific places, individuals and organizations.

   . . . [Y]ou should adopt a particularly cautious approach to planning and licensing matters. Membership of a group that campaigns for or against a particular planning or licensing application may well constitute a prejudicial interest. You should avoid committing yourself on any matter that may fall to be decided by you as a member of a planning or licensing committee. (Standards Board, 2004: 4–5)

This guidance is unfortunate and may be driven as much by an attempt to 'judge-proof' decisions as to ensure ethical behavior. The Board has conflated the rules on bias and remaining free of prejudice with the rules on interests, which may become so significant as to be prejudicial. The two sources of prejudice (prejudgment and personal interest) are separate, but the Board appears to have 'read backwards' and concluded that if a councillor is prejudiced (or a well-informed member of the public might reasonably think so), then they must have a personal interest. But even if such biases are, as Stark (2000: 148–51) suggests 'self-generated encumbrances', they are very different from the sorts of interest that give rise to conflict of interest concerns.

Moreover, in making sure that councillors retain an open mind, one may undermine the value attached to campaigning; one may also undermine the value attached to electing officials if, once in power, the very fact that they have been elected to pursue a policy is an obstacle to them pursuing that policy. Consider a real-life scenario from the Standards Board:

If you were a vocal member of the *No More Incinerators* group, and sat on a planning committee to determine an application for a new incinerator, you would have a personal and prejudicial interest in the matter.

One might equally argue that if you were a vocal member of *No More Incinerators*, had been elected on that platform, and had been appointed to the planning committee by your colleagues on that basis, it would be invidious to prevent you from participating on that basis. Your opposition to incinerators does not represent a 'private' interest, it represents your view of the public interest and no problems of conflict of interest thus arise.

The point is that local councils are not simple administrative units – as the 'decision-maker' approach of the courts would have it. They are very deliberately democratic bodies – their members are elected, and represent local interests.

Surprisingly, the Board also suggests

> if you made a particular issue a centrepiece of your election campaign, or were elected on the basis of a single-issue campaign, but are not a member of a related lobby group, you will not have a personal or prejudicial interest under the Code of Conduct. However, you still need to consider whether you are genuinely open to persuasion about the matter. (Standards Board, 2004: 9)

It would appear that membership of the group, not the individual's own opinion, is determinative of whether the individual is genuinely open-minded. But this is frankly ridiculous: one is no more nor less prejudiced because one is a member of *No More Incinerators* than if one's election slogan was 'No More Incinerators'. Being a member of a group is neither here nor there – except that membership of a group is an 'interest' under the Code of Conduct, whereas campaign slogans are not.

If treating positions as interests is questionable, the problem is exacerbated in the 'skateboard' scenario, where the Board tried to argue that the councillor's mother's 'interest' as an objector, amounted to a 'family' interest extending to the councillor. There was a strong case for saying that the fact that the lead campaigner was one councillor's mother was relevant, and a potential source of influence, and should have been declared. She did not have a direct, financial interest; nor did it affect her personal well-being. As the adjudicating tribunal found, if she did not have an interest, then neither could her son. Problematically, however, the Board had tried to argue that the mother had an interest because she would want her campaign to be successful, therefore success would affect her well-being. As the tribunal noted, any position to which a person became publicly committed would therefore constitute an 'interest'. The clerk advising the planning committee in question had gone further – advising that any councillor who had been lobbied should withdraw. Apart from circumscribing participation to an impractical extent, such a stance would turn 'autonomy' into 'decision making in a vacuum'; and risk removing vital political activity from political decision-making.

Treating political positions as encumbrances becomes even more perverse when confronted with 'dual-hatted members', that is, those who sit on more than one body. (In local government this may happen because one body nominates members of another.) In many countries, such 'incompatibilities' are the basic stuff of conflict of interest legislation. What is perhaps more problematic is when such relationships are permitted but regulators attempt to squeeze them into an unsuitable ethical straitjacket.

Consider this example:

> The Code of Conduct does not automatically prevent you from considering the same issue at more than one tier of local government, including speaking and voting in both tiers . . .
>
> So, for example, if an issue comes up for discussion at both the parish and district level, and you sit on both authorities, you should:
>
> - at the parish level, make it clear that you will reconsider the matter at the district level . . .
> - at the district level, declare a personal (but not prejudicial) interest arising from your membership of the parish council which has already expressed a view on the matter, and make it clear that the parish council's view does not bind you and that you are considering the matter afresh. (Standards Board, 2004: p. 15)

This position is neat theoretically – the primacy of deliberation in both assemblies is maintained – but hardly tenable in practice. A simple statement that one will keep one's mind open is valueless: as the *Locabail* ruling concluded, such a statement is made worthless by the 'insidious nature of bias'. It is suggested here that the correct answer to the problem of dual-mandates could well be that adopted at Westminster – to ignore them. Membership of local councils and the European Parliament require disclosure but do not trigger any recusal provisions. This strikes a balance between the administrative need to ensure open, transparent decision-making, and the democratic arguments for allowing representatives to represent their constituents' interests.

## CONCLUSION

It should not be concluded from all this that imposing ethical rules on legislators is futile or counterproductive. There is a place even within the most politically charged environments for ethical rules. Nor is it the case that any restriction on the ability or choice of candidates for a particular constituency is inherently anti-democratic. To go back to Burke [1774], constituents elect not a member of Bristol but a member of Parliament – legislators exercise power generally and collectively, not locally and individually. This gives non-constituents a legitimate interest in the behavior of others' representatives. To hold otherwise would be to legitimate the worst excesses of clientelism.

However, it is suggested that conflict of interest regulation requires a finely balanced matching of risks to regulation – nuanced enough to catch most problematic behavior without embracing its counterpart, and simple enough to comprehend and implement.

In ethics discourse, compliance is often seen as the 'low road' to ethics, to be compared with the arguably softer strategies of integrity assessment. But in the regulation literature compliance is often identified with crime-control strategies that aim to eliminate or at least reduce a proscribed activity, or conversely to ensure a prescribed activity. In contrast, regulation involves 'sustained and focused control . . . over activities that are valued by a community' (Selznick, 1985). By implication those activities also give rise to concerns that necessitate regulation. In that sense, once it is recognized that 'conflict of interest' may be a necessary evil, regulation seeks to mitigate, to control, to manage but not to eliminate it.

Ethical norms must start from an understanding of legislators as individuals, what they do, and their professional and personal roles. The rules must work to augment and buttress the normative environment in which politicians work, not to counter and undermine it. In the UK both Members of Parliament and local councillors are elected. They are there to represent, to respond, to articulate and aggregate interests; they are politicians. The rules for MPs generally recognize this fact. The rules applying to local councillors, especially the archaic Common Law rules on bias, treat councillors as apolitical administrators. They set standards for local representatives that differ little from those for judges. But councillors are not judges. They are politicians and the ethics infrastructure needs to take account of their need to politick.

## NOTES

1. It should be recognized that the reforms implemented have on a number of occasions differed considerably from the CSPL's proposals.
2. Heidenheimer's distinction between 'black', 'gray' and 'white' corruption is based on elite and mass attitudes. I use the term here to refer to situations that are ethically objectionable but qualitatively and quantitatively less severe – and less 'clear cut' – than outright bribery, such financial relationships that reinforce an official's existing disposition to a particular decision; or payments designed to foster a degree of mutual obligation rather than an explicit *quid pro quo*.
3. 2001/02: HC 1147, Appendix, Annex A.
4. House of Commons, *The Code of Conduct for Members of Parliament and the Guide to the Rules*.
5. For clarification, 'the House of Lords' in this context means the Judicial Committee of the House of Lords, composed of senior British and Commonwealth judges, sitting as a court.
6. *Porter v Magill* [2000] 2WLR 1444 (CA).
7. *Porter v Magill* [2000] 2WLR 1449 (CA).
8. *Porter v Magill* [2001] UKHL 67, para. 21 (HL).
9. *Porter v Magill* [2001] UKHL 67, para. 144 (HL).
10. *Porter v Magill* [2001] UKHL 67, para. 154 (HL).
11. Porter won a pyrrhic victory on this point, pyrrhic because Scott pointed out that five valid votes would be insufficient to win without the casting vote of the Chairman, which

was tainted because he was privy to the secret policy. There was, therefore, no valid autonomous vote by the Committee to break the chain of causation between Porter and the losses caused by the policy.

12. *Porter v Magill* [2000] 2WLR (CA).
13. *Porter v Magill* [2000] 2WLR (CA).
14. 2001/02: HC 1147, Appendix, para. 4.
15. *Locabail (UK) Limited v Bayfield Properties Limited* [2000] 2WLR 870.
16. *Timmins v Gormley* [2000] 2WLR 870.

# REFERENCES

Anechiarico, F. and J.B. Jacobs (1996), *The Pursuit of Absolute Integrity: How Corruption Control Makes Government Ineffective*, Chicago, IL and London: University of Chicago Press.

Bauer, R.F. (1996), 'Professional ethics and the concept of the "merits" ', *Journal of Applied Philosophy*, **13**, 21–30.

Burke, E. (1854 [1774]), 'Address to the electors of Bristol', in E. Bohn, *The Works of the Right Honourable Edmund Burke*, vol. 1, pp. 446–8, republished in P.B. Kurland and R. Lerner (1986), *The Founders' Constitution*, ch. 13, document 7, Chicago, IL: University of Chicago Press, also accessed at http://press-pubs.uchicago.edu/founders/documents/v1ch13s7.html.

Burke, E. (1792) 'On the subject of the Roman Catholics in Ireland', letter to Sir Hercules Langrishe, accessed at www.ourcivilisation.com/smartboard/shop/burkee/extracts/chap18.htm.

Heidenheimer, A. (1978), *Political Corruption: Readings in Comparative Analysis*, Brunswick, NJ: Transaction.

Johnston, Michael (1996), 'The search for definitions: the vitality of politics and the issue of corruption', *International Social Science Journal* (English version) **149**, 321–36.

Johnston, Michael (1997), 'Private officials, public interests, and sustainable democracy: when politics and corruption meet' in K.A. Elliott, *Corruption and the Global Economy*, Washington, DC: Institute for International Economics, pp. 61–82.

Key, V.O. (1936), *The Techniques of Political Graft in the United States*, Chicago, IL: University of Chicago Press.

Mackenzie, G. Calvin and M. Hafken (2002), *Scandal Proof: Do Ethics Laws Make Government Ethical?*, Washington, DC: Brookings Institution Press.

Madison, J. (2006 [1788]), *The Federalist 57*, Atlanta, GA: Emory University School of Law.

Nye, J.S. (1967), 'Corruption and political development: a cost-benefit analysis', *American Political Science Review*, **61**(2), 417–27.

Philp, M. (1997), 'Defining political corruption', *Political Studies*, **45**, 436–62.

Philp, M. (2001), 'Access, accountability, and authority: corruption and the democratic process', *Crime, Law and Social Change*, **36** (4), 357–77.

Reeve, A. and A. Ware (1991), *Electoral Systems: A Comparative and Theoretical Introduction*, London: Routledge.

Selznick, P. (1985), 'Focusing organisational research on regulation' in R. Noll (ed.), *Regulatory Policy and the Social Sciences*, Berkeley, CA: University of California Press, pp. 363–8.

Standards Board for England (2004), *Lobby Groups, Dual-hatted Members and the Code of Conduct*, London: Standards Board for England.

Stark, A. (2000), *Conflict of Interest in American Public Life*, Cambridge, MA and London: Harvard University Press.

Thompson, D. (1987), *Political Ethics and Public Office*, Cambridge, MA and London: Harvard University Press.

Thompson, D. (1993), 'Mediated corruption: the case of the Keating Five', *American Political Science Review*, **87**(1), 369–81.

Thompson, D. (1995), *Ethics in Congress: From Individual to Institutional Corruption*, Washington, DC: Brookings Institution Press.

# 13. Perceptions of corruption as distrust? Cause and effect in attitudes toward government

**Steven Van de Walle**

## INTRODUCTION

A foreigner moves to Belgium, and needs a telephone line in his new apartment. His Belgian friends wish him good luck, telling him it will take months, unless he has some connections in the public telephone company, or knows a politician who could intervene for him. The foreigner, not being well-connected, reluctantly decides to follow the standard procedure, and visits the telephone company's office the next day. To his surprise, he is the only customer there and is able to file his application within 20 minutes, helped by a very friendly employee. One day later, his telephone is connected. His friends are amazed. Pleasantly surprised about this fast service, he goes back to the telephone company's office, taking a bottle of his native country's wine for the friendly and helpful employee, and asked the employee how comes his telephone was connected that fast, while everyone told him it would take months. The employee smiles and tells him, 'well, you know, you were the first customer in weeks following the normal procedure, and not having some local politician call us. We really appreciated that, and decided to connect your telephone right away.'

This joke, emergent from the 1980s, illustrates how political and other 'connections' have been a central element in the functioning of public services in Belgium. Belgium has had an image of being a corrupt country for a long time (Maesschalck, 2002; De Winter, 2003). A number of high-profile corruption scandals in the 1980s and 1990s has contributed to this image, and the structure of the party-political system has been a major factor in some of these cases (De Winter, 2000). Recently, however, there appears to have been a positive evolution (Van de Walle, 2004b).

In this chapter, we use a representative survey of 3168 Flemish citizens to analyse the determinants of perceptions of administrative and political corruption. We will show that citizens' perceptions of corruption are embedded in general attitudes toward government and that subjective corruption indicators may be heavily influenced by predispositions toward government, and therefore do not reflect the respondents' personal experience with corruption. Because many citizens do not have frequent personal experience with corrupt practices, the answer they give in surveys is influenced by other factors. The absence of an experiential basis allows respondents considerable freedom to take certain other attitudinal aspects into account. This creates problems of comparability and invites respondents to broaden their frame of reference to whatever factor they wish when giving an opinion on corruption. Perceptions of administrative corruption, hence, both contribute to the general attitudes toward administration and government as well as being a consequence of them (Van de Walle, 2004c).

In the first section we briefly present some of the available survey material on citizens' perception of public sector corruption in Belgium. Using data from a general survey administered in Flanders in 2003, we subsequently analyse determinants of general perceptions of corruption and unethical behavior. We show that these perceptions are to a large extent influenced by feelings of political alienation and general attitudes toward government. It is therefore difficult to distinguish cause and effect between trust in government and perceptions of corruption. We then will show that general perceptions of corruption should not be seen as an expression of individual experience. Parallels become apparent with how citizens evaluate government services, where a disconnection seems to exist between generally positive personal bureaucratic encounters and more negative attitudes toward public services in general. We end by reviewing possibilities for avoiding 'contamination' of perceptions of corruption by general attitudes toward government, and for developing indicators that better measure actual corruption.

## PERCEIVED CORRUPTION IN BELGIUM

By means of an introduction, we briefly present some of the available survey data on citizens' perception of corruption in Belgium. The 1995 ISPO General Election Study (Beerten *et al.*, 1997) revealed that 29 percent of Belgians thought politicians to be more corrupt than other individuals, while 65.5 percent did not see a difference. This study also revealed that citizens have more problems with politicians who demand bribes or payments for granting government contracts than with politicians who accept money for a contract. A politician using bribes for funding his or her personal election campaign is considered more reprehensible than is a politician who

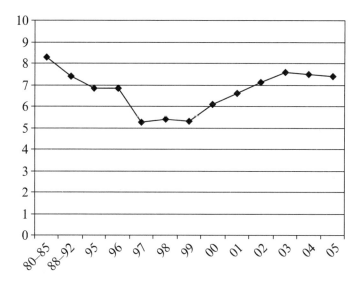

*Source:* Transparency International: Corruption Perceptions Index.

*Figure 13.1 Belgium in the Corruption Perceptions Index*

transfers the money to his or her political party, although 73.9 percent of respondents overall viewed accepting bribes as unacceptable.[1]

The best-known source for corruption indicators is the Transparency International (TI) Corruption Perceptions Index (CPI) (Figure 13.1). This index ranks countries based on perceived corruption among politicians and public officials.[2] Even though the CPI does not lend itself to making time-series comparisons, the trend for Belgium in recent years is quite clear: Since 1999 there has been an unambiguous positive trend (the lower the score, the higher perceived corruption). The score does not return to the 1980s level, but this is probably due to changes in the method of measurement and the fact that data for Belgium and Luxembourg have not always been disaggregated. Luxembourg generally ranks higher than Belgium.

In 2005, Belgium ranked 19th among the least corrupt countries (in a total of 133 countries). This puts the country on a par with Ireland and higher than, for example, Spain and Japan. Still, Belgium performs worse than many other EU15 countries, including its neighboring countries. Compared to 2004, the country declined in the rankings, even though this change is probably not large enough to be significant.

Additional information on Belgian citizens' attitude toward corruption can be found in the 1999–2000 European Values Study. One question was about the perceived occurrence of taking bribes. Table 13.1 shows the

*Table 13.1    According to you, how many of your compatriots do the following? Accepting a bribe in the course of their duties?*

|     | Almost all (%) | Many (%) | Some (%) | Almost none (%) |
|-----|---------------|----------|----------|-----------------|
| BE  | 4.8           | 23.0     | 63.5     | 8.7             |
| AT  | 2.4           | 30.4     | 63.3     | 3.9             |
| DE  | 5.1           | 27.9     | 61.2     | 5.8             |
| FI  | 2.3           | 20.3     | 64.5     | 13.0            |
| IT  | 7.4           | 43.8     | 46.5     | 2.3             |
| LU  | 0.9           | 9.7      | 38.1     | 33.0            |
| UK  | 1.8           | 29.4     | 60.0     | 8.7             |

*Source:*   European Values Study, only results for EU15 countries (Halman, 2001).

answers in a series of European countries and indicates significant differences between countries. In Belgium, 27.8 percent of the respondents report that almost all or many of their compatriots accept bribes. This percentage is comparable to that in Austria, Germany and the UK, yet higher than that found in Finland or Luxemburg. In Italy, however, this percentage peaks at 41.2 percent.

Another question was asked as to what extent citizens considered it justified for someone to accept a bribe in the course of his or her duties. The percentage of respondents that considered accepting a bribe to never be justified was 77.7 percent in 1981, 78.6 percent in 1990 and 84.1 percent in 1999. Figure 13.2 illustrates how the Transparency International and European Values Study findings are related.

Considering bribes to be unjustified does not lead to perceptions of corruption to be lower in a particular country, though there are exceptions. Perceptions regarding accepting bribes is actually quite similar across most countries, despite differences in CPI scores. In only a few Central-European countries is accepting bribes considered to be somewhat more justified, yet the differences remain small.

## WHAT DETERMINES PERCEPTIONS OF CORRUPTION? AN ANALYSIS

For this section, we use data from the *Werken aan de Overheid* survey (WADO-Working on Government), which was administered as part of a research project commissioned by the ministry of the Flemish Community (2000–4, www.kuleuven.be/trust). The questionnaire dealt with citizens' attitudes toward the public sector and contained items on socio-demographics,

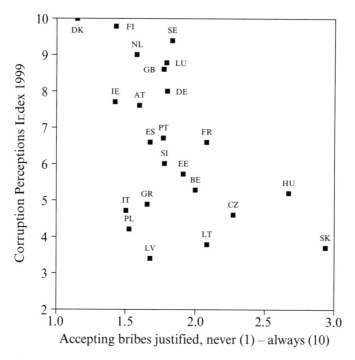

*Source:* Transparency International Corruption Perceptions Index 1999, where '10' means that corruption is perceived to be very low; European Values Study (1999–2000 wave). 'Please tell me for each of the following statements whether you think it can always be justified, never be justified, or something in between. Someone accepting a bribe in the course of their duties.' Scale 1 (never) to 10 (always), mean score (Halman, 2001).

*Figure 13.2    Perceptions of corruption (TI) and justifiability of accepting bribes (EVS) in the EU countries*

citizens and public services, citizens and politics, and citizens and society. Participants were inhabitants of the Flemish Region (aged 18–85). Three surveys were administered: a face-to-face survey (2002, $n = 1248$, response rate 68.2 percent), an initial mail survey (2002, $n = 2166$, response rate 63.5 percent), and a second mail survey (2003, $n = 3168$, response rate 61.9 percent).[3] We will only report data from the 2003 survey here (Van de Walle *et al.*, 2004). Questionnaires were sent with two-week intervals. Fifteen successive waves covered a period of half a year (third and fourth quarters of 2003). In this way the impact of events on citizens' opinions could be measured and long-term impacts and evolutions analysed. We do not, however, analyse trends in this chapter. Respondents each received three mailings: an introductory letter, the questionnaire with postage-paid return envelope and

*Table 13.2    Perceptions of unethical behavior in the public sector in Flanders*

|  | Totally disagree (%) | Disagree (%) | Not agree, not disagree (%) | Agree (%) | Totally agree (%) |
|---|---|---|---|---|---|
| Civil servants are more corrupt than other people | 8.4 | 28.7 | 38.2 | 19.0 | 5.7 |
| Politicians are more corrupt than other people | 3.0 | 18.4 | 36.2 | 29.4 | 13.1 |
| You need 'connections' to get something done by government or the public administration | 2.1 | 11.3 | 30.5 | 40.5 | 15.7 |
| All users of public services are treated equally | 10.9 | 40.2 | 26.1 | 16.7 | 6.1 |
| Users of public services always get what they're entitled to | 7.8 | 35.4 | 35.5 | 18.6 | 2.7 |

*Source:*   Werken aan de Overheid (WADO) 2003, *n* = 3168.

a reminder. As an incentive, a limited number of gifts (approx. 0.5 to 1 percent of respondents) was given to respondents by means of a lottery.

The survey contained a number of issues related to corruption and favoritism, five of which are analysed here in greater detail. Three of these are articulate corruption-related issues, the other two focus on issues of equal treatment.

Surprisingly, 56.2 percent of the respondents believe an individual needs connections to get something done from government or public administrators; only 13.3 percent disagree. The results are somewhat more encouraging in response to the question regarding corruption: just under a quarter of respondents believe that civil servants are more corrupt than other people. Politicians, however, are perceived to be more corrupt than other people by 42.4 percent of participants in the survey. Responses to these three questions are strongly correlated.

The correlation table along with a factor analysis confirm that the items are measuring different dimensions of ethical treatment. While opinions on corruption are quite moderate, there is evidently something wrong with

*Table 13.3    Perceived ethical treatment of citizens, correlations*

|  | Users get what entitled to | Civil servants corrupt | Need connections | Politicians corrupt |
|---|---|---|---|---|
| Users treated equally | 0.51[a] | −0.08[a] | −0.17[a] | −0.13[a] |
| Users get what entitled to |  | 0.07[a] | −0.16[a] | −0.11[a] |
| Civil servants corrupt |  |  | 0.43[a] | 0.40[a] |
| Need connections |  |  |  | 0.36[a] |

*Note:* [a] Correlation is significant at the 0.01 level; Kendall's tau b.

equal treatment. Just one out of five respondents agrees that users of public services are treated equally and get what they're entitled to, while over half of the respondents disagree.

In the next step, we attempt to explain these attitudes by socio-demographic characteristics, social attitudes, voting behavior, and media exposure. Socio-demographic variables are gender, level of education (six levels), and age (six categories from 18–24 to 65+). Social attitudes are individualism (based on two items: 'Humanity, brotherhood and solidarity are all nonsense. Everybody has to take care of themselves first and defend their own interests' and 'People should always pursue their personal pleasure, and shouldn't think too much about others'), and authoritarianism (also based on two items: 'Obedience and respect for authority are the two most important virtues children have to learn' and 'What we need is strong leaders who tell us what to do'). Voting behavior is based on the question 'Suppose there are national elections next Sunday. Which would be your preferred political party?' This variable has been recoded into seven dummies, each referring to one of the main parties; AGALEV (greens), CD&V (Christian-democrats), N-VA (Flemish nationalists), SP-A (social democrats), Spirit (Flemish nationalist and social democrat), Vlaams Blok (extreme right) and VLD (liberals). The three media variables measure whether an individual reads reputable newspapers, watches the news on public television, and/or watches news on commercial television. The five dependent variables have been recoded into trichotomous variables. Table 13.4 gives the results of the multivariate ordinal logit regression models.

The strongest models are these explaining attitudes towards the items 'civil servants are more corrupt than normal people' and 'politicians are more corrupt than normal people'. Opinions about political corruption are strongly influenced by party preference. Extreme right wing voters are more likely to think that politicians are more corrupt than other people. Just 8 percent of extreme right wing voters disagree with the statement that

*Table 13.4    Determinants of perceptions of ethical behavior: ordinal regression models*

|  | Civil servants corrupt | Politicians corrupt | Need connections | All treated equally | Get what entitled to |
|---|---|---|---|---|---|
| SEX (0=male, 1=female) | **0.185*** | **0.050** | **0.21**** | **−0.024** | **0.143*** |
|  | (0.074) | (0.074) | (0.077) | (0.074) | (0.073) |
| EDUCATION | **−0.128**** | **−0.082*** | **−0.115**** | **−0.020** | **−0.073*** |
|  | (0.033) | (0.032) | (0.033) | (0.032) | (0.032) |
| AGE | **0.021** | **0.012** | **−0.001** | **0.007** | **0.032** |
|  | (0.027) | (0.027) | (0.028) | (0.027) | (0.027) |
| AUTHORITARIANISM | **0.041**** | **0.025** | **0.038**** | **0.047**** | **0.050**** |
|  | (0.014) | (0.014) | (0.014) | (0.014) | (0.014) |
| INDIVIDUALISM | **0.159**** | **0.142**** | **0.096**** | **−0.002** | **0.048**** |
|  | (0.014) | (0.014) | (0.015) | (0.014) | (0.014) |
| PARTY: agalev | **0.041** | **−0.027** | **−0.514*** | **0.036** | **0.266** |
|  | (0.23) | (0.225) | (0.229) | (0.232) | (0.228) |
| PARTY: cd&v | **−0.348**** | **−0.174** | **−0.297*** | **0.193** | **0.233** |
|  | (0.132) | (0.132) | (0.139) | (0.133) | (0.131) |
| PARTY: n-va | **−0.103** | **0.152** | **0.009** | **−0.258** | **−0.080** |
|  | (0.213) | (0.213) | (0.221) | (0.223) | (0.215) |
| PARTY: sp-a | **−0.172** | **−0.475**** | **−0.392**** | **0.373**** | **0.343**** |
|  | (0.131) | (0.132) | (0.138) | (0.132) | (0.131) |
| PARTY: spirit | **0.356** | **−0.128** | **0.174** | **0.201** | **0.361** |
|  | (0.212) | (0.217) | (0.238) | (0.212) | (0.208) |
| PARTY: vlaams blok | **0.393**** | **0.617**** | **0.265** | **−0.067** | **−0.241** |
|  | (0.142) | (0.152) | (0.16) | (0.146) | (0.144) |
| PARTY: vld | **−0.188** | **−0.671**** | **−0.238** | **0.115** | **0.167** |
|  | (0.129) | (0.131) | (0.138) | (0.132) | (0.129) |
| QUALITY NEWSPAPERS | **−0.166** | **−0.190** | **−0.240*** | **0.009** | **−0.098** |
|  | (0.108) | (0.105) | (0.107) | (0.107) | (0.106) |
| TV NEWS public TV | **−0.137** | **0.019** | **−0.233** | **0.185** | **−0.064** |
|  | (0.134) | (0.138) | (0.145) | (0.135) | (0.133) |
| TV NEWS commercial TV | **0.152** | **0.295*** | **0.087** | **0.252** | **0.043** |
|  | (0.132) | (0.135) | (0.141) | (0.133) | (0.132) |
| *valid N* | 2742 | 2747 | 2749 | 2731 | 2735 |
| Nagelkerke pseudo $R^2$ | 0.148 | 0.143 | 0.098 | 0.017 | 0.040 |

*Note:*   Standard errors in parentheses; * $p<0.05$, ** $p<0.01$, *** $p<0.001$

politicians are more corrupt than normal people. Social-democrats and liberals are less likely to think politicians are more corrupt than other individuals. At the time of data collection, these were the two main parties in the regional and federal governments, but an alternative explanation could be that certain traditional voter segments of these parties have defected rather early to the extreme right. Respondents with individualistic attitudes are more likely to label politicians as corrupt, as is a lower education, and a propensity to watch the TV news on a commercial TV channel, rather than on public TV.

Perceptions of administrative corruption tend to be influenced by being female, lower educated, scoring higher on individualism, and a somewhat higher authoritarian attitude. As is the case for perceptions of political corruption, a party preference for the extreme right leads to a higher perceived corruption. Voting for Christian-democrats leads to lower perceived administrative corruption. Despite the number of explanatory variables, the models for political and administrative corruption explain just 14.3 and 14.8 per cent of total variation.

The models for equal treatment and for getting what one is entitled to have very low $R$ squares, yet there are a number of significant relationships. Stronger authoritarian attitudes co-exist with stronger beliefs in equal treatment. Individualism leads to a higher belief that everyone will in the end get what they're entitled to when interacting with public services. Perceptions and expectations of equal treatment are higher among supporters of the social-democratic party, a party whose ideology stresses equality. There are some effects of education and gender: females and lower educated persons are somewhat more inclined to believe that public service users will get that to which they are entitled.

Christian-democrats, Greens and Social-democrats are less inclined to believe connections are needed to get something done, while individualism and lower education leads to a higher perceived need of connections, just as does being female. Those reading reputable newspapers do not agree that connections are needed. Overall, again, the model's explanatory power is quite low.

When we look at only the three models directly dealing with corruption (administrative and political, and the perception that connections are needed), lower education, high individualism and a preference for the extreme right are important determinants. All these variables are frequently encountered in the research on political alienation. It is thus likely that, instead of reflecting opinions on or experiences with corruption, the dependent variables could in fact be considered as expressions of this alienation. Stating that connections are needed, or that civil servants are corrupt may therefore be the result of actual experienced corruption, but it may also be part of a general (negative) predisposition toward government. We expand our model, to include a number of political alienation variables. All alienation variables load on a single factor:

- voting is useless; the parties do what they want to do anyway;
- most politicians promise a lot, but don't do anything;
- most of our politicians are competent people, who know what they are doing;
- parliament can best be abolished, since it does not solve any problem;
- the present political system is rotten; and
- to what extent do you trust government?

All variables have been recoded from five to three categories. Because media exposure was not relevant in the basic model, we drop it here.

In all three cases, almost all alienation variables are significant determinants for the corruption and ethics perceptions. In one of the two cases where relationships are not significant at the $p<0.05$ level, there is border significance. Adding the alienation variables leads to a substantial and even sometimes very substantial increase in explained variance ($R^2$). Together with some party preference variables, alienation accounts for most of the variance in the corruption and ethics perceptions. The impact of extreme right voting, which was relevant in the basic models, disappears, possibly due to the fact that this voting behavior is partly determined by alienation.

## WHAT ABOUT CAUSALITY?

The classical, mechanistic explanation for this kind of finding is that citizens feel alienated from their political or administrative system because they perceive it as being corrupt. In this chapter however, we defend the hypothesis that perceptions of corruption are in fact expressions of a more general attitude towards government. A further implication of this viewpoint is that the attitudes as measured in our survey cannot be considered as adequate reflections of actual corrupt practices. We briefly return to this second point toward the end of the chapter.

In previous research on citizens' perceptions of public services and on citizens' trust in institutions we have shown that there is a substantial degree of generalization in respondents' answers to quite general questions (Van de Walle, 2004c). Trust in a certain institution quite often coincides with trust in most institutions. Dissatisfaction with government in general often coincides with dissatisfaction with a broad range of issues. A person with a negative attitude toward government is also more likely to complain about high taxes, corruption, or administrative inefficiency. Certain general predispositions toward government influence most attitudes toward government-related aspects.

This has important implications for the interpretation of survey findings like the ones we have presented above, and for building explanatory models. Failing to recognize this generalization of negative or positive attitudes toward government often results in models that are very good at proving what one wanted to prove in the first place. Correlations between general negative attitudes toward government and more specific elements of dissatisfaction (taxes, corruption . . .) do not necessarily mean that high taxes or high levels of perceived corruption are to be seen as causes of or explanations for this dissatisfaction. Instead, these specific elements could be interpreted as expressions of this general attitude. It would thus be premature to look at the models in Table 13.5 and to consider citizens' political alienation as resulting from high levels of corruption. Instead, perceived corruption and perceived unethical behavior are an expression of this political alienation. By presenting the perceptions of corruption and unethical behavior as dependent variables, we have further illustrated our point.

Proving causality, however, is not common in social methodology, and often is simply impossible. Yet, causal constructions are an important rhetorical device. Hence Ruscio's criticism on the all-too-easy prescriptions for restoring citizens' trust in government:

> Reactions to the decline *(of trust, . . .)* have certainly not been lacking, but they typically follow a predictable formula: an analyst's alarmed response which is used to justify a set of prescriptions favored by the analyst. Trust can be restored by – take your pick – term limits, balanced budgets, regulatory reform, reinventing government, campaign reform, responsible journalism, stronger political parties, a third political party, vigorous state and local government, constraints on lobbying or an end to divided government. (Ruscio, 1997: 454).

Limiting corruption and the introduction of an ethics infrastructure could easily be added to this list.

## DO GENERAL PERCEPTIONS REFLECT PERSONAL EXPERIENCE?

For citizens, it is not easy to base their perceptions about or attitude toward corruption on personal experience. Fragmented evidence suggests that actual individual acts of corruption are quite limited in most Western countries. In the International Crime Victims Survey for instance, a question is included on actual experienced corruption in relation with, for example,

*Table 13.5    The effects of political alienation on corruption, ordinal regression models*

|  | Civil servants corrupt | Politicians corrupt | Need connections |
|---|---|---|---|
| *SEX (0=male, 1=female)* | **0.233**\*\* | **0.108** | **0.244**\*\* |
|  | (0.074) | (0.078) | (0.079) |
| EDUCATION | **−0.108**\*\* | **−0.025** | **−0.072**\* |
|  | (0.031) | (0.033) | (0.032) |
| AGE | **−0.049** | **−0.035** | **−0.061**\* |
|  | (0.027) | (0.028) | (0.029) |
| AUTHORITARIANISM | **0.044**\*\* | **0.012** | **0.041**\*\* |
|  | (0.014) | (0.015) | (0.015) |
| INDIVIDUALISM | **0.116**\*\*\* | **0.078**\*\*\* | **0.041**\*\* |
|  | (0.015) | (0.015) | (0.016) |
| PARTY: agalev | **0.400** | **0.621**\* | **−0.156** |
|  | (0.232) | (0.241) | (0.231) |
| PARTY: cd&v | **−0.112** | **0.055** | **−0.088** |
|  | (0.132) | (0.139) | (0.141) |
| PARTY: n-va | **0.029** | **0.244** | **0.140** |
|  | (0.215) | (0.224) | (0.225) |
| PARTY: sp-a | **0.322**\* | **0.302**\* | **0.124** |
|  | (0.134) | (0.141) | (0.143) |
| PARTY: spirit | **0.726**\*\* | **0.359** | **0.547**\* |
|  | (0.214) | (0.228) | (0.244) |
| PARTY: vlaams blok | **0.238** | **0.283** | **0.001** |
|  | (0.142) | (0.158) | (0.161) |
| PARTY: vld | **0.329**\* | **0.090** | **0.301**\* |
|  | (0.131) | (0.138) | (0.141) |
| VOTING USELESS | **0.093** | **0.207**\*\*\* | **0.146**\* |
|  | (0.051) | (0.053) | (0.054) |
| POLITICIANS PROMISE | **0.205**\*\* | **0.894**\*\*\* | **0.264**\*\*\* |
|  | (0.066) | (0.068) | (0.065) |
| COMPETENT | **−0.226**\*\*\* | **−0.426**\*\*\* | **−0.120** |
|  | (0.056) | (0.060) | (0.061) |
| ABOLISH PARL. | **0.344**\*\*\* | **0.255**\*\*\* | **0.250**\*\*\*\* |
|  | (0.058) | (0.063) | (0.065) |
| SYST. ROTTEN | **0.245**\*\*\* | **0.595**\*\*\* | **0.404**\*\*\* |
|  | (0.062) | (0.064) | (0.065) |
| TRUSTGOV | **−0.512**\*\*\* | **−0.347**\*\*\* | **−0.607**\*\*\* |
|  | (0.069) | (0.071) | (0.071) |
| *N* | 2840 | 2852 | 2842 |
| Nagelkerke pseudo $R^2$ | 0.256 | 0.421 | 0.238 |
| $R^2$ increase[a] | 0.118 | 0.286 | 0.149 |

*Notes:*    [a] increase compared to basic model without media variables.
Standard errors in parentheses: \* $p<0.05$, \*\* $p<0.01$, \*\*\* $p<0.001$.

customs officers, police officers and inspectors or other government officials.[4] Frequencies for these items are generally low to extremely low (Van Kesteren *et al.*, 2000). In our own survey, we included an item on politicians' constituency service and the extent to which citizens have approached a politician during the last four years for solving a personal problem.[5] Just 2.5 percent of respondents mentioned more than one contact, while 9.6 percent of respondents admitted having approached a politician in the four preceding years. Using politicians' constituency service does not equal corruption. Other methods frequently used to measure actual corruption rather than perceptions are household surveys, where personal stories of corrupt experiences are shared and recorded within specific groups. The method is less often used in developed countries, probably because of the lower occurrence of corrupt acts, and costs of collecting meaningful data.

Absence of personal experience forces survey respondents in general surveys to relate to other elements or information to form their opinion on corruption. The number of respondents whose answers are related to corruption based on recently experienced corruption is likely to be extremely low. Reactions to a statement such as 'you need connections to get something done from government' do not necessarily have a specific referential basis, but more probably refer to information about government in general that is present in the respondent's mind (Zaller, 1996). Most probably this information concurs with general attitudes towards government and with the general stereotypes of government and administrations (Van de Walle, 2004a).

Here, a parallel with research on citizens' perception of public services surfaces. For several decades, scholars have repeatedly stumbled on a number of apparent contradictions in citizens' opinion about public services. One contradiction deals with process. Citizens dislike inefficiency but are equally dissatisfied when delivery of services is ruthlessly efficient (Blau, 1956: 14). Citizens complain about cumbersome red tape and paper-based interaction, but wouldn't like either that the official would forget precious details about the specific encounter (du Gay, 2000). Both vices and virtues of bureaucratic systems are used to fuel the traditional dislike of the bureaucracy (Hill, 1992): corruption itself as well as the bureaucratic impersonality that results from anti-corruption measures may give rise to dissatisfaction. An inefficient police force creates dissatisfaction, but so does a police force that is too eager issuing parking tickets. Two dominant images prevail: the lazy, incompetent bureaucrat versus the power-hungry, manipulative civil servant. It is not quite obvious how these two images may reasonably co-exist.

The other contradiction, perhaps more important here, deals with evaluation. While many citizens dislike public administration in general, they are actually quite satisfied with many concrete services. Citizens generally evaluate specific and concrete services in a more positive way than is the case for government in general or for general concepts such as 'the public administration'. The general image of bureaucracy does not correspond to the evaluation citizens make about their own experience with public services ('bureaucratic encounters'). Public administration scholars started to write about this in the 1970s. One of the earliest extensive studies on the issue was a large-scale study by Katz *et al.* (1977) on differences in the evaluation of public and private services. They asked respondents to evaluate public and private sector services in general, as well as a recently used public and private sector service. When respondents had to compare public and private sector services, they indeed rated private sector services higher. However, when the comparison concerned the private and public sector service that was used most recently, differences between the evaluation of public and private sector services disappeared. Goodsell devoted an entire book (*The Case for Bureaucracy* (1983)) to the issue of divergence between evaluations of concrete bureaucratic encounters and the general public attitude *vis-à-vis* bureaucracy. Most of Goodsell's observations are echoed in other research and articles as well (Grunow, 1981), and his theoretical explanations do not differ greatly from Katz *et al.*'s research on bureaucratic encounters. Klages (1981) referred to German research indicating differences in citizens' evaluation of civil servants in general and employees who provide specific public services. Hill (1992: 20), in his chapter entitled 'Taking bureaucracy seriously' wants to know why citizens state they were treated fairly by the administration, while they don't think governmental offices are giving fair treatment. Although Hill uses some new survey material, his approach does not introduce much more than Goodsell. Hill's evidence found that citizens tend to agree with negative statements about bureaucracy when these are unrelated to bureaucratic performance and vague enough to serve as an outlet for the stereotypical anti-bureaucratic images (Hill, 1992: 22). The explanation lies therefore not in the degree of generalization, as can be concluded from reading Goodsell, but rather on the symbolic content of concepts and objects and not on the level of abstraction:

> The conventional wisdom in political science and social psychology has been that abstract attitude objects are processed differently than concrete ones. The simple symbolic politics view assumes that processing of political symbols depends on the evaluations associated with them, not on the symbol's level of abstraction (Sears, 2001: 20).

The abstract objects studied in public administration (government, bureaucracy, civil servants) often bear negative symbolic content, and this content is being reflected when respondents are asked to give an opinion on the administration or bureaucratic ethics and corruption. Because of the high level of abstraction of the concept (public administration) or the low level of personal experience (corruption), respondents form an answer that is plausible because it is compatible with the general symbolic content and their own general attitude toward government.

## WHAT ABOUT PERCEPTIONS OF CORRUPTION?

How do we find these processes in perceptions of corruption? In our WADO survey, we also asked respondents to indicate their level of trust in a series of institutions (1 = very little; 5 = a lot). At the beginning of the questionnaire, a general item on trust in government was also included.[6] Table 13.6 shows how the general opinion on corruption correlates quite strongly with trust in government in general and with trust in more general and diffuse institutions, while correlations with rather specific institutions are considerably weaker. The correlation between perceptions of corruption and general trust in government is the highest, directly followed by the quite generally phrased items such trust in the Flemish administration, Federal administration and municipal administration. At the bottom of

*Table 13.6   Trust and corruption: correlations*

| You need connections to get something done | | | |
| --- | --- | --- | --- |
| Trust | Correlation coefficient | Trust | Correlation coefficient |
| Government (general) | −0.31 | European Commission | −0.17 |
| Flemish administration | −0.26 | Police | −0.17 |
| Federal administration | −0.25 | Courts/justice system | −0.15 |
| Municipal administration | −0.23 | Educational system | −0.12 |
| Flemish Parliament | −0.20 | Public transport (bus, tram) | −0.11 |
| Flemish Government | −0.20 | Flemish employment agency | −0.10 |
| Belgian Parliament | −0.20 | Public television | −0.10 |
| Belgian Government | −0.20 | Refuse collection | −0.08 |
| Flemish political parties | −0.18 | Army | −0.06 |
| Walloon political parties | −0.18 | Postal service | −0.06 |
| College of mayor and aldermen | −0.17 | Railway company | −0.05 |

*Source:*   Werken aan de Overheid (WADO) 2003, *n* = 3168, Kendall's Tau b, all correlations significant.

the list are very specific services such as the railway company, the postal service and so on, where correlations are very small, yet still significant. A traditional explanation would be that citizens tend to associate institutions such as the Flemish or Federal administration more with corruption than is the case for services such as the postal service or the national railways.

It would be incorrect however to infer from these findings that citizens experience or have experienced more frequent occurrences of corruption in these non-specific institutions ('the administration', 'government'). In fact, these correlations merely confirm what we have described earlier. Even though we have not measured perceptions of corruption in very specific and concrete governmental institutions, we can quite confidently state that survey respondents will report lower corruption in many specific institutions than they will for the public administration or government in general. Exceptions to this 'general rule' will then probably be services where there have recently been corruption scandals or services that traditionally had a very negative image. This means that the opinion on corruption is probably part of a general opinion about government and not so much the result of actual experience. General surveys do not distinguish whether these opinions are part of the general attitude towards government or resultant from actual experienced corruption.

The relationship between general opinions about corruption, and general attitudes towards government are also visible in a more international analysis. Figure 13.3 shows the levels of confidence in the civil service in the EU countries (excluding Malta and Cyprus), as measured in the European Values Study, and these countries' scores on the Transparency International Corruption Perceptions Index in the same year. Even though imperfect, there is a strong correlation between both indicators (Pearson correlation = 0.506).

Again, this figure may be seen as indicating that corruption drives down confidence in the civil service, but it can also be interpreted as supporting our view that both perceptions of corruption, and confidence in the civil service, are derived from a general view of government. There are no reliable criteria however, to decide whether and when a corruption perception indicator reflects generalized views of government or actual experience with corruption.

## A NEED FOR BETTER MEASUREMENT OF CORRUPTION?

While perceptions of corruption as a factor of general attitudes toward government are an interesting indicator for researchers, most practitioners

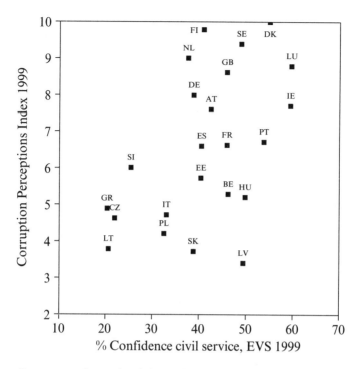

*Source:* Transparency International Corruption Perceptions Index 1999 and European Values Study 1999: % 'a great deal' and 'quite a lot' of confidence.

*Figure 13.3: Confidence in the civil service and perceptions of corruption*

and policy-makers are interested in actual corruption. This chapter clearly showed that general items on perceived corruption risk to be 'contaminated' by general predispositions toward government. Generally, there are two possibilities for isolating citizens' perceptions of corruption from general predispositions toward government. One is to avoid broad and general questions and instead to focus on specific and concrete situations. The other is to do away with measuring perceptions altogether and to step up efforts to develop objective indicators of corruption.

**Specific Measurement**

We have shown that general perceptions of corruption correlate with levels of trust in quite general institutions. The more specific an item in a questionnaire, the narrower the respondent's framework of reference for answering the question becomes. This may help in filtering predispositions.

A general question such as 'is the public administration corrupt' invites respondents not only to think about recent experience, but also to think about all possible administrations, about bureaucratic stereotypes, even about politicians, and so on. A more narrowly defined question such as 'did you personally experience corruption in service Y during the past three encounters' drastically confines the framework of reference to service Y and helps to exclude many of the general predispositions toward government or administrations. Specific measurement of corruption should therefore disaggregate the general corruption items and ask questions on corruption with regard to many different specific services and with regard to many different expressions of corruption. Some examples are the Transparency International Global Corruption Barometer, where respondents were asked to give their opinion on the presence of corruption in a series of sectors. They also could indicate the amount of bribes paid by one's household, and the reason why this was done (www.transparency.org). The barometer did not, however, link actual behavior to specific sectors. Even more detailed are household surveys, some also conducted by Transparency International. In these surveys, detailed questions about corrupt practices and experiences are included. These questions refer to concrete interactions with government services and officials. For policy makers such a specific measurement is also important, because it shows them where and how corruption is manifest and hence facilitates action. Policymakers who use general corruption indicators can in fact only use this information to decide on general measures to combat corruption, without being able to establish priorities for action. Most of these very detailed surveys are conducted in developing countries. Lower occurrence of corrupt practices in developed countries would require very large samples to gather significant data, thus rendering them somewhat more impractical.

**Objective Measurement**

Possibilities for measuring corruption objectively are sparsely reported in the literature. One approach counts the number of cases related to corruption before the courts. In Belgium, Yante (2003) analysed the number of lawsuits related to corruption. Despite the often-defective judicial statistics, he did find a decrease and also observed a tendency for more severe punishment in corruption cases. This relatively easy approach negates certain aspects, because corruption is essentially an illegal and hidden activity (Kaufmann, Kraay *et al.*, 2003). A falling number of lawsuits may also suggest decreasing judicial oversight or more hidden corruption. Essentially, effectively measuring corruption is *de facto* combating corruption.

Kaufmann *et al.*, in their *Governance Matters III* working paper, refer to a small number of studies that attempted to measure corruption directly. They mention Di Tella and Shargrodsky (2003), who measure variation in procurement prices for medical supplies, where high variation suggests there is corruption involved, and Golden and Picci (2005), who compare expenditures for public infrastructure with existing inventories, where high discrepancies may hint at corruption.

A third approach is to map incentives and opportunities for corruption (Rose-Ackerman, 1999), influenced by the demand and supply in the citizen-official encounter. Opportunities for asking or giving bribes may be influenced by the level of discretion exercised by civil servants or political decision-makers. Incentives are influenced by factors such as the likelihood of being caught, and the savings in time and money to be had by circumventing customary procedures, especially when the customary procedure is long and expensive with unpredictable outcomes.

## CONCLUSION

In this chapter, we analysed determinants of subjective perceptions of corruption in Belgium. Belgium, a country with a somewhat corrupt image, seems to have made some progress in dispelling such negative perceptions during the last decade, as demonstrated by the country's Transparency International rankings. In an analysis of survey data, we found political alienation to be one of the main determinants of citizens' perception of political and public sector corruption and of unethical behavior in the administration. This had important implications for both the interpretation of the causal link between corruption and other attitudes toward government, and for the practice of measuring corruption. General surveys revealed that opinions on corruption and unethical behavior are embedded in more general attitudes toward government. Unlike the reportedly widespread personal experience with public corruption in Belgium, citizens of Western countries hear about corruption but research has demonstrated that firsthand experiences remain limited, thus emphasizing the geographical and cultural limitations of this study.

Still, general perceptions of corruption are often used as measures of corruption in a country. These general perceptions are useful indicators for attitudinal research, and also have a value in mapping a country's image. There is a need however for the development of more objective indicators of corruption, and when surveys are used, very specific questions are to be asked, rather than general queries. Finally, because perceptions of corruption seem to be an expression of general attitudes toward government, we can no longer simply use surveys to prove that low levels of trust are a consequence of corruption. Rather, high levels of perceived corruption are probably a reflection of low trust. An implication of this is that declines in actual corruption will not immediately have an impact on citizens' general perceptions of the occurrence of corruption.

## NOTES

1. 'Hardly acceptable' and 'never acceptable'. Of the remaining respondents, 17.8 percent stated this is 'sometimes acceptable', and 5.4 percent stated that accepting money and giving it to one's party is 'completely acceptable'.
2. www.transparency.org, note that CPI scores cannot just be compared on a year-to-year basis, as composition has changed a number of times.
3. In the 2003 survey, ages 25–44 are underrepresented, ages 45–60 tended to return the questionnaire more often, and the +70 category is again underrepresented. Response was higher in rural areas.
4. Q290: 'In some countries, there is a problem of corruption among government of public officials. During 1999, has any government official, for instance a customs officer, a police officer or inspector in your country asked you, or expected you to pay a bribe or his or her services?' Answer = yes/no. In Belgium there were nine 'yes' answers on 2501 respondents in the 1999 survey.
5. 'People sometimes call on politicians for solving personal problems. Did you during the last four year call on a politician's constituency service for solving some personal problem?' We use the Dutch word 'dienstbetoon', which is generally translated as constituency services, but which is in fact something more specific. 'Dienstbetoon' refers to the waning Belgian politicians' habit for holding office every week or month somewhere in their constituency to meet individual citizens. Traditionally, this practice has been associated with corruption, for example because citizens visited politicians to arrange jobs for family members or to get building permits. Nowadays, however, the practice has evolved into some kind of front-office social work, where politicians are considered easier to approach than are certain national administrations. Politicians are now believed to limit their 'dienstbetoon' to showing citizens the correct administration they should contact with a certain problem or to referring citizens to the ombudsman. Of the respondents in our survey who had approached a politician, 33.9 percent stated it helped solving the problem, while 49.9 percent declared it did not. The others (29.9 percent) took a neutral position.
6. General question near the start of the survey: 'To what extent do you trust government' (1–5 scale).

## REFERENCES

Beerten, Roeland, Jaak Billiet, Ann Carton and Marc Swyngedouw (1997), *1995 General Election Study Flanders-Belgium: Codebook and Questionnaire*, Leuven, Belgium: ISPO.

Blau, Peter, M. (1956), *Bureaucracy in Modern Society*, New York: Random House.

De Winter, Lieven (2000), 'Political corruption in the Belgian partitocracy: (still) an endemic disease?', EUI working paper RSC No. 2000/31.

De Winter, Lieven (2003), 'Political corruption in Belgium', in Martin J. Bull and James L. Newell (eds), *Corruption in Contemporary Politics*, Houndsmills: Palgrave Macmillan, pp. 93–105.
Di Tella, R. and E. Shargrodsky (2003), 'The role of wages and auditing during a crackdown on corruption in the city of Buenos Aires', *Journal of Law and Economics*, **46** (1), 269–92.
du Gay, Paul (2000), *In Praise of Bureaucracy*, London: Sage.
Golden, Miriam and Lucio Picci (2005), 'Proposal for a new measure of corruption, and tests using Italian data', *Economics and Politics*, **17** (1), 37–75.
Goodsell, Charles T. (1983), *The Case for Bureaucracy: A Public Administration Polemic*, Chatham: Chatham House Publishers Inc.
Grunow, Dieter (1981), 'Client-centered research in Europe', in Charles T. Goodsell (ed.), *The Public Encounter: Where State and Citizen Meet*, Bloomington, IN: Indiana University Press, pp. 223–41.
Halman, Loek (2001), *The European Values Study: A Third Wave Source Book of the 1999–2000 European Values Study Surveys*, Tilburg, Netherlands: WORC, Tilburg University.
Hill, Larry B. (1992), 'Taking bureaucracy seriously' in Larry B. Hill (ed.), *The State of Public Bureaucracy*, Armonk, NY: M.E. Sharpe, pp. 15–57.
Katz, Daniel, Barbara A. Gutek, Robert L. Kahn and Eugenia Barton (1977), *Bureaucratic Encounters: A Pilot Study in the Evaluation of Government Services*, Ann Arbor, MI: Institute for Social Research.
Kaufmann, Daniel, Aart Kraay and Massimo Mastruzzi (2003), *Governance Matters III: Governance Indicators for 1996–2002*, Washington, DC: World Bank.
Klages, Helmut (1981), 'Das Verhältnis zwischen Staat und Bürgern in der Bundesrepublik Deutschland', in Michael Buse and Horst Burschmann (eds), *Bürgernahe Verwaltung und der Verwaltungsausbildung*, Baden-Baden, Germany: Nomos Verlaggesellschaft, pp. 24–43.
Maesschalck, Jeroen (2002), 'When do scandals have an impact on policy making? A case study of the police reform following the Dutroux scandal in Belgium', *International Public Management Journal*, **5** (2), 169–93.
Rose-Ackerman, Susan (1999), *Corruption and Government: Causes, Consequences, and Reform*, Cambridge: Cambridge University Press.
Ruscio, Kenneth P. (1997), 'Trust in the administrative state (book review)', *Public Administration Review*, **57** (5), 454–8.
Sears, David O. (2001), 'The role of affect in symbolic politics', in James H. Kuklinski (ed.), *Citizens and Politics*, Cambridge: Cambridge University Press, pp. 14–40.
Van de Walle, S. (2004a), 'Context-specific images of the archetypical bureaucrat: persistence and diffusion of the bureaucracy stereotype', *Public Voices*, **7** (1), 3–12.
Van de Walle, S. (2004b), 'Kan er iets geregeld worden? Corruptie bij de overheid in cijfers', *Vlaams Tijdschrift Voor Overheidsmanagement*, **9** (4), 39–45.
Van de Walle, Steven (2004c), *Perceptions of Administrative Performance: The Key to Trust in Government?*, dissertation, Leuven, Belgium: Instituut voor de Overheid.
Van de Walle, Steven, Jarl K. Kampen, Bart Maddens and Geert Bouckaert (2004), *Sourcebook, Veldwerkverslag en Materiaal bij de 'Werken aan de Overheid' Surveys*, Leuven, Belgium: Instituut voor de Overheid.

Van de Walle, Steven, Jarl K. Kampen and Geert Bouckaert (2005), 'Deep impact for high impact agencies? Assessing the role of bureaucratic encounters in evaluations of government', *Public Performance and Management Review*, **28** (4), 532–49.
van Kesteren, John, Pat Mayhew and Paul Nieuwbeerta (2000), *Criminal Victimisation in Seventeen Industrialised Countries: Key-findings from the 2000 International Crime Victims Survey*, The Hague: Ministry of Justice, WODC.
Yante, J.-M. (2003), 'La Corruption dans l'Administration belge aux XIXe et XXe Siècles', in Seppo Tiihonen (ed.), *The History of Corruption in Central Government*, Amsterdam: IOS Press, pp. 65–82.
Zaller, John (1996), *The Nature and Origins of Mass Opinion*, Cambridge: Cambridge University Press.

# PART V

# Conclusion

# 14. Global perspectives on good governance policies and research

## Leo W.J.C. Huberts, Jeroen Maesschalck and Carole L. Jurkiewicz

## INTRODUCTION

Moral challenges have confronted every society, regardless of locale or state of industrial development. Every political institution and civil society has had to contend with questions of ethicality. The failure to effectively resolve these challenges is not new. What is novel, as suggested here, is a shift in the public's capacity and desire for scrutiny and insistence upon adherence to moral standards defined by appropriate behaviors from those holding public authority and the public trust. These individuals are being held to increasingly higher standards in the past decade and this has fueled a concomitant interest in public ethics research.

This chapter will reflect on both the practice and study of ethical governance from a global perspective. The intent is to provide an overview of common dilemmas as well as a framework for continued theory development and empirical research. First, a synopsis of the scope and breadth of current research in this area will be examined along with its impact on policy development and its beneficiaries will be presented. Second, a overview of what aspects of good governance comprise the focus of current research, what areas are under-analysed, and how efforts should be directed in order to address these inadequacies in theory development. Further, this research will be examined within the context of practical application to countries experiencing a range of corruptive factors at all governmental levels; what does and can research do to address these problems directly, in a manner that is of value to those administrators faced with these challenges on a daily basis.

This purview of inquiry is important not only on a circumscribed level, but is essential to the international policy debate as well. It is frequently presupposed that there is agreement on the basic values of governance characterizing liberal democracies with private enterprise and market economies, though this remains to be proven. Similarly, the effectiveness of anti-corruption and integrity policies and institutions shares a presumed agreement without substantiation. These underlying assumptions beg to be examined in light of current and future research. The trend toward culturally integrative and empirically-based research is encouraging and will no doubt play an essential role in further articulation of both the issues and the methods of inquiry used to examine them.

# ETHICS AND INTEGRITY IN INTERNATIONAL POLICY

It can be argued that increasing attention has been paid to issues of ethics and integrity in politics, administration, economy and society on a global scale. Following the cyclical nature of such things, good governance appears to be back on the agenda of politicians, administrators, managers, interest groups, the citizenry and members of the research community in general. Stimulated by widespread reports of corruption typifying the era beginning in the 1990s, few countries have escaped the intensified oversight. The Italian political party system exploded in the early 1990s because of revelations of corruption. The regimes of Marcos in the Philippines and Suharto in Indonesia imploded for the same reasons (Klitgaard, 1988; Rose-Ackerman, 1999), as is happening explosively today in Bulgaria, Thailand, and to a lesser extent among factions in the United States. In point of fact scandal seems the norm and ethicality the exception, and the only variances among nations appears to be scope, size of impact and novelty of the violation. As few countries have been untouched by public scandals in the twenty-first century it must be asked whether corruption and scandal are endemic to all governmental systems and, if so, is it possible to enact change. Certainly there are no easy answers and any solutions must address the issue from both a macro- and micro-level. There are a number of global and international initiatives tackling this problem that are worthy of note.

**United Nations**

The United Nations General Assembly Resolution on Corruption in 1997 reaffirmed its commitment to address the problem of the adoption of the International Code of Conduct for Public Officials. The effort was expanded in 2001 during the UN Convention against Corruption at the Second Global Forum on Fighting Corruption and Safeguarding Integrity at the Hague. Adopted by the General Assembly in October 2003, it completed the ratification process and was entered into force in December 2005, to be monitored and evaluated by the United Nations Office on Drugs and Crime (UNODC).[1] As United Nations Secretary-General Kofi Annan said in his statement on the adoption by the General Assembly of the United Nations Convention against Corruption:

> Corruption hurts the poor disproportionately by diverting funds intended for development, undermining a government's ability to provide basic services, feeding inequality and injustice, and discouraging foreign investment and aid.

Readers can access the full text of the Convention at http://www.unodc.org/unodc/en/corruption.html. The points included in the Convention are intended to be both comprehensive and a statement of international consensus. These include a description of the values to be promoted among public officials, policies for prevention, legal remedies for violations and a clause promoting asset recovery from individuals convicted of using public funds for personal gain.

Annexed to a General Assembly Resolution of 12 December 1996 was the Code of Conduct for Public Officials,[2] whose general principles include:

1. A public office, as defined by national law, is a position of trust, implying a duty to act in the public interest. Therefore, the ultimate loyalty of public officials shall be to the public interests of their country as expressed through the democratic institutions of government.
2. Public officials shall ensure that they perform their duties and functions efficiently, effectively and with integrity, in accordance with laws or administrative policies. They shall at all times seek to ensure that public resources for which they are responsible are administered in the most effective and efficient manner.
3. Public officials shall be attentive, fair and impartial in the performance of their functions and, in particular, in their relations with the public. They shall at no time afford any undue preferential treatment to any group or individual or improperly discriminate against any group or individual, or otherwise abuse the power and authority vested in them.

Other articles of this Code encompass conflicts of interest, disclosure of assets, acceptance of gifts or other favors, handling confidential information, and engaging in political activities. Collectively, this effort on behalf of the UN is an optimistic initiative in combating a deeply entrenched global problem, that of mandating ethics and integrity in governance.

Yet the ubiquitous nature of corruption is, sadly ironically, evidenced in the administration of the United Nations itself as the subject of accusations of corruption and various integrity violations (Rosett, 2006). The most prominent of these was the 1996 Oil-for-Food Program scandal ensuing when, under UN auspices, over $65 billion worth of Iraqi oil was sold on the world market in violation of the provisions that it was to be sold in quantities necessary only to exchange for food, medicine and other humanitarian needs. The Program was discontinued in late 2003 amidst allegations of widespread abuse and corruption when it was revealed by the Volcker investigation that the excess sales allowed the regime to rebuild its military in the wake of the first Gulf War. The Program director was suspended and then resigned from the UN when it was concluded he had accepted bribes from the Iraqi regime.

Beyond the UN in toto, Kofi Annan's son was implicated for allegedly procuring UN Oil-for-Food contracts on behalf of a Swiss company, Cotecna, in exchange for personal gain and India's foreign minister was removed from office because of his alleged direct role in the scandal.

Ethical policy developments almost always consequent to scandal and, true to form, the UN established an Ethics Office in 2006 with independent external oversight and auditing, as well as expanded provisions governing whistle-blowing and staff financial disclosures. Announcing the new office, Mr Annan stated:

> Staff members expressed concern about the ethics climate within the United Nations in the 2004 integrity perception survey. Similar concerns were raised by the report of the Independent Inquiry Committee on the oil-for-food programme. In addition, recent events have created the imperative to establish new mechanisms to improve ethics within the organization. The creation of an ethics office is central to this effort.

The ethics office would foster a staff culture of transparency and accountability and set standards for training and appropriate professional conduct, the report adds. It would lead and manage the UN ethics infrastructure by taking such steps as administering the financial disclosure program, which would encompass about 1000 staff members, and protect the staff against retaliation for reporting misconduct.

### The Word Bank and IMF

Mirroring ethics growing importance in the world of politics, major international financial and economic institutions like the World Bank and the International Monetary Fund[3] have also embraced corruption-prevention techniques as central criteria when determining questions of developmental aid and debt release in international relations. Essentially, the focus is on whether assisting a country will ultimately facilitate profiteering of the elites through bribery and fraud. The WB, in concurrence with the IMF, has identified corruption as among the greatest obstacles to economic and social development, distorting the rule of law, and weakening the institutional foundation on which economic growth depends.[4] As corruption sabotages policies and programs that aim to reduce poverty, confronting it is critical to the achievement of the WB's overarching mission of poverty reduction. The WB's anticorruption strategy builds on five key elements: increasing political accountability, strengthening civil society participation, creating a competitive private sector, mandating institutional restraints on power, and improving public sector management. As summarized by former World Bank President, Paul Wolfowitz[5] in April 2006:

> In the last half-century we have developed a better understanding of what helps governments function effectively and achieve economic progress . . . It is essentially the combination of transparent and accountable institutions, strong skills and competence, and a fundamental willingness to do the right thing. Those are the things that enable a government to . . . raise their national incomes by as much as four times . . . The World Bank first acknowledged corruption as a major impediment to development only ten years ago. But since then, it has been leading the development community in coming to grips with this very serious, but long-ignored problem. Fighting corruption is a long-term commitment, and results will not come overnight . . . That is why fighting corruption requires a long-term strategy that systematically and progressively attacks the problem, and . . . requires the commitment and participation of governments . . . citizens, and . . . businesses alike.

In 2006 the World Bank brought together 'over 250 leaders, thinkers, development practitioners, and youth from over 70 developed and developing countries' for what was termed a World Ethics Forum.[6] Discussions focused on strategies to promote ethical leadership and public integrity as tools for better governance and accelerated development. Its goal was to develop, empower and support leaders at all levels who are committed to integrity. By raising awareness of and enhancing the capacity to recognize the issues, forming action coalitions across nations and sectors, engaging in capacity-building for ethical, effective leadership, and providing resources to facilitate these ends the Forum sought to operationalize many of the over-arching goals first articulated a decade earlier. The Global Integrity Alliance is but one of many products emerging from the Forum. Said Sanjay Pradhan, Director for Public Sector Governance in the Poverty Reduction and Economic Management Vice Presidency at the World Bank: 'The dynamics of ethical leadership are under-analysed, under-appreciated, and under-emphasized by the international community. Ethics and integrity are critical factors for development, and the World Ethics Forum allowed the exchange of views among public, private, and civil society leaders to create new joint initiatives and partnerships.'

## OECD

The Organisation for Economic Co-operation and Development, comprised of 29 Member States representing the industrialized world, has made anti-corruption initiatives and ethics and integrity policies an important aspect of its work. Its main contribution has been the 1997 OECD Convention on Combating Bribery of Foreign Public Officials in International Business Transactions. The Convention, signed by all member countries and a number of non-members, came into force in 1999 and for the first time made bribing a foreign public official a criminal offense. Another area of focus is evident in the OECD Guidelines for Managing Conflict of Interest in the Public Service which offers the first international benchmark in the field. A 'conflict of interest' was concretely defined as involving 'a conflict between the public duty and private interests of a public official, in which the public official has private-capacity interests which could improperly influence the performance of their official duties and responsibilities'.[7] The Guidelines state that the proper objective of an effective Conflict of Interest policy is not the simple prohibition of all private-capacity interests on the part of public officials, but rather to maintain the integrity of official policy and administrative decisions and of public management generally, recognizing that an unresolved conflict of interest may result in abuse of public office. To achieve this objective public bodies must possess and implement relevant policy standards for promoting integrity. These include effective processes for identifying risk and dealing with emergent conflicts of interest, appropriate external and internal accountability mechanisms, aggressive management approaches that ensure that public officials take personal responsibility for complying with both the letter and the spirit of such standards.

### Civil Society

Transparency International, based in Berlin, is the best known and most ubiquitous example of an international non-governmental organization fighting corruption. With branches in 99 countries (2006), TI favors a holistic approach to a national integrity system (Pope, 2000; Transparency International, 2001). Although each country or region is unique in its own history and culture, its political system and its stage of economic and social development, similarities do exist and experience and lessons are often transferable. TI proposes a National Integrity System as a comprehensive method of fighting corruption. It comprises eight interdependent pillars for research, action and dialogue: public awareness, public anti-corruption strategies, public participation, watchdog agencies, the judiciary, the media, the private sector and international cooperation. Emergent from this initiative is the popular Corruption Perception Index, whereby countries are scored on a continuum based upon surveys among business persons and analysts. Additionally, TI monitors a Corruption Barometer which tracks public opinion on bribery and corruption and issues an annual report (TI, 2005). Collectively, those measures offer a glimpse of both the breadth and awareness of corruption in a sampling of countries across the globe. According to TI, the sectors most affected by corruption are political parties (especially in high income countries), and the legislature and the police (in many low income countries). When asked if corruption had gotten better or worse in their countries over the past three years, 57 percent of respondents stated corruption had increased, and 27 percent said it had stayed the same. While some regions (for example Africa) appear to be optimistic about the future, overall 44 percent of respondents expect corruption will increase over the next three years.

### Conclusion

To the extent it is possible to summarize this sampling of initiatives and to generalize from those findings, one might conclude the following. First, international organizations over the past ten years have demonstrated a growing commitment to fight corruption. The topic holds a prominent agenda position in international politics and administration and is seen as essential in safeguarding integrity to promote political and economic progress. Second, an extensive framework of conventions, rules, monitoring guidelines and sanctions has been built and continues to grow. Third, these policies and practices are exercising increasing influence among the decision-making bodies determining who receives financial assistance, debt reduction, developmental aid, and political and economic favors; countries who seek such support and do not abide by nor recognize these anti-corruption initiatives are regarded much less favorably on the whole. Fourth, there appears to be a growing awareness among the international community that issues of integrity and ethics of government and governance encompass aspects beyond curbing and sanctioning corruption. Expanded interest in defining what good governance is on a global scale, integrating principles of ethical leadership across cultures and sectors and overcoming political and economic barriers to acceptance of global initiatives characterizes work in this field today and into the foreseeable future. The anti-corruption effort is in its infancy and as such is widely flawed, but areas seen as lacking are viewed as more urgent in the current move to align economic, political, and ethical philosophies.

# CRITICISM OF THE DOMINANT GLOBAL POLICY FRAMEWORK

While efforts to combat corruption and enhance ethicality and integrity are growing in scope and popularity, criticism regarding who has the right to establish such precepts and who really benefits from the intended outcomes abounds (Caiden *et al.*, 2001; Fijnaut and Huberts, 2002).

A key question is whether the UN, WB, and IMF are the right organizations to address these questions, especially given the scandals those organizations face themselves; they advocate transparency, accountability, disclosure standards, and so on yet appear to violate their own dictates (Everett *et al.*, 2006: 8). Is it possible or even desirable to seek global consensus on what constitutes ethical political and public administrations? Since much of the existing research in this area was derived from Western thought, the frameworks may or may not represent the political and social best practices of the rest of the world (Benaissa, 1993; Punch *et al.*, 1993; Pieth and Eigen, 1999). While the moralist approach contends that all corruption is undesirable, the functionalist approach argues that there are conditions when bribing and corruptive acts are good for a society and that political, economic and social relationships might suffer if such behaviors are extinguished (Johnson, 2004: 155–63; Bardhan, 1997). Certainly more objective data is needed to make these determinations.

On the question of who are the beneficiaries of such efforts, one group states it is a win-win outcome for everyone from rich industrialized nations to developing countries. The other side of the argument states that institutions like the World Bank and the International Monetary Fund contribute to the development of a global free market capitalism which ultimately harms the poor and powerless and, thus, address the ethicality of forcing a developing country in the direction of a market economy and private enterprise (Heidenheimer and Johnston, 2002; Pieth and Eigen, 1999; UNDP, 1998). Doubt also exists regarding the purity of interest in anti-corruption efforts from countries with varying political agendas, from developing nations where dictators control public funds to international super-powers who use their economic might for political and military ends, to those in the middle of the global hierarchy who seek advantage over others of their ilk seeking economic development assistance. Are anti-corruption efforts simply a new, seemingly virtuous packaging of tools to exercise individualized agendas? Table 14.1 addresses that question in part.

The table presents the Corruption Perception Index scores of the first 30 countries among the full 159 to ratify the UN Convention against Corruption. The CPI score ranges from 10 (highly clean) to 0 (highly corrupt). Perhaps surprisingly, only two countries have a score above 5.0

*Table 14.1  CPI score of the 30 first countries that ratified the UN Convention*

| Country | 2005 CPI score | Country rank |
| --- | --- | --- |
| Algeria | 2.8 | 97 |
| Belarus | 2.6 | 107 |
| Benin | 2.9 | 88 |
| Brazil | 3.7 | 62 |
| Croatia | 3.4 | 70 |
| Djibouti | Not on list | |
| Ecuador | 3.5 | 117 |
| Egypt | 3.4 | 70 |
| El Salvador | 4.2 | 51 |
| France | 7.5 | 18 |
| Honduras | 2.6 | 107 |
| Hungary | 5.0 | 40 |
| Jordan | 5.7 | 37 |
| Kenya | 2.1 | 144 |
| Libya | 2.5 | 117 |
| Madagascar | 2.8 | 97 |
| Mauritius | 4.2 | 51 |
| Mexico | 3.5 | 65 |
| Namibia | 4.3 | 47 |
| Nigeria | 1.9 | 152 |
| Paraguay | 2.1 | 144 |
| Peru | 3.5 | 65 |
| Romania | 3.0 | 85 |
| Sierra Leone | 2.4 | 126 |
| South Africa | 4.5 | 46 |
| Sri Lanka | 3.2 | 78 |
| Togo | Not on list | |
| Turkmenistan | 1.8 | 155 |
| Uganda | 2.5 | 117 |
| United Republic of Tanzania | 2.9 | 88 |

(France and Jordan), and only five belong to the 50 least corrupt countries in terms of CPI. The more corrupt a country is perceived, the more quickly it acted to ratify the anti-corruption measure. Is this because the effort was viewed as a legitimate method to combat a pervasive evil in their society, or because the mechanics of ratification under a dictatorship are decidedly more efficient than under democratic regimes, or because these countries are eager to adopt a veil of proactivity in order to position themselves favorably in requesting economic relief?

Another key point of criticism lies in the anti-corruptive methodology. At the forefront in this regard is the Corruption Perception Index of Transparency International (Johnston, 2005; Sampford *et al.*, 2006). As these reputational scores are primarily based on the impressions of international business persons and risk analysts it is necessarily imprecise. Skeptical by nature, these individuals may not register as significant a country's effort to combat corruption with new policies or legislation, but may relatively overreact to new reports of scandals or convictions.[8] Additionally, as the countries are ranked, an increase in one country's score forces a reduction in the score of another country although the downward placement and concomitant negative effect on economic aid may not be warranted. Further, most proposals and frameworks are based upon firsthand reports by anti-corruption practitioners rather than scientific evaluation. Although empirically-based knowledge in this area is increasing, rational policy choices simply cannot be supported at this time in the field of good governance[9] (Andvig and Fjeldstad, 2001; Everett *et al.*, 2006).

## ETHICS, INTEGRITY AND CORRUPTION THEORY

Theoretical models addressing the concepts and processes of ethical administration in the public sector are developing concomitant with the research in best practices referenced above. Cooper (2004), stresses that in order to frame the significant research questions and allow for sustained and systematic inquiry, the following precepts need to be clarified:

1. What are the normative foundations for PA Ethics? (constitutional thought, social equity, virtue or the public interest).
2. How do American administrative ethical norms fit into a global context?
3. How can organizations be designed to support ethical conduct?
4. When is it acceptable to treat people equally and when unequally?

While research in this area has generally adopted this set of unifying themes, the global intellectual community has understandably taken issue with the second question as posed by Cooper, an American. The question itself provides fodder to those who criticize efforts of the WB, IMF and UN as being simply the implementation arm of Western ethical culture. Setting aside that argument for the moment the question will be rephrased to one asking if there is a global context with which all countries' administrative reforms align.

Toward that end Cooper and Yoder (2002, 2005) examined a large number of international treaties, pacts, agreements, conventions and programs going back to the 1970s. They attempted to identify the core values explicitly advocated or implicitly assumed and examined the reasoning underlying such values. They surmised their findings suggested an 'emerging global standard for public ethics' that consists of five core values:

1. The right to self-determination (with transparency as a requisite for people to secure this right individually and collectively).
2. Freedom (including freedom of information, autonomy of economic choice, and autonomy of political choice).
3. Honesty by government (making accountability possible).
4. Trust as the essential glue that holds democratic governance and market economies together (in essence a product of freedom and honesty).
5. Stability (and predictability), as a by-product of freedom, honesty, and trust.

Recognition of an increasingly interdependent world and a growing global commitment to market economies and democratic governance were the reasons given to support the five recurring core values.

Other scholars heeded Cooper's call and strove to replicate and expand this research in other venues. Menzel (2005) reviewed and assessed the research on ethics and integrity in governance published in ten US print journals from 1999 till 2004. He identified five interrelated themes: ethical decision-making and moral development; ethics laws and regulatory agencies; organizational performance; ethics management; and the ethical environment.

Frederickson's and Ghere's (2005) book, *Ethics in Public Management*, organized the seminal research to date in this area into four clusters: organization designs that support ethical behaviour; market forces that compromise administrative ethics; unintended outcomes of anticorruption reforms; and administrative ethics in global perspective. The themes indicate that greater attention is being paid to the interconnection between market and government ethics, and that further development of integrity and ethics policies is needed. Ghere (p. 352) concludes:

> the prospect of adopting a global ethic – a framework for defining right and wrong that knows no social, economic, or political borders – remains far in the future. In the meantime, public administrators can reprofessionalize their ethics in a manner that incorporates global humanitarian concern. To do so, practitioners need researchers to map globalization's ethical terrain and to recommend approaches for globally pertinent actions that are just, prudent, and feasible.

Lawton and Doig (2006) reviewed the body of European ethics research much in the same way Menzel did, focusing on journals articles published between 1999 and 2003.[10] Common themes identified were the public service ethos; regulation of individual (ethical) behavior; role of professionals; and cultural and political influences. They found the literature rife with real-world accounts (by the European Commission, the OECD and others), contributing to a plethora of descriptive studies on a broad range of topics. They concluded that what is needed for the next step is enhanced comparative research and a method of unifying the knowledge thus far collected, such as is being enacted by the EGPA Study Group established in 2003.[11]

Bossaert and Demmke's (2005) effort mirrored in part that of Cooper and Yoder in their examination of EU member policies regarding ethics and integrity. Their main conclusions address the challenges faced in the microcosm of assimilation EU states are experiencing with attempts to develop a uniform European Code of Ethics. Issues regarding reconciliation of differing views, who has the authority to oversee the effort, and what force should be incorporated into any potential code are all questions facing such a project. They advocate that a first step might be to establish a voluntary, non-legally binding European code of ethics to increase awareness of the issues at hand and stimulate dialogue. One surprising similarity they report is that, despite differences in general ethical perceptions, the obligations of civil servants regarding ethical behavior are remarkably similar in all 25 national public services of the enlarged EU. This is evident in the ethical requirements determined by laws as well as in disciplinary actions. Moreover, the traditional values of national civil services (neutrality, respecting the rule of law, confidentiality, impartiality, avoiding conflicts of interest, etc.) have remained unchanged for decades. These values are echoed in Palidauskaite's (2006) research on Eastern European countries that concludes the values purported for public servants are legality, serving the public, loyalty to the constitutional government, impartiality, competence, professionalism, honesty, integrity, disinterestedness, political neutrality, transparency and openness.

The study of ethics is not, of course, limited to US and EU researchers and it would be informative to have a global perspective on these and other issues (the significant contributions of Australian scholarship, to name just one additional country, such as Miller *et al.* (2005); Preston and Sampford (2002); Sampford and Preston (1998); Sampford *et al.* (2006) should be noted here). This text, however, will not attempt to speak for the worldwide community but does offer some unique insights into integrating a cross-Atlantic dialog on ethics in the public service. Those insights have emerged from a conference in 2005 jointly sponsored by the

EGPA group and the Section on Ethics of the American Society for Public Administration.[12]

## PERSPECTIVES ON ETHICS AND INTEGRITY OF GOVERNANCE

An overview of the research presented at this joint conference offers the following new perspectives to add to the summaries of research and action provided above.

First, the international academic dialog on these subjects has become more cooperative, intellectually challenging, vigorous, and substantive. The field is yet dominated by American scholars and American themes (Cooper, 2001; Frederickson and Ghere, 2005), although a shift toward greater balance is evident. This bent toward American research is in part a reflection of the sheer number of scholars at work in that area in comparison to the European academic community, as well as the history of scholarship on which the Americans can build. But it is also a function of the international academic community where English is the dominant language, American journals proliferate, and the American ethos of publish or perish motivates US authors to aggressively pursue publications in the few international journals that do exist. This book and other like-minded symposia (Menzel and Jurkiewicz, 2006), we hope, effectively demonstrate that the non-American voice is essential in advancing scholarship for all ethics researchers. As the World Ethics Forum and the Global Integrity Alliance illustrate, there is a trend toward global networks and the international academic community is well-positioned to be in the forefront of developments involving politics, economics, health, education and ethics.

In addition to bridging geographical and cultural boundaries, creating a collective knowledge base requires the integration and clarification of some key dimensions. One is the integration of varying disciplines into the ethics arena, as illustrated in (Figure 14.1). The need to speak a common language goes beyond English to the nuances a specialized vocabulary of terms if ethics researchers are to be able to unify their work and generalize their findings. Some examples here may accentuate this need.

Kaye, a political scientist, wonders why ethics researchers neglect the significance of politics, while Lewis searches for the foundations of ethics in a rich variety of disciplines, and Vandenabeele and Horton are historians and institutional theorists, Hoekstra *et al.* symbolize the link between public and proprietary administration, and Emery and Wyser focus on integrity in governance. Each of these scholars is engaged in related research yet each area of study is defined by a separate paradigm and

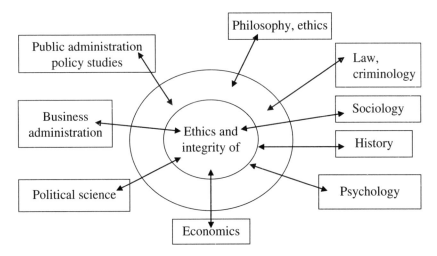

*Figure 14.1    Many related disciplines and aspects*

bodies of publication and theoretical concepts. Speaking English is clearly not enough to bring these different theoretical dialects together and in synchronicity moving in the same direction. It is that goal toward which the efforts presented in this book as well as at the conference focus, to advance a multidisciplinary and eventually interdisciplinary cumulative theory of ethical administration. It is the challenging conclusion of the scholars and practitioners previously cited to do just that.

So, how to begin? First, it is necessary to reach an agreement upon which of the many research topics available should be chosen for intensified international and multi-disciplinary cooperative work. Thus, initiatives such as the 'Transatlantic Dialogues' have been undertaken, but much more needs to be done in this regard. Second, the collective research process needs organization and resources, meaning that individual researchers need to reach out to colleagues in other disciplines and countries to work together on mutually beneficial projects. Again, conferences such as the Transatlantic Dialogue meetings provide an opportunity to meet potential fellow researchers and discuss commonalities of interests and resources. Interestingly, in Lawton's and Doig's (2005) synopsis one would expect that European scholars at this conference would focus on theoretical, conceptual, and definitional issues, and based upon Menzel's (2005) claim we would anticipate American scholars would emphasize the empirical. Yet as Figure 14.2 illustrates the scholars' contributions to this book contest that theory. Europeans in this book are more focused on empirical research while the Americans seek to explain and develop theory. Not to say that

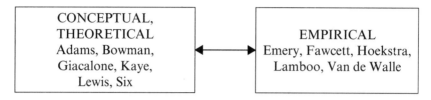

*Figure 14.2   Research orientation*

observation is problematic. On the contrary, it offers greater evidence of the need for cross-dialog and a shedding of preconceived limits on what we need to know and how we should go about knowing it.

## A SHARED LANGUAGE: TOWARD CONCEPTUAL CLARITY

Fruitful social science requires that the problem first be delineated and, given the ambiguous nature of ethical studies, this must begin with a definition of terms. Communication can be challenging enough when speaking the same language, and to be able to forge a common rubric for research and dialog the field needs to come to an agreement regarding terms. Conceptual clarity is essential for public debate, policy-making and theory development in ethics on an international level, particularly with the commonly relativistic interpretations of concepts such as corruption, integrity and governance. A review of the more commonly used terms and their definitions is useful here.

The concept of corruption is often at the heart of the debate about the moral quality of government and it can be understood to mean any number of things. The legal definition states it is acting in the interest of an actor because of the advantages promised or given. Pope (2000) suggests it should include all abuses of office for private gain, such as fraud and theft. Yet another defines corruption as synonymous with all types of wrongdoing by functionaries, thus encompassing all vices, maladies, and weaknesses of politics and bureaucracy. Referring to bureaucracies, Caiden once distinguished 179 types of what he called bureaupathologies, including corruption, deceit, discrimination, fraud, injustice, mediocrity, red-tape and waste (Caiden, 1991: 490).

Employing the word integrity can represent a range of perspectives by both the author and the reader (Montefiore and Vines, 1999; Dobel, 1999).[13] Integrity can be seen as 'wholeness' or completeness, as one specific value (incorruptibility or righteousness), as acting in line with constitutional or regime values (Rohr, 1989), as complying with the relevant moral values and norms, or as complying in an exemplary way with moral standards. Typologies of integrity violations are frequently used as well, resulting from theoretical and empirical analyses of particular professions. Such typologies generally include behavior both internal and external to the organization and contain a range of relevant (laws, rules, codes, informal norms). Table 14.2 illustrates an integrity typology for police conduct, with nine distinct clusters. Each integrity violation is associated with a continuum of behaviors from most to least serious, as determined by how far these behaviors are from normative value expectations. Corruptive behavior such as bribing, for instance, can vary from cents to billions, and also the impact of the decisions taken in exchange for the bribe can differ enormously (for example, from doing a friend a favor by sharing

*Table 14.2   Types of integrity violations related to police behavior*

---

*Corruption: bribing*
   misuse of public power for private gain; asking, offering, accepting bribes
*Corruption: favoritism (nepotism, cronyism, patronage)*
   misuse of public authority to favor friends, family, party
*Fraud and theft*
   improper private gain acquired from the organization (with no involvement of external actors)
*Conflict of (private and public) interest*
   personal interest (through assets, jobs, gifts and so on) interferes (or might interfere) with public interest
*Improper use of authority* (for noble causes)
   to use illegal/improper methods to achieve organizational goals (within the police for example illegal methods of investigation and disproportionate violence)
*Misuse and manipulation of information*
   lying, cheating, manipulating information, breaching confidentiality of information
*Discrimination and sexual harassment*
   misbehavior towards colleagues or citizens and customers
*Waste and abuse of resources*
   failure to comply with organizational standards, improper performance, incorrect or dysfunctional internal behavior
*Private time misconduct*
   conduct in one's private time which harms the publics trust in administration/government

---

*Source:*   Huberts *et al.*, 1999: 449–51.

a tidbit of information, to shoddy policies and projects with disastrous economic consequences for populations). Sexual harassment, for example, can vary between a sexist remark and rape.

Typologies can be especially useful in comparative research. For instance, central integrity problems in the Netherlands might be very different from those in Italy or the US (or the UK as Fawcett and Wardman clarify Chapter 8 of this book). By applying a typology, scholars can define the integrity issues such that even while speaking cross-culturally apples are being compared to apples and oranges to oranges, so to speak.

The word governance is frequently used in contemporary social sciences with a general understanding that it refers to something broad in scope and includes a division of power and authority (Van Kersbergen and Van Waarden, 2004; Pierre and Guy Peters, 2000; http://europa.eu.int/comm/governance). Frederickson and Smith (2003: 210) summarized as the central question of governance as being 'how can public-sector regimes, agencies, programs and activities be organized and managed to achieve public purposes?' Common agreement surrounding the term is that it speaks to the political and administrative process and institutions and does not encompass policies and results. The ethics and integrity of governance addresses the morality of those who govern rather than evaluating the quality of the decision or policy. To use a current example, questions of governance do not concern themselves with whether the invasion of Iraq was ethical, but instead examine the decision-making processes that led to the invasion of Iraq and make determinations as to whether the decision-makers and involved public servants acted with integrity.

Integrity is but one aspect of governance, although one that permeates almost every other aspect. It is necessary, for the sake of scientific inquiry, to separate the application of moral principles to the conduct of officials in organizations and other areas of competence such as financial, legal, or democratic principles (Thompson, 2001: 79, 91). This framework for the qualities of governance is summarized in Figure 14.3 (based on Bovens *et al.*, 2001). We realize that integrity is interconnected with democracy, lawfulness and economy, but the attractiveness of the framework as a heuristic device is that it points out a number of dilemmas in the study of the integrity of governance. Such a model enables practitioners and scholars to reflect more systematically on the limitations as well as possibilities of the mentioned criteria, including integrity.

Underpinning this model is the presumption that those who govern can make errors and demonstrate incompetence in any one of the four criteria, but violations in only one of the four areas constitutes the potential for evil (Adams and Balfour, 2004). Simply put, an individual can do wrong

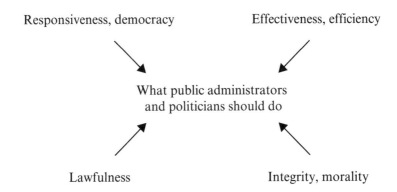

Responsiveness, democracy              Effectiveness, efficiency

What public administrators
and politicians should do

Lawfulness                              Integrity, morality

*Figure 14.3    Quality of governance criteria*

without committing an integrity violation. Blurring this distinction is not uncommon, particularly in cultures where politics and religion are inter-twined, but doing so can lead an organization to lose sight of what is morally important and what is not. This can have very negative conse-quences such as employees becoming so afraid to take any risk for fear of committing a moral violation and are thus paralyzed into inaction. No one wants their integrity questioned on the basis of a technical inefficiency. They are also more likely to cover up errors when they occur, potentially compounding the problem for the organization into the long-term, but pro-tecting their individual reputation at the time.

As a consequence, organizations need to clearly define their central moral values and norms; these will serve as the basis for determining whether or not to initiate an integrity investigation. This is never an easy endeavor, but it is an important one for organizations that take ethics and integrity seri-ously. As a start for those organizations to whom this is foreign, Caiden (1999) had elucidated principles such as the provision of public benefits, enforcing the rule of law, ensuring public responsibility and accountability, setting an example, improving professional performance and promoting democracy that may prove helpful. Reviewing these or those suggested by OECD, ASPA, or another associative body, or by engaging in a dialog with your organization (Jurkiewicz, 2001), the process can provide key elements in the development of a mission, goals and ethical standards that reflect the organization as a dynamic and honorable institution.

Some of the questions that frustrate ethics researchers can be interpreted in terms of this framework. In this book for example, Adams, Balfour, Reed, Emery and Wyser concentrate on the possible tension between economy and effectiveness (including technology) and integrity. Kaye points out the limitations of integrity when the logic of politics and responsiveness is taken seriously. Bowman and West confront the logics of politics and integrity regarding employment and appointment in the public sector. Six and Huberts attempt to relate the norms of the public, legal norms, and the norms of the political system with the integrity of public functionaries. In all cases, clarity of language can serve as a common denominator in discussing and measuring these variables which can lead to new directions in the study of ethics and governance.

## NEW DIRECTIONS: INTEGRITY AND ETHICS MANAGEMENT

Management issues have been among the topics most extensively researched and debated in administrative ethics. What strategies and instruments are available to protect the integrity of an organization and its members? What institutions succeed in curbing corruption within and stimulating the integrity of a country's civil service system? Questions regarding leadership and management styles; codes, procedures and rules; training and education (the pedagogy of ethics); and national integrity institutions were all addressed at the Leuven Conference. Additionally, a number of chapters in this book describe and evaluate the development of integrity policies, such as Hoekstra *et al.*, Maesschalck, Lamboo *et al.*

How to evaluate the state of the art in ethics management research? After numerous attempts to present inventories of policies and policy instruments, the time seems ripe to move into the study of the effectiveness of those policies. What has caused changes in values, views and behaviors? How have changes in the actual integrity of a public organization, a politician or a civil servant impacted the trust of the people in the individual and his or her organization?

These are key questions for the future. Research models will need to be developed that separate the strategic and effectiveness dimensions. Strategies can be compliance or value based (to simplify the types of intervention), and effectiveness can be assessed by recording values and views as well as actual behavior.

One of the important issues here is the relationship between the integrity of governance and the public trust in governance. Van de Walle's chapter in this book demonstrates that this relationship is complex and that the directionality of effect remains unknown: do perceptions of trust determine views on integrity and corruption or does corruption and disintegrity determine level of trust? Fawcett and Wardman give voice to the commonsensical notion that inappropriate behaviors by those who govern can damage public confidence.

## NEW DIRECTIONS: LINKING THE GLOBAL POLICY AND RESEARCH AGENDA'S

A lot has been said to this point regarding global integrity *policies* on the one hand and the development in the *research* on (global) ethics and integrity of governance on the other hand.

These two developments are interconnected, as evidenced by the fact that international organizations do or subsidize much of the empirical research that has been done. This relationship of course encourages reflection on whether we as researchers tailor our questions or methodologies and findings to address their concerns or do we speak truth to power. This question is becoming more urgent now that the international community seems to realize, more than in the past, that the integrity and ethics of government and governance has other implications beyond curbing and sanctioning corruption. There is more interest in attempting to define what good governance is as more than simply a lack of corruption. Attempts to focus more on integrity, values, and leadership are indicative of this development.

Given the above, four clear areas of research present themselves. First is what constitutes good governance in an international context. The research to date assumes the universality of the values of western democratic market economies and has been used to justify a top-down approach. This is in line with much criticism on cultural relativism as a justification of corruption in 'non-western' contexts. International treaties, conventions, policies and conferences have been studied to establish a basis for common values and principles, and has concluded that much commonality is present. Not surprisingly, then, research on the values of the elite has led to support for the values articulated by that elite. Although cultural relativism is not adequate in itself to frame the discussion of what constitutes good governance, credible evidence for cultural monism let alone cultural imperialism is lacking as well. As some chapters in this volume argue, we will have to explore further what the populations, ideologies, and religions of this world really see as good governance. Bottom-up research is necessary, with empirical as well as theoretical work. What do people in developing countries see as good governance when they are able to decide themselves?[14] What of Asian nations? We know that Europeans appear to be more pluralistic than Americans in their orientation toward good governance, which should not be surprising given the diversity of countries (transitional in Eastern Europe, varying political systems in Western Europe, and fundamental differences in political systems and administrative traditions between the North and the South). These differences need to be acknowledged and addressed in moving forward toward a synthesis of understanding.

Second, is the measurement of corruption and integrity (Sampford *et al.*, 2006). It is rather easy as well as justified to criticize the corruption perception index, but what might replace that score? What would be a more accurate way to determine the content of a national iceberg of integrity violations? (Huberts et al., 2006).

Third, the extensive framework of international conventions, rules, monitoring and possibly sanctioning that has been built over the past decade needs to be examined. The number of instruments that have been produced to measure corrupt practices and regimes is impressive, but no objective study has been done on their validity, reliability, or effectiveness. Clearly there are times when policies with good intentions resulted in bad outcomes, but why this is the case remains unexamined. Studies on the effectiveness of anti-corruption and integrity institutions and policies are very much needed in the present state of policy development.

The fourth topic concerns what is known about the extent of corruption in countries and the effectiveness of national anti-corruption methods and strategies. Most proposals and frameworks are based on the experiences and knowledge of anti-corruption practitioners and not on scientific evaluation. Although systematic inquiry has intensified, what scant evidence there is available does not seem to permit or support rational policy choices in the field of national, regional and local good governance. This, of course, stands in contrast to the far-reaching policy prescription to which international organizations adhere.

## CONCLUSION

In summary, research on public sector ethics is essential to the understanding and practice of good governance. Further, such research is dominated by the American perspective and, although progress has been made, much more effort is required on both sides of the Atlantic to achieve a balance between the European and American perspectives and beyond to include the voice of nations across the globe. Finally, we need a common language as a basis to bring about this fusion of ideologies and epistemologies toward the end of substantive, generalizable research. Summarized here is a reflection on the practice and study of good governance from a global perspective as it exists today, along with suggestions on where it needs to move into the future.

Anti-corruption activities were a reactionary and necessary first step to address ethics in governance on a global scale. The discipline must now move beyond that toward collective theory-building based on empirical evidence. The most important first step in this regard is to connect the international policy and research agendas more explicitly. The communities of researchers and policy makers are committed to contribute toward curbing corruption and safeguarding integrity. For researchers it is at the same time important to keep some distance from policy makers and institutions, to protect their independence and to be eager to question what seems obvious.

## NOTES

1. http://www.unodc.org/unodc/en/corruption.html.
2. http://www.un.org/Depts/dhl/resguide/resins.htm with *Conventions, Declarations and Other Instruments Found in General Assembly Resolutions.*
3. While both organizations are significant to the global shift in corruptive awareness, the emphasis given the World Bank herein over the IMF is due to their scope of operations: 'The IMF places great emphasis on good governance when providing policy advice, financial support, and technical assistance to its 184 member countries. It promotes good governance by helping countries ensure the rule of law, improve the efficiency and accountability of their public sectors, and tackle corruption. In so doing, the IMF limits itself to economic aspects of governance that could have a significant macroeconomic impact. The IMF also has strong measures in place to ensure the integrity of its own organization.' Since 1996, the IMF's role in promoting good governance has expanded considerably, while still being limited to economic aspects of governance that could have a significant macroeconomic impact. http://www.imf.org/external/np/gov/guide/eng/index.htm (15 May 2006). Significant macroeconomic impact. http://www.imf.org/external/np/gov/guide/eng/index.htm (15 May 2006).
4. www.worldbank.org -> anticorruption website.
5. http://web.worldbank.org/WBSITE/EXTERNAL/NEWS/0,,contentMDK: 20883752~pagePK:34370~piPK:42770~theSitePK:4607,00.html.
6. Forum details can be accessed at: http://web.worldbank.org/WBSITE/EXTERNAL/NEWS/0,,contentMDK:20885902~menuPK:34463~pagePK:34370~piPK:34424~theSitePK:4607,00.html.
7. OECD Guidelines Art. 10.
8. Alternatives such as the Public Integrity Index of the Centre for Public Integrity cannot really compete with the TI Index for only a limited number of countries are indexed (www.publicintegrity.org).
9. For an interesting exception with an evaluation of World Bank strategies concerning African countries, see: Klein Haarhuis, 2005 and Klein Haarhuis and Torenvlied, 2006.
10. For more on this topic see: Chapman (2000); Della Porta and Vanucci (1999); Heywood (1997); Lawton (1998).
11. For more information on the Study Group on Ethics and Integrity of Governance of the European Group on Public Administration (EGPA), see: www.egpa-ethics.eu.
12. The conference program and presented papers are accessible through: www.egpa-ethics.eu (go to previous conferences, Leuven, 2005) as well as through http://soc.kuleuven.be/io/ethics/ (May 2006).
13. See Six and Huberts (Chapter 5 this volume).
14. Within administrative ethics more attention is being paid to the relationship between ethics and religion or spirituality (Giacalone and Jurkiewicz, 2003) but this is much less the case for the exploration of the relationship between non-Christian and non-western religion and spirituality on the one hand, and views on good governance on the other.

# REFERENCES

Adams, G.B. and D.L. Balfour (2004), *Unmasking Administrative Evil*, revised edn, Armonk, NY and London: M.E. Sharpe.

Agha, Hussein and Robert Maley (2006), 'Hamas: the perils of power', *The New York Review of Books*, **53** (4), accessed at www.nybooks.com/articles/18789.

Andvig, J.C. and O. Fjeldstad (2001), *Corruption: A Review of Contemporary Research*, Oslo: Norsk Utenrikspolitisk Institut.

Anechiarico, F. and J.B. Jacobs (1996), *The Pursuit of Absolute Integrity. How Corruption Control Makes Government Ineffective*, Chicago, IL and London: University of Chicago Press.

Annan, K. (2006), Statement to the General Assembly of the United Nations Convention against Corruption, accessed at www.unodc.org/unodc/corruption.htm.

Bardhan, Pranab (1997), 'Corruption and development: a review of issues,' *Journal of Economic Literature* **35** (September), 1320–46.

Benaissa, Hamdan (1993), 'Corruption and the socio-cultural context', in M. Punch, E. Kolthoff, K. van der Vijver and B. van Vliet (eds), *Coping with Corruption in a Borderless World*, Deventer, Netherlands: Kluwer Law and Taxation Publishers, pp. 59–72.

Bossaert, Danielle and Christoph Demmke (2005), *Main Challenges in the Field of Ethics and Integrity in the EU Member States*, Maastricht, Netherlands: European Institute of Public Administration, accessed at www.eipa.nl.

Bovens, M.A.P., P. 't Hart, M.J.W. van Twist and U. Rosenthal (2001), *Openbaar bestuur. Beleid, organisatie en politiek*, 6th revised edn, Alphen aan den Rijn, Netherlands: Kluwer.

Caiden, G.E. (1991), 'What really is public maladministration?', *Public Administration Review*, **51** (6), 486–93.

Caiden, G.E. (1999), 'The essence of public service ethics and professionalism', in L.W.J.C Huberts and J.H.J. van den Heuvel (eds), *Integrity at the Public-Private Interface*, Maastricht, Netherlands: Shaker, pp. 21–44.

Caiden, G.E., O.P. Dwivedi and Joseph Jabbra (2001), *Where Corruption Lives*, Bloomfield, CT: Kumarian Press.

Chapman, Richard A. (ed.) (2000), *Ethics in Public Service for the New Millennium*, Aldershot: Ashgate.

Cooper, Terry L. (ed.) (2001), *Handbook of Administrative Ethics*, 2nd edn, New York and Basel: Marcel Dekker.

Cooper, Terry L. (2004), 'Big questions in administrative ethics: a need for focused, collaborative effort', *Public Administration Review*, **64** (4), 395–407.

Cooper, Terry L. and Diane Yoder (2002), 'Public management ethics in a transnational world', *Public Integrity*, **4** (4), 333–52.

Della Porta, Donatella and Alberto Vanucci (1999), *Corrupt Exchanges. Actors, Resources, and Mechanisms of Political Corruption*, New York: Aldine de Gruyter.

Dobel, J. Patrick (1999), *Public Integrity*, Baltimore, MD and London: Johns Hopkins University Press.

Doig, Alan and Robin Theobald (1999), *Corruption and Democratisation*, London: Routledge.

Everett, James, Dean Reu and Abu Shiraz Rahaman (2006), 'The global fight against corruption: a Foucaultian, virtue-ethics framing', *Journal of Business Ethics*, **65**, 1–12.

Fijnaut, Cyrille and Leo Huberts (eds) (2002), *Corruption, Integrity and Law Enforcement*, Dordrecht, Netherlands: Kluwer Law International.

Frederickson, H. George and Kevin B. Smith (2003), *Public Administration Theory Primer*, Boulder, CO: Westview Press.

Frederickson, H.G. and R.K. Ghere (eds) (2005), *Ethics in Public Management*, New York: M.E. Sharpe.

Giacalone, R.A. and C.L. Jurkiewicz (2003), *Handbook of Workplace Spirituality and Organizational Performance*, New York: M.E. Sharpe.

Government of Malaysia (2004), *National Integrity Plan*, Putrajaya: Integrity Institute of Malaysia.

Heidenheimer, Arnold and Michael Johnston (eds) (2002), *Political Corruption. Concepts & Contexts*, 3rd edn, New Brunswick, NJ and London: Transaction.

Heywood, P. (ed) (1997), *Political Corruption*, Blackwell: Oxford.

Huberts, L.W.J.C., D. Pijl and A. Steen (1999), 'Integriteit en corruptie' ['Integrity and corruption'], in C. Fijnaut, E. Muller and U. Rosenthal (eds), *Politie. Studies over haar werking en organisatie*, [*The Police. Studies on its Activities and Organisation*], Alphen aan den Rijn, Netherlands: Samsom, pp. 433–72.

Huberts, L.W.J.C. (2002), 'Global ethics and corruption', in J. Rabin (ed.), *Encyclopedia of Public Administration and Public Policy*, New York: Marcel Dekker, pp. 546–51

Huberts, L.W.J.C. (2005), *Integriteit en Integritisme in Bestuur en Samenleving. Wie de schoen past . . .*, 23 February, Amsterdam: Oratie Faculteit der Sociale Wetenschappen.

Huberts, Leo, Karin Lasthuizen and Carel Peeters (2006), 'Measuring corruption: exploring the iceberg', in Charles Sampford, Arthur Shacklock, Carmel Connors and Fredrik Galtung (eds), *Measuring Corruption*, Aldershot, UK and Burlington, VT: Ashgate, pp. 265–93.

Johnson, Roberta Ann (ed.) (2004), *The Struggle Against Corruption*, New York, and Basingstoke: Palgrave Macmillan.

Johnston, Michael (2005), *Syndromes of Corruption. Wealth, Power, and Democracy*, Cambridge: Cambridge University Press.

Kersbergen, K. van and F. van Waarden (2004), 'Governance as a bridge between disciplines: cross-disciplinary inspiration regarding shifts in governance and problems of governability, accountability and legitimacy', *European Journal of Political Research*, **43**, 143–71.

Klein Haarhuis, Carolien (2005), *Promoting Anti-corruption Reform. Evaluating the Implementation of a World Bank Anti-corruption Program in Seven African Countries (1999–2001)*, Utrecht, Netherlands: ICS Dissertation Series.

Klein Haarhuis, Carolien and René Torenvlied (2006), 'Dimensions and alignments in the African anti-corruption debate', *Acta Politica*, **41** (1), 41–67.

Klitgaard, R. (1988), *Controlling Corruption*, Berkeley, CA: University of California Press.

Lawton, A. (1998), *Ethical Management for the Public Services*, Buckingham, UK and Philadelphia, PA: Open University Press.

Lawton, A. and R.A. Doig (2005), 'Researching ethics for public service organizations: the view from Europe', *Public Integrity*, **8** (1), 231–43.

Maesschalck, J. (2005), 'Approaches to ethics management in the public sector: a proposed extension of the compliance-integrity continuum', *Public Integrity*, **7** (1), 21–41.

McKinney, J.B. and M. Johnston (eds) (1986), *Fraud, Waste and Abuse in Government*, Philadelphia, PA: ISHI.

Menzel, D.C. (2005), 'State of the art of empirical research on ethics and integrity in governance', in H.G. Frederickson and R.K. Ghere (eds), *Ethics in Public Management*, New York: M.E. Sharpe, pp. 16–46.

Menzel, Donald C. and Carole L. Jurkiewicz (2006), 'Introduction to the symposium on ethics and integrity in governance', *Public Integrity*, **8** (1), 5–9.

Miller, Seumas, Peter Roberts and Edward Spence (2005), *Corruption and Anti-Corruption. An Applied Philosophical Approach*, Upper Saddle River, NJ: Pearson Prentice Hall.

Montefiore, Alan and David Vines (eds) (1999), *Integrity in the Public and Private Domains*, London: Routledge.

Organisaton for Economic Co-operation and Development (OECD) (2002), *Trust in Government. Ethics Measures in OECD Countries*, Paris: OECD.

Organisation for Economic Co-operation and Development (OECD) (2000), *No Longer Business as Usual. Fighting Bribery and Corruption*, Paris: OECD.

Organisation for Economic Co-operation and Development (OECD) (2004), *Managing Conflicts of Interest in the Public Service. OECD Guidelines and Country Experiences*, Paris: OECD.

Palidauskaite, Jolante (2006), 'Codes of ethics in transitional democracies', *Public Integrity*, **8** (1), 35–48.

Pierre, J. and B. Guy Peters (2000), *Governance, Politics, and the State,* Basingstoke: Macmillan.

Pieth, Mark and Peter Eigen (eds) (1999), *Korruption im internationalen Geschäftsverkehr. Bestandsaufnahme. Bekämpfung. Prävention*, Neuwied and Kriftel, Germany: Luchterhand.

Pope, J. (2000), *Fighting Corruption: The Elements of a National Integrity System (TI Source Book 2000)*, Berlin: Transparency International, also accessed at www.transparency.org.

Preston, Noel and Charles Sampford, with Carmel Connors (2002), *Encouraging Ethics and Challenging Corruption. Reforming Governance in Public Institutions*, Sydney: The Federation Press.

Punch, M., E. Kolthoff, K. van der Vijver and B. van Vliet (eds) (1993), *Coping with Corruption in a Borderless World. Proceedings of the Fifth International Anti-Corruption Conference*, Deventer, Netherlands: Kluwer Law and Taxation Publishers.

Rohr, John A. (1989), *Ethics for Bureaucrats. An Essay on Law and Values*, 2nd edn, New York and Basel: Marcel Dekker.

Rose-Ackerman, Susan (1999), *Corruption and Government. Causes, Consequences and Reform*, Cambridge: Cambridge University Press.

Rosett, Claudia (2006), 'How corrupt is the United Nations?', *Commentary*, April, accessed at www.commentarymagazine.com/article.asp?aid=12104031_1.

Sampford, Charles, Noel Preston, with C-A Bois (eds) (1998), *Public Sector Ethics. Finding and Implementing Values*, Annandale, Australia: The Federation Press, and London: Routledge.

Sampford, Charles, Arthur Shacklock, Carmel Connors and Fredrik Galtung (eds) (2006), *Measuring Corruption*, Aldershot, UK and Burlington VT, USA: Ashgate.

Thompson, Dennis F. (2001), 'The possibility of administrative ethics', in Willa Bruce (ed.), *Classics of Administrative Ethics*, originally published in 1985, Boulder, CO: Westview, pp. 79–92.

Transparency International (TI) (2001), *The National Integrity System. Concept and Practice*, report by Transparency International for the Global Forum II on Fighting Corruption and Safeguarding Integrity, prepared by Alan Doig and Stephanie McIvor, Berlin: Transparency International.

Transparency International (2005), *Report on the Transparency International Global Corruption Barometer 2005*, Berlin: Transparency International Policy and Research Department.

United Nations Development Programme (UNDP) (1998), *Corruption & Integrity Improvement Initiatives in Developing Countries*, New York: UNDP.

United Nations Office on Drugs and Crime (UNODC) (2005), *Compendium of International Legal Instruments on Corruption*, New York: United Nations.

Williams, R. and A. Doig (eds) (2000), *Controlling Corruption*, Cheltenham, UK and Brookfield, VT: Edward Elgar.

Yoder, Diane E. and Terry L. Cooper (2005), 'Public-service ethics in a transnational world', in H. George Frederickson and Richard K. Ghere (eds), *Ethics in Public Management*, New York: M.E. Sharpe, pp. 297–327.

# Index